New Directions in Latino American Cultures

A series edited by Licia Fiol-Matta and José Quiroga

NEW CONCEPTS IN LATINO AMERICAN CULTURES

A series edited by Licia Fiol-Matta and José Quiroga

VIRAL VOYAGES

Tracing AIDS in Latin America

Lina Meruane

Translated by

Andrea Rosenberg

First published in Chile as *Viajes virales: La crisis del contagio global en la escritura del sida* by Lina Meruane. Copyright © Fondo de Cultura Económica S.A., 2012.

First published in English in 2014 by
PALGRAVE MACMILLAN®
in the United States—a division of St. Martin's Press LLC,
175 Fifth Avenue, New York, NY 10010.

Where this book is distributed in the UK, Europe and the rest of the world, this is by Palgrave Macmillan, a division of Macmillan Publishers Limited, registered in England, company number 785998, of Houndmills, Basingstoke, Hampshire RG21 6XS.

Palgrave Macmillan is the global academic imprint of the above companies and has companies and representatives throughout the world.

ISBN: 978–1–137–39498–9

Library of Congress Cataloging-in-Publication Data

Meruane, Lina, 1970–
    [Viajes virales. English]
    Viral voyages : tracing AIDS in Latin America / by Lina Meruane ; translated by Andrea Rosenberg.
        pages cm. — (New directions in Latino American cultures)
    Includes bibliographical references and index.
    ISBN 978–1–137–39498–9 (hardback : alk. paper)
        1. Latin American literature—20th century—History and criticism.
    2. Latin American literature—21st century—History and criticism.
    3. AIDS (Disease) in literature. I. Title.

PQ7081.M4413 2014
860.9'3561—dc23   2013045795

A catalogue record of the book is available from the British Library.

Design by Newgen Knowledge Works (P) Ltd., Chennai, India.

First edition: May 2014

The translation of this book has been supported by

Fondo Nacional de Fomento del Libro y la Lectura, Chile, 2013

New York University's Humanities Initiative, 2013

To my parents, tireless travelers

CONTENTS

ACKNOWLEDGMENTS

I am grateful to the many people who offered me a hand or a text during the long period in which *Viral Voyages* was written, first in Spanish, and then in the English version. I am deeply indebted to the two scholars who believed in this project when it was nothing but an idea: Sylvia Molloy, who offered me a constant, compelling conversation about literary self-fashioning, queerness, and disease, and who taught me, through my reading of her extraordinary work on dissidence, that scholarship is not just about intellectual alertness but also about the pleasure of writing; and Mary Louise Pratt, whose sharp, thought-provoking questions helped me identify the ideological route of the disease and who, through her brilliant books and essays, inspired my own work. I thank professors Jo Labanyi and Gerard Aching for their insightful observations and their ever-so-generous enthusiasm, as well as my scholar friends Gabriel Giorgi, for the ongoing conversation on contemporary queer communities, and Arnaldo Cruz-Malavé, for his original and stimulating ideas, and for that unique sense of humor, always so handy. I would also like to express my gratitude to those who sent me citations and articles, even before they had been published: Dieter Ingenschay in Berlin, Tim Frasca in New York, Blanca Figueroa in Lima, Henri Billard in Poitiers, Francisco Javier Hernández-Adrián in Durham, and Ximena Riesco and Claudia Ortega in Santiago de Chile. I am grateful, too, for the collaboration of three astute readers of the manuscript at different points in its revision: Velebita Koričančić (Mexico City/Zagreb), Alia Trabucco Zerán (New York/Santiago), and Guillermo Astigarraga (New York/Córdoba). For this edition, many thanks to scholars and editors Licia Fiol-Matta and José Quiroga for their enthusiastic endorsement of my book, as well as to Andrea Rosenberg for her careful and inspiring translation of *Viajes virales*. A very special thanks to my longtime friend, Chilean artist Marcela Trujillo, for turning deadly viruses into lively planets for the cover of both editions of this book. I am most thankful to my parents for their unconditional support of my writing, and also to the friends and family who make up my convivial New York and Santiago communities. And to Jose, my partner in this and so many other journeys in life—to him I am especially grateful.

The material aid I received was also crucial. All along, this book was granted support from New York University: a fellowship to complete my doctoral studies; the Dean's Dissertation Fellowship that allowed me to finish the first draft; and the Research Challenge Grant provided by Fred Schwarzbach, dean of Global/Liberal Studies, to put the finishing touches on the Spanish-language manuscript. The translation of this book was funded by two additional grants: one from New York University's Humanities Initiative and another from Chile's Consejo Nacional de la Cultura y de las Artes. For all this invaluable support, I am truly indebted.

Beginning the Journey

All books bring together several stories, their seams like invisible scars. The fine thread that runs through these *Viral Voyages* binds together two of my oldest obsessions: literature as a meandering expression of the real, and the disciplinary discourse surrounding illness. These obsessions arose in my own biography through circumstance some time ago. Because of them, I have fixed my gaze on the imagined achievements and real misfortunes that so many bodies experienced in public hospitals and domestic spaces, as well as on the streets, where the military made civilian bodies its target. Chile's dictatorship slowly began to weaken in the 1980s, but it was in the years of its liberating collapse that acquired immunodeficiency syndrome (AIDS) appeared. The curfews were already becoming a thing of the past when a close friend, almost as young as I was back then, told me that his test had come back positive. He would now live with the constant certainty of death—that same fear that I, too, had grown up with. The fear of an expected death was a terminal condition, I thought. And it was perhaps there that this book began to be written: in our shared knowledge of human fragility.

I think, now, that perhaps it was no coincidence that three important Latin American AIDS novels (*El color del verano* by Reinaldo Arenas, *Pájaros de la playa* by Severo Sarduy, and *Salón de belleza* by Mario Bellatin) as well as the chronicles of Pedro Lemebel came into my hands the same year that I left Santiago, Chile, to begin a doctorate in literature in New York City. With those books tucked in my suitcase, I arrived in capitalism's world headquarters, which had been—and in a way continued to be—the epicenter both for the movements of sexual dissidence and for that horrific crisis. With those texts, and in that city full of contradictions, I began to set the central ideas of this book down on paper.

Viral Voyages also began in encounters and conversations with pilgrims of the disease, and thanks to stories that various people transmitted to me from afar: through email or the post, or simply relayed orally with ineffable enthusiasm. Back then, the numerous books that appear in these pages still circulated in silence. Critics did not review them, or they did so without referring to the virus, much less to the sexual transgressions of the books' protagonists; they refused to talk about AIDS. It was as if the mere mention of the syndrome would infect them with the iconic illness of the end of the twentieth century. As if it would cause widespread suspicion about their own sexual identities. As if choosing to differ from the norm were still a punishable criminal offense and not an essential act of political resistance and solidarity. AIDS, which had appeared in Latin American literature as a surreptitious sign, began increasingly to be *written* on the page, expressed in a more irreverent, almost exhibitionist way, its authors compelled by the urgent need to bear witness; and this sign was gradually deciphered by readers. In the public spaces of Latin America, however, it remained mysteriously hidden. And this book comes, too, from the desire to unveil this enigma.

I decided to use Latin American accounts of the epidemic produced in different locations around the world to trace the trajectories of this terrible virus and the way it was represented—its literary translations, its iterations in discourse. I plotted its movement across the globe by following the routes of a number of authors who wrote about the epidemic. In the texts of narrators who lived out their final years in exile in New York or Paris, who recounted the crisis from Chile or Cuba, from Argentina or Peru, from Colombia or Mexico, I glimpsed a set of circumstances that were shared in common and yet irretrievably individual, shaped by singular political situations and by the subjective experience of the disease.

I choose to term this corpus *HIV-positive* because of the presence, whether explicit or not, of the virus, and especially because the corpus uses AIDS as the platform for its critique. It is a literary system that marks points of convergence and divergence; it is a potential corpus, always incomplete and mutating (having become immeasurably large), that speaks of fear and death but also of fierce survival and of pleasure. These narratives have taken on the task of documenting the complexity of the tragedy over the course of the three uncertain decades that constitute this book's temporal boundaries: spanning from the beginning of the crisis in 1980 until the first years of the current century. They reflect the internal contradictions of a dissident community that is best expressed in the plural, because only thus can its great internal heterogeneity be evoked.

This corpus allows us to note the transformations that have taken place in communities that are both anchored in their respective territories and yet also extraterritorial and undergoing a shift that is as much historical as it is cultural: the much-debated processes of change in Latin American capitalist culture as a backdrop for sexual emancipation. These changes in the culture of capitalism and its new technologies of communication and travel would allow dissident sexualities to articulate a utopian notion of freedom beyond the borders of the repressive, homophobic nation. It would be first a feat of the imagination and, soon thereafter, a result of the deliberate construction of a diverse, cosmopolitan community. This mobile utopia would expand under neoliberalism, which was accompanied by a celebration of the supposedly egalitarian and democratic possibilities of the globalized world. But the beginning of the contemporary epidemic and its tragic consequences, symptomatic of a shift in the social paradigm, would be a warning sign, marking a breach in the surety of freedom and suggesting that the progressive community had fallen into a new trap. Globalization (driven by neoliberal policies and shaped by the new capitalism) would not only fail to fulfill the promised conditions of democratic or economic equality among continents, but it would also offer the lethal journey of the virus as a symbol of this failure.

It is from this idea that *Viral Voyages* begins. The cataclysm known as AIDS is examined here from two vantage points—one offering an overview, and the other a more particularized perspective—that together create a chamber in which the different voices that murmur throughout these pages reverberate. The first part ("Logbook of an HIV-Positive Voyage") is an interdisciplinary exploration of the global space of the epidemic and the drifting destinies of its protagonists, both within fiction and outside of it. This part examines the cultural, social, and political context inscribed in the discursive production of the epidemic, outlining the global and local displacements of its metaphors (their connections, recurrences, and divergences) and the relationship among the writings of the cosmopolitan communities that have shaped the central themes of this calamity. The second part ("Viral Voyagers") has a localist impulse that uses the literary text as evidence; it moves away from the sociopolitical perspective, focusing instead on what the writings about the illness actually report or conceal. Examining narrative works—some hailed as emblematic, others still marginal—this part is broken into five chapters, organized chronologically, that reflect on what I perceive to be recurring themes in the representation of the crisis in Latin America.

I begin—in chapter 1 of the second part—with a reflection on the traditional link between homosexuality and notions of moral and physical infirmity that in the first half of the twentieth century drove sexual dissidents to travel outside the nation, becoming an itinerant community fleeing the obsessive diagnoses of medicine and the repressive norms of the homeland. These flights toward freedom and the utopian possibility of establishing a community outside the nation allow us to examine how this community would imagine itself over the course of the following decades: first in the celebration of its cosmopolitan liberation, and then, once the epidemic hit, in the certainty of a new sort of extermination or in the survival of a virtual HIV-positive diaspora.

The book offers—in chapter 2—an analysis of the travels of the infection and of infectious travelers, arguing that the stigmatized imagining of the sick person coincided with the urgent search for the epidemic's origin and the vain effort to find the foreign patient zero. The chapter underscores the claim of Latin American dissidents, who, far from accepting the prevailing interpretations, drew their own map of the infection using the virus as a metaphorical weapon to question the capitalist system firmly established on the continent.

Next, chapter 3 examines return journeys to the homeland, a space that is symbolically both a place to die and one that demands an end to state repression of dissidence, inclusion in the national project, and reestablishment of the state's caretaking functions. It is here that the crisis becomes nationalized. But it is precisely in the local sphere that we find a competition for representation in the crucial moment, activating destructive gender-based tensions that lead the affected groups to mutually exclude each other.

In HIV-positive writing, this social dynamic—in chapter 4—is reflected in the restoration of older sexist models that reject any sign of the feminine and problematically celebrate the normative return to a masculinity identified with the biological and political health of the body. The final chapter, which examines the uncertain step from terminal to chronic illness, observes how the community of AIDS survivors continues to be shaped by fear of contact and contagion. In the community's longed-for return to sex and affection, communicative technologies are used as a safe zone for *being* in a virtual community but perhaps no longer for actually *living* together. The incredible liberation mediated by globalization's favorite technology reaffirms, at least in literature, a contradictory step backward.

The varieties of displacement discussed in these pages are multifarious. In the imaginative journeys bravely undertaken in so many AIDS texts, the afflicted dissident does not think of himself as embodying a globalization that could have been—and even briefly appeared to be—liberating. Rather, he sets himself up as its inverse, its negative figuration, as that which threatens that old cosmopolitan utopia. The

Latin American community's place among the least fully globalized regions and communities of the planet allows us to read the carrier of the virus, the sufferer of AIDS, as the deceptive subject of that dream—as "one of the dystopian harbingers of the global village" (Sontag 181). This lucid insight, offered by Susan Sontag at the close of her well-known essay on the disease, is confirmed by the narrative path of many of the texts that compose the Latin American HIV-positive corpus. It must be said, nevertheless, that this is only one reading of the crisis, one that should be joined by others to do justice to the complexity of a representation that is still in development. I do hope, however, that this work will provide keys for interpreting a tragic story that even now, three decades after the epidemic began, remains unfinished.

PART I

Logbook of an HIV-Positive Voyage

Yo he pasado lo que llaman una vida errante, que consiste en no vegetar en una sola de las dependencias de esta posesión nuestra que viene a ser el mundo.

[I have lived what they call a wandering life, which means refusing to stagnate in place in this possession of ours that becomes the world.]

Augusto D'Halmar,
El hermano errante (The wandering brother)

Traveling Epidemics, Rhetorical Infections

I will begin with a well-known fact: every epidemic crosses multiple boundaries. Ruled by an expansionist mandate, it breaches the protective barriers of the organism that involuntarily serves as its host. From there, it travels to other bodies near and far, from the known community to the imagined one.[1] In its clandestine compulsion to travel, this unfortunate companion in any geographic journey rapidly spreads across the vast territories of the planet. The impenitent nomadism of disease is seen again and again throughout history. Leprosy in the eleventh century was carried by humans over hundreds of years to every corner of the known world. The black plague, perhaps the worst epidemic in history, traveled the Orient in rodents that accompanied merchants traveling by sea and on foot and, in frequent and regular outbreaks, devastated fourteenth-century Europe.[2] Many of the old

---

[1] The reference here is to Benedict Anderson's well-known formulation in *Imagined Communities* (1991).

[2] At the time, with the cause of the epidemic (also known as the bubonic plague and the black death) still unknown, Jews were accused of poisoning the water wells, which provoked violent attacks against those communities.

continent's diseases, such as smallpox, yellow fever, and syphilis, benefited from the invasive movement of the European colonizers and decimated the indigenous populations of the Americas and Africa; in the opposite direction, like a furtive form of vengeance, cholera spread destructively across Europe in the nineteenth century through British colonists who brought the disease from India. In the next century, the great viral onslaught came from the so-called Spanish flu, which was neither originally nor exclusively from Iberia but from Europe and the United States. It was extremely lethal, even for a pandemic.[3] The movement of infection never stopped: polio spread slowly but surely, with regular outbreaks and immediate *exportation*. All these epidemics extended to every corner of the mapped world.

Yet its effects were never as widespread nor as synchronic in their assault as those of acquired immunodeficiency syndrome (AIDS), a disease that spread across broader territories than any other epidemic and that has produced a vertiginous upward slope of infections and deaths—a million a year over the past three decades—in an era that has boasted shamelessly of enormous advances in prolonging survival.[4] The HIV virus must have begun making its way around the globe in the mid-1970s, evading possible medical obstacles.[5] Because of its

[3] It is unclear precisely how many people died of the Spanish flu, but it appears to have been between 50 and 100 million people in two years. Unlike the press in other countries, the Spanish press was not censored in the period between the two world wars; the flu was therefore much more widely covered in that country and came to be known as the Spanish flu. For a history of all of these epidemics, see Watts (1999).

[4] It is estimated that the black plague caused 75 million deaths in the fourteenth and fifteenth centuries. This is a remarkable figure, given the population at the time, but relatively speaking the disease had less of an impact than AIDS. In three decades (1980–2010), the syndrome has caused 30 million deaths, and it is estimated that some 35 million people are carriers of HIV. Despite antiretroviral medications, calling this disease *chronic* is a relative matter: some 90 percent of HIV-positive people live in so-called developing countries, where access to medication is often limited or even nonexistent. For up-to-date statistics, see the following official sites: <http://www.avert.org/worldwide-hiv-aids-statistics.htm> and <http://www.unaids.org/en/>.

[5] Recent genealogical studies suggest that the virus must have appeared in Central Africa around 1930, but that in the 1960s it began to circulate more widely thanks to various forms of migration in different directions: tourism, military invasions, and humanitarian efforts, as well as the deployment of international troops to Angola in 1975. See Leiner (1994), de Gordon (2000, 2006), and Gilbert (2007). American scientists currently argue that at the end of the 1970s, HIV infections were entering the immune systems of various groups in the United States, a claim bolstered, in hindsight, by the so-called junkie pneumonia that began to afflict New York heroin addicts starting in 1977. See Epstein (1995).

long incubation period and its multiple possible manifestations, the virus passed from person to person unnoticed or masked by the symptoms of other unusual illnesses that were later dubbed *opportunistic*.[6] It was aided by travel technologies that facilitated movement and left their high-speed mark on the twentieth century. Its vast expansion now unimpeded, HIV spread silently for years across the continents, colonizing new territories and new bodies until its lethal debut in society at large in 1981. The diagnosis fell like a deadly blow, one that was felt simultaneously in the great capitalist metropolises and would reverberate in hundreds of cities around the world. The virus's geographic reach, the speed with which it spread, the slow presentation of its symptoms, and the simultaneity of its appearance across the globe all reinforced the perception of a world in which distances seemed to have shrunk and in which human beings were more connected, *hyperlinked*, a world that evoked unprecedented proximity and the unsettling conviction that we exist in an infinite web of relationships of inevitable infection. Not only did this connectivity (called *global* because it is that term that has most famously captured or capitalized on the shortening of distances and the supposedly equalizing multidirectional flow) make transmission possible, but it also catalyzed the frenetic, uncontrollable spread of this contemporary illness.

Yet we should note, before outlining this complex history, that the virus's accelerated propagation was not merely geographic, following the routes of infection mapped out with careful precision and perhaps with prejudice by epidemiologists. It would not stop at the viral mutations that take place in the spread of any infection. The travels of this virus, like those of all epidemics before it, did not just trace a route through geographic space; their movements have not just had a geopolitical impact but also generated other shifts in meaning: new or renewed cultural significations of illness that both explain the society that produces them and shape its collective imagination. Soon no longer simply an epidemic, the virus became a pandemic[7] of significations. This infection of the

---

[6] This is the term used for the various infections that appear when the immune system collapses. The strangest of these are Kaposi's sarcoma, a viral cancer, and pneumocystis jirovecii, a form of pneumonia caused by a fungus; others include herpes and toxoplasmosis. An opportunistic infection can be any illness that takes advantage of a weakened immune system.

[7] To clarify terms, an *endemic* disease is one that remains within a community; *epidemic* and *pandemic* indicate a greater quantitative, but especially geographic, impact. For the purposes of this book, I use the terms *epidemic* and *pandemic* interchangeably to refer to AIDS.

discourse began with the first hint of the mysterious disease. AIDS and the death that rippled out around it did not just trigger a need for narratives that would attempt to explain the epidemic within the old parameters of movement that had been used for diseases in the past. The production of metaphors for the syndrome also attempted to restrict it rhetorically; to instrumentalize it for ideological ends, whether moralizing and repressive or, in more resistant subcultures, progressive and subversive; to defuse the stigmatizing processes of power over the affected. This process would make new associations, new metaphors, possible. The disease gave rise to a metaphorical language among scientists and doctors, politicians, and the church and its representatives that would be deployed in the mass media. It would appear in testimonial accounts and, somewhat later, in fiction. This language adds, superimposes, or contrasts previous representations of the infected (considered holy and demonic, repulsive and seductive, always endowed with special powers that must be destroyed) with other more contemporary ones, provoking, in the words of insightful medical linguist Paula Treichler, the "chaotic assemblage of our understandings of AIDS" (*How to Have Theory* 11). As Treichler explains it, AIDS, as an epidemic of signification, requires an attentive gaze: the language of metaphor less reflects the reality of the disease than it symbolically constructs it. To put it another way, every illness expressed in language becomes a discursive construction, a powerful cultural artifact, a rhetorical mechanism that can produce adverse social realities. The *plague* (one of those dangerous metaphors)[8] is also a device that generates complementary and contradictory significations, reorganizing past ideas that have traveled to us (from very long ago and very far away) and placing them in the present. In the desperate search for explanations that characterizes any epidemic, other scholars argue,[9] there arise discursive formulations that establish a continuity of meaning that transcends the particularities of the epidemic itself. In its representation, there converge not only previously codified cultural elaborations but also new interpretations taken from the historical context in which the pathology appears. Images from the past are exhumed, and existing or even borrowed prejudices are brought back to life.

---

[8] The word *plague* indicates an invasion of insects or animals, and its impact is agricultural, but Susan Sontag argues that the term has become a negative way to refer to epidemics.

[9] See Rosenberg (1989) and Gilman (1984, 1988).

The set of established metaphors—which is centuries old but always up to date, local but shaped by ideas from beyond a community's borders—is produced by a rhetorical process that is extremely contagious: the metaphors of an epidemic are transmitted with the same intensity as the disease itself and, in becoming a narrative, acquire their own *spatial trajectories*.[10] It is in these trajectories of the language of AIDS, of HIV-positive writing, and of its complex discursive construction that my own reflections begin.

The Impatient Expansion of the Epidemic

It is essential to trace the context of textual production for this epidemic. Unlike the epidemics of the past, this syndrome and the narratives around it have crossed the world, connecting organic, geographic, political, and cultural territories as well as a range of disciplines. Its sudden and simultaneous appearance and the ease of its communicability on a large, even global, scale, as well as the near-immediate mutation and circulation of meanings that confirm it as a discursive epidemic—all of these were secondary effects of a new mobile culture. The decreasing cost of travel and the appearance of new communication technologies that had not been available to previous diseases were part of the long process of capitalism's structural and institutional transformation that began at the end of the nineteenth century. Early industrial capitalism had been a static body: it was controlled from the top by paternalistic-minded magnates who thought of the company as a large family or a vast government bureaucracy, or even as an enormous rigid army, and they took pride in offering jobs in exchange for unconditional loyalty that facilitated worker exploitation. But the more social aspect and especially the bulky bureaucratic structure of that style of capitalism, modeled around large institutions, would become obsolete by the middle of the twentieth century.

---

[10] Michel de Certeau has suggested that the Greek roots of the word *metaphor*—from *metastás* (beyond or after) and *phorein* (to pass or to carry)—contain the idea of mobility. The word brings together both the possibility of story and that of travel: "In modern Athens, the vehicles of mass transportation are called *metaphorai*. To go to work or come home, one takes a 'metaphor': a bus or a train. Stories could also take this noble name: every day, they traverse and organize places; they select and link them together; they make sentences and itineraries out of them. They are spatial trajectories" (115).

The winds of neoliberal logic that would sweep these structures away were echoed in society's new desire for freedom.[11] This cultural shift began, writes a skeptical Richard Sennett, "in the 1960s, that fabled era of free sex and free access to drugs, [when] serious young radicals took aim at institutions, in particular big corporations [of paternalistic capitalism] and big government [of bureaucratic organization], whose size, complexity, and rigidity seemed to hold individuals in an iron grip" (9). These young radicals worked to free the company from its bureaucratic structure and adapt it to the scientific and technological revolution of the 1970s, and to consolidate a new, flexible capitalism, a capitalism that Sennett calls *impatient.* That decidedly radical young person (*so serious,* Sennett emphasizes) emerges as the preferred subject of this new (postindustrial, late, neoliberal, savage, impatient) capitalism: a man (women are never mentioned) who makes impatience his watchword. An adaptable man, ready to let go of the past, of acquired experience; a man who is comfortable with constant change, with endless movement; one who aspires neither to belong nor to stay in one place. Like all of the ideals invoked by the social sciences, this subject who exemplifies the era is a necessary figure, a social construction in which cultural principles acquire a face, a body. Being young, not having significant responsibilities, being able to take risks, wanting to always take the initiative—these were the new professional ideals. Outside of the company, the ideal citizen would also be one who was free to consume, one with an insatiable appetite for new objects and—why not come out and say it?—new bodies. This ideal citizen's consumption would also be governed by the premise of impatience: the Marxist notion of accumulation would be left behind. The new consumer would no longer be a *collector* of things that represent him; he would no longer be entranced by objects. The consumer/collector of yore would become a consumer/tourist who jumps endlessly from one place to another. He would be stimulated not by the object but by the process of acquiring it; desire would die as soon as it was consummated.

So let's tie this all together: the cultural transition from old, static capitalism to impatient capitalism would be the appropriate context in which to cultivate a culture associated with the (equally impatient) expansion of the epidemic, mediated by a new figure linked to the

---

[11] In his book *The Culture of the New Capitalism* (2007), Richard Sennett examines the changes in contemporary free-market culture and concludes that "these changes have not set people free" (13). In this book we can come to the same conclusion: the epidemic is the symptom—both literal and literary—of the free market.

consecration of the movement, speed, and freedom of consumption: the young radical, the *most serious* of the capitalist avant-garde. Though Sennett's image is compelling, it turns out to be incomplete or inadequate: in speaking of the idealized self of the young go-getters, of feverish consumers who are opposed to dependence and to being tied down but who have enormous networks of contacts—that self, whether real or imagined, that tends to think about relationships in terms of transactions—Sennett forgets one possible aspect of their radicalism. After all, who would be the most *serious* in their radicalism? Who carries the lightest communal burden? Who would historically be most willing or even eager to take on risk? These are, of course, rhetorical questions, but it is nevertheless surprising that the sociological narrative makes no note of one group of young people who were more radical than anyone—first known as *homosexuals*, then as *gays*, and now falling into the broad category of *dissidence*.[12] Without stretching the argument too far, I venture to

[12] Naming sexual dissidences or nonnormative sexualities has a complex history. It has been subject to the ebbs and flows of the semantic tide, where each word is marked by local and temporal limitations. The term *homosexual* was coined in the mid-nineteenth century by combining the Greek roots *homós* (equal) and *sexualis* (sexual); thus it etymologically included men and women who were attracted to people of the same sex. Popularized at the end of the nineteenth century for diagnostic purposes, the word came to replace more colloquial and derogatory words, but it remained linked to its punitive medical origins. In the 1980s the word (along with the notions of *masculine* and *feminine*) was gradually called into question and replaced by terms that politicized sexuality while taking into account the wide range of ways in which dissidence was expressed: *gay, lesbian, bisexual, transvestite*, and soon also *transsexual* or *transgender* and, referring to those who oppose any form of assimilation, *queer*. By extension, the abbreviation that brings them together as a political movement has become longer and longer: from LGBT in the 1980s to LGBTTQ at the end of the 1990s. In recent years other groups have arisen—intersex, undecided, asexual—as have variations within different cultures that have been incorporated in a number of local ways into this abbreviation. Because of this linguistic difficulty in a moment of multiplying terminologies, this book will employ generic terms such as *dissidence* or *nonnormative sexuality*, as well as *homosexuality*, a term favored, as will be seen later, by many of the authors cited in this book. According to the nomenclature of each era, *homosexual* referred to those men who maintain erotic and even emotional relationships with men without politicizing or deconstructing their sexuality, while *gay, identidad gay*, or *cultura gay*, terms adopted in Latin America during the transitions to democracy but also problematized in more radical sectors because of their colonial connotations, were used to refer to dissidence that had its origin in the United States, or that distanced itself from the transvestite or transsexual community and attempted to assimilate into socially acceptable conventions. Variations of the local slang (*pájaro, loca, bugarrón*) would be adopted in particular cases, and they would use *lesbiana* to refer to the few dissident women who appear in textual representations of AIDS. (See notes 22, 59, and 104.)

suggest that those young people who escaped the social norm were the ones who paradoxically embodied the system's ideal. Free of matrimonial limitations. Without children to raise or support. Young people whose aimlessness made it difficult for them to map out their future but allowed them to take advantage of the freedoms of the new capitalism. Those dissidents came closer than anyone else to the representation—perhaps stereotyped and reductive yet in many ways accurate—of the community upon which the virus would seem to focus its fury. That community, burdened with a historic stigma but beginning to become liberated, paradoxically fit the shoes of neocapitalist culture better than anyone. Which was why they would also be blamed afterward, when the epidemic and panic began to spread: for exercising that freedom, for their supposed insatiability (the display of which corresponded to the construction and celebration of the most repressed aspects of their collective identity). These men would be blamed, in short, for satisfying a logic of excess that the economic system itself promoted.

The Global as a Fiction of Liberation

But we will leave this thesis, which is not Sennett's but a possible extension of it, unfinished for now; we will pause instead to note that it was only beginning in the 1970s, a decade in which the AIDS virus was already in circulation, that changes in transportation and communication, as well as new financial, economic, and political technologies, came fully into force. These structural and cultural changes that made the epidemic possible were so radical that the era and its spatial and temporal configuration or compression could be given a brand-new name: *the globalized world*. That auspicious and, for a long time, indisputable label (globalization as orthodox truth, as ineluctable destiny, notes Zygmunt Bauman) was widely promoted as an effect and especially as a cause of a shift that was presumed to be democratizing. The initial celebration of the term was based on that utopian aspect, impervious to doubt: that of a finite planet, one that was integrated and accessible to all, of a world order that could no longer be adequately understood using past models such as development versus underdevelopment, center versus periphery, north versus south. Instead, at first, there was a dream of a current of riches that would *flow* globally, in all directions (in the worst-case scenario, the excess of capital would trickle fluidly down[13]—that is, toward the poor) and where wealth would cross borders that were more and more unnecessary, even irrelevant, and reach every corner of the planet. An invisible global hand would parcel out the earnings of the market in a transparent and absolutely free way. The fluidity of the new institutional structures and of capital would be joined by the fluidity of personal communications and of movement, eventually eliminating differences and their segregating effects.

That chimerical vision, promoted by a model of fluidity that acclaimed the freedoms achieved during those years and promised even greater future freedoms of movement (mobility as a coveted value), was only a 1980s-era ideal: while certain globalized intellectuals used the discourse to support their communitarian dreams or consolations, that fiction of increasing freedom gradually proved to be an affliction. Wherever the system had created a degree of economic liberalization, problematic symptoms of crisis appeared: the end of welfare policies, eradicated by neoliberalism; growing economic inequality between and within nations; the enrichment of international elites who were becoming more unified, and the impoverishment of vulnerable economic sectors and the people who lived and worked in them; inverse migration patterns, driven by economic necessity and sometimes by a region's political or sexual violence. The so-called global order was order for some and disorder for others. Or worse, an implacable order that placed some in a position of advantage over others. In the advanced stage of capitalism, globalization came to articulate, legitimize, and consolidate the economic control of the developed world and especially of the unlimited power of multinational corporations, whose headquarters and decision making tend to be located in the most powerful nations. Through trade agreements that defended the free market, these corporations achieved the opposite of economic liberation, limiting the earnings of their counterparts in less influential countries, protecting their own interests, and maximizing their benefits at the expense of other less fortunate nations and workers who were not free to negotiate better terms as a group.

---

[13] Trickle-down theory was an economic program based on tax cuts and other benefits for companies and the upper class, on the assumption that these measures would end up benefiting the population as a whole. Although it is a long-standing economic policy, it tends to be associated with the neoliberal period because it was then that it was most widely disseminated and discussed. Keynesian economists were the most ardent opponents of this theory.

The rightward turn evidenced in the elections of Ronald Reagan and Margaret Thatcher, as well as by the continuation of the Latin American dictatorships, meant an effort to eliminate the welfare state and its social programs, which were gradually being weakened by the antigovernment ideology of neocapitalism, companion of and accomplice to the globalist model. The rhetoric of freedom promoted a logic of ceaseless consumption of goods that favored private companies to the detriment of public institutions, reducing taxes so as to strangle the state and its caretaking functions. The private sector was liberated above the public one, but other freedoms, physical or moral, were also restricted, ones that had been achieved by movements representing vociferous minorities: feminists fighting for the Pill and abortion and divorce; the various communities of sexual dissidents transgressing all the norms of so-called decency. In the rigid conservative mindset, carrying economic freedom to the extreme required repression in more public contexts of liberation. Emancipation unleashed anxieties about lack of control, as if one form of freedom could lead to others—because, in fact, the free market should loosen all restrictions; that was its calling card. For the moralistic right, freedoms related to promiscuity were unacceptable. Conservatives identified them with a communitarianism apparently synonymous with communism, with social decay and degeneration. But those dissident groups were situated, at least in sexual terms, far beyond the norms of the Left, which turned out to be just as moralistic: although there were local interpretations of dogma, for a long time the Left considered homosexuality a bourgeois aberration.

THE DECEPTIVE SEMANTICS OF GLOBAL FLOW

Various sectors of critical thought—from antiglobalization groups that appeared at the end of the 1980s to political scientists, sociologists, anthropologists, postcolonial theorists, travel writers, and cultural critics—sounded the alarm and attempted to decode, point by point, the deceptive semantics of globalization: not just what was hidden beneath the media celebration of its asymmetrical achievements but also its strategic use in maintaining neoimperial political and economic interests. Though aware of the profound technological, economic, political, and cultural changes that linked every area of the planet—even those far removed from the economic benefits that globality seemed to promise—critics still highlighted the political calculus behind these dramatic exclusions. They denounced the global theory and practice that had been created, packaged, and exported (under the marketing label of neoliberalism) to Latin America,[14] historically a space subject to political and economic intervention from the United States. In a polemical early statement, Keynesian economist John Kenneth Galbraith poured water on the happy talk: "We North Americans invented [globalization] to disguise our program of economic intervention in other countries" (qtd. in Pratt, "Why" 277). In a similar vein, the sociologist John O'Neill suggested in 1990 that the global order contains clear hierarchies: "Some nations may consider themselves to be the prime agents in this world order, while others can only maintain an aligned status" (332), their role to defend the very order that works against them.

The responses to the critiques confirmed the problem: in the centers of power, every rejection of that form of intervention was seen as a threat to the global system and was combated through the production of an alarmist discourse. This intimidation strategy was reinforced and made into a spectacle by the mass media, which dismissed any form of resistance, caricaturing any *antiglobalization* movement as *global panic*. And among all the possible political, economic, and social *panics* of capitalism (because capitalism as a system is plagued by a series of crises that paradoxically serve to buttress it), there appeared the emblematic disease of this turn of the century. AIDS would seem to be a most unusual system failure: one social ill, biological in nature, highlighting another that undermined the legitimacy of the state and of aid possibilities in the international order.[15]

Yet the outbreak of the virus-turned-syndrome in the most powerful world capitals was symptomatic of the moment. It took place in an era permeated by the rhetoric of globalization. Science would soon echo the terminology in use, combining notions from other fields—dissolved economic barriers, transgressed national borders, battered military defenses—in a single statement that described multiple vulnerabilities: The syndrome is caused by a joint attack by a number of different agents that from within the body (guerrilla warfare is the model here) take advantage of a defensive system that has been weakened by an invading retrovirus (the model here is war but also foreign invasion). The immune system is the scientific object of the twentieth century, the icon in which "the principal systems of symbolic

---

[14] Henceforth, I will refer only to Spanish-speaking Latin America. I will be discussing neither the unique history of AIDS in Brazil nor its HIV-positive literature.
[15] The link between AIDS and the processes of globalization was suggested, perhaps for the first time, by O'Neill in "AIDS as a Globalizing Panic" (1990).

and material 'difference' in late capitalism" can be seen (Haraway 204), and it is precisely this system that is under threat. The virus, according to medicine's authoritative discourse, does not just penetrate that system but also multiplies rapidly within its cells until they explode, spreading out again through the body, which is more and more defenseless, and transmitting itself to others. This destructive operation is carried out through bodily *fluids*—blood, semen, saliva, tears—fluids that are very much of a piece with the new semantics of the economic system. The nomenclature includes all this but also shifts between a military vocabulary created for the past (yet still all too relevant) and "an infectious language of leakage and containment" (Epstein 6) born of the global logic.

Susan Sontag writes in a brilliant essay that the syndrome's narrative production made use of the long-established repertoire of metaphors of illness, precariously balanced between the idealization of the patient and the stigmatization of the ill, and soon leaned toward the more negative representation, borrowing images from its own era. Examining the metaphorization of various illnesses—the plague as divine punishment, the mark of the sacred in leprosy, the excess of passion and artistic distinction of tuberculosis and its subsequent identification with poverty, the frigidity of women with cancer— Sontag notes that AIDS ended up reinforcing the most dangerous metaphor: the infected person as a threat to society and the illness as a form of political aggression by something that is able to cross borders. A sophisticated reader of metaphor, Sontag clearly sees that updated and exaggerated image in the early metaphors of AIDS: the body/nation invaded or assaulted by a foreign virus that would defeat the defensive army or, in other versions, the AIDS patient as a Third-World guerrilla fighter or terrorist threatening the imagined health of the nation. In these warlike interpretations of the syndrome (sometimes glamorized but always ominous), the critic adds, the attack is always the result of a foreign incursion, of an invasive movement. Sontag objects to the stigmatizing use of language that identifies illness with an infectious agent that must be suppressed, metonymically identifying the sick person with an enemy to be eliminated. And yet she too employs expressions and ideas that are linked to or come from economics (moralistic *inflation*, metaphorical *inflation*, and, most problematically, the image of the infection as *liquid*: the health of the body defined by its fluids and not, as in antiquity, by its humors). Sontag claims, in an authoritative scientific tone, that "one gets [AIDS] from the blood or sexual fluids of infected people or from contaminated blood products" (105). This way of seeing the body owes a debt to the new metaphorical articulation of the global world, connected by flows. Sontag stumbles into the rhetorical trap of the moment when she contrasts the mobility of AIDS with cancer as the effect of physical and especially emotional stagnation,[16] of repressed and domestic sexuality indicated by a slow growth within the body (a vivid image of unwanted pregnancy) that perhaps explains the marked gender difference in the representation of the two diseases: cancer is seen as a feminine, noncontagious disease, while AIDS is seen as the result of the transmission of fluids between masculine bodies.

The distinction is clearly a product of its context, of the ideas prevailing at the time that each illness entered the public discourse. It is evident in texts written at the same time as Sontag's essay, such as the poem "Autoepitafio" (Auto-Epitaph) by the Cuban writer Reinaldo Arenas, a prominent victim of the disease. His dying voice is raised not just in denunciation but also as a clear affirmation of pleasure when he writes, "(Ni después de muerto quiso vivir quieto). / Ordenó que sus cenizas fueran lanzadas al mar / donde habrán de fluir constantemente" [(Not even after death did he wish to live quietly.) / He ordered his ashes thrown into the sea / where they would flow constantly][17] ("Autoepitafio"). In this final poem, Arenas vitally identifies himself with incessant movement; he chooses to *flow* eternally. The liquidness of the sea becomes a metaphor for identity itself, the emancipation of desire against the oppressive stability of the homeland: the sea refers not just to the Mariel boatlift that allowed him to escape into exile from Cuba but also, more abstractly, to fluidness as a utopia of emancipation even beyond death. It is that infectious rhetoric of freedom borrowed from globalization that Sontag uses, without noticing fluidity's own contradictions. But Sontag is merely employing the vocabulary that her era put at her disposal, a rhetoric normalized by hegemonic thinking; it is as if power had managed to impose its system of values, normalizing its standards and its terms until they became imperceptible. It was perhaps for that reason that when her essays on illness appeared, Sontag was criticized not for the use of these terms but for her warning about the use of metaphor. In *AIDS and Its Metaphors* (1989), written soon after the syndrome

---

[16] Emotional repression is particularly associated with women, as if cancer were a reincarnation of the symptoms of hysteria, an illness in which the sufferer expresses too much but reveals very little.

[17] *Translator's note*: Unless otherwise indicated, all translations are mine.

had acquired an official, definitive name[18] and a decade after *Illness as Metaphor* (1978), Sontag would respond to her critics by claiming that language requires metaphors, that they are inevitable, that it is impossible to think or speak without them; it was nevertheless necessary, she insisted, to constantly tweak that rhetorical device to minimize its damaging effects and to refrain from constructing distorted realities for those affected.[19] It is curious, then, that Sontag criticizes the rhetorical manipulation of infection—its harmful and fluid images of war—but does not stop to examine the semantics of economics—the fluid image of viral transmission that echoes that of *flow*, the ultimate metaphor of globalization—and its clearly colonialist overtones. The notion of a world theorized in economic terms and reconsidered by intellectuals from a variety of disciplines was not, after all, a neutral one;[20] but only later would the admittedly incisive metaphor of flow be called into question. Zygmunt Bauman would argue that *liquid* modernity is characterized by the provisional nature of social relationships in the contemporary world; postcolonial theorist Mary Louise Pratt had an even more political take on that liquidness, pointing out that this fluidity did not *flow* well: it did not move equally in all directions. Its movement was not accidental, nor were the interests that guided it—the supposedly incorporeal hands of the market. But these scholars provided neither an alternative image or metaphor, nor threadbare and possibly reductive geopolitical conceptualizations (north-south, center-periphery). What they

---

[18] The syndrome was initially called GRID (gay-related immune deficiency), but the name was replaced in 1982 by the more neutral HIV/AIDS. The discarded acronym is, perhaps not surprisingly, a noun commonly used in the globalization debate, as *grid* refers to a supposed communicative blanket that would cover the world. As Pratt (2006) indicates, its reach is in fact limited because the weakened neoliberal state cannot provide what companies will not give if they do not see potential profits in extending communications to less densely populated areas (that is, areas where the market is limited).

[19] It is important to note here that Sontag sees the sick person as being always in a position of weakness, without imagining that he, too, produces language and appropriates metaphors. An example of this process is apparent in literature, especially AIDS literature, in which authors give new meanings to many metaphors, such as the animal metaphors used to stigmatize them.

[20] From progressive literary critic Susan Sontag to the presumably descriptive approach of Arjun Appadurai's cultural anthropology, globalization has been thought of as a dynamic process, as simultaneous flows of people, information, technologies, capital, and ideology that move in space and time, shaping and even transforming culture. Among these linked flows, Appadurai claims, AIDS is just another manifestation (50).

offered instead was a denunciation: globalization as a reformulation of trickle-down economics, but now without even considering a future distribution of excess wealth. Pratt aimed her critical gaze at imperialism once more, recalling an endless list of subjects ravaged by innumerable economic and, by extension, human abuses. Those subjects, Pratt argues, refute the imaginary flow of the system and therefore, adds Richard Sennett, "the sick...can be stigmatized for showing their neediness" (62), which works against the idea of flow.

We should return to Sontag on this point: the problem is not that she avoided the evident lethal expansion of the syndrome or did not perceive the clear connection between the breakneck speed of infection and the contemporary velocities of inequality. It is, rather, that her reading offers no critical alternative to the language of globalization. Her gaze is determined by the place in which the epidemic was produced, and there does not appear to be enough distance, either spatial or temporal, to detect the degree to which the prevailing ideology influences every context. Even undermining her own ideas, Sontag seems to be immersed in the hegemonic discourse of capitalist freedom or perhaps permeated by a sort of 1970s-era progressive utopianism. She makes her argument convinced that the society of new global capitalism and its white, heterosexual citizens will rush to the rescue of those marginalized subjects in crisis. And I say "crisis" in multiple senses: as organic collapse, as an instance of social dissent, as political disorder. For Sontag and other American thinkers who follow her, if the syndrome is the effect of a relationship of flows between bodies, between nations and continents, if it is an epidemic of global proportions, then the response must be as well. As Sontag puts it, "the AIDS crisis is evidence of a world in which nothing important is regional, local, limited; in which everything that can circulate does, and every problem is, or is destined to become, worldwide" (180). This line of thinking could suggest, in short, that nothing carries any weight if it does not bear the insignia of globalism. The epidemic event has an impact and broad significance because it transcends its own limited geography: it is not just another natural disaster in Africa or Latin America; instead, it involves the citizens of the whole world. Sontag does not wonder, however, how the local is defined or why the millions of affected Africans are local while the millions of Americans count as global. The model for entering the current of world concerns is not called into question; Sontag does not contemplate what ethereal hands control the strings of relevance. She seems to accept (because if there is irony there, Sontag does not show it) the logic of a system in which some citizens are more visible than others, circulate more than others, are more citizens of the world than others. She then concedes that the global trumps the infinite localities that constitute it. And that concession anticipates another that is even more troubling: if the crisis stops afflicting particular citizens from particular countries, will the problem of AIDS disappear from the global agenda?

We can conjecture, in retrospect, that the numberless HIV-positive inhabitants of the poor countries managed to slip into the *global* concerns of the richer countries precisely because they were part of the narrative of the crisis, the necessary explanatory or causal element, and because they shared the same symptoms. The loss of interest in the origin and transmission of this disease, once they were understood, and the discovery in the mid-1990s of the combination of medications that would control the illness marked the beginning of the disappearance from the media of poor countries and their affected citizens. It could even be surmised that AIDS attained the world stage because it appeared in highly visible areas of the world such as the densely populated cities of the United States—Los Angeles, San Francisco, and New York, as well as Washington and Miami—and because the meager information about the topic was an immediate sensation in the media, confirming intense social prejudices about the sexual freedom of minorities during a period of renewed conservatism. The virus detected in the United States, like everything American, acquired immediate international relevance. The panic spread to the rest of the world when it became clear that the syndrome was invariably fatal, that its long, silent latency period delayed carriers' discovery of their infection and hindered the containment of the infection, that diagnoses of the disease were appearing in countless cities and villages in different countries: from Switzerland to Tanzania and other parts of Africa; from Haiti to Paris to some areas of Asia, Brazil, and the Spanish-speaking Americas. The United States and, to a lesser extent, France became centers for disseminating news about the disaster that would soon be associated exclusively with those *strange* men who, one suspected or even knew, had sex with other men.

A Dissident Wandering

Before moving any further, to read this *epidemic of globalization* we must identify the main actors involved: those *different* men, with secret private lives, who were called *homosexuals* or called themselves *gays*, who flew the rainbow flag in the years of the transition to democracy, transvestites who sometimes regarded them with suspicion, transsexuals and queers, and the multiple communities—whether unified or scattered to the winds, nomadic, virtual, or imaginary—that would play a starring role in and document the crisis. That diverse group of sexual dissidents, all driven by an impulse to wander, would in the 1980s be faced with an epidemic that tragically revitalized the early link between homosexuality, pathology, and displacement. Pathologized by normative narratives that deemed them dangerous, denied the privilege of belonging—except, claims Sylvia Molloy, when they made of their gender posing a political statement—and faced with a national project of inclusion that excluded them or even pushed them to leave, these ever-suspect men would be identified with the figure of the exile, he who is *out of place*, the stranger, the foreigner.

In fact, the journey—whether real or imaginary—represented the only way to escape the stigma of moral and mental illness imposed on them for centuries by modern judicial and scientific systems. The figures of the *invert* and the *Uranian*[21] (the latter, according to Néstor Perlongher, being a more poetic expression) already existed and coexisted, but medicalization took place in the form of a neologism (*homosexual*) that was not at all poetic. This term was coined in Europe in 1869 by an eccentric Hungarian doctor who answered to the names Károly Mária Kertbeny and Karl-Maria Benkert; the medical category was exported to the rest of the Western world at the end of the nineteenth century, generating, according to Gabriel Giorgi, a renewed obsession with diagnosis that would be scrupulously exercised on those suspected of engaging in unspeakable acts. The corrective power of the sciences came to supplement or even supplant the powerful religious fictions of heresy and unnatural sin in Latin America—sin was made flesh by science, pathologized, producing strategies of systematic intervention designed to *cure* that evil and eliminate it from the social imaginary, as if it were a source of infection for the nation.[22] The nightmares of isolation, persecution, and extermination experienced by homosexuals of the time has marked

---

[21] This nineteenth-century term referred to people who have a female psyche in a male body (that is, men who are attracted to people of the same biological sex). It would later be extended to so-called transgender women.

[22] The proposed nomenclature traveled to Latin America and was recycled there, though with some differences in meaning: in many places *homosexual* was—and still is—reserved for effeminate men, also called *passive* or *penetrated*; the imported medical-legal taxonomy was never used for *active*, *penetrating*, or *virile* men. See Guerra Cunningham (105). (See notes 12, 59, and 104.)

fiction—from very early on and until very recently—with a tragic out-look, doomed to isolation or even annihilation. Augusto D'Halmar's anguished *Pasión y muerte del cura Deusto* (1924; The passion and death of Father Deusto), perhaps the first Latin American novel to deal with a sexual relationship between men; the gloomy figure of Manuela in José Donoso's *El lugar sin límites* (1966; *Hell Has No Limits*); Molina in Manuel Puig's *El beso de la mujer araña* (1976; *Kiss of the Spider Woman*), jailed as a sexual dissident and then murdered in his only moment of political and romantic courage—these are simply variations on a single scenario that offers no way out. These fictions of annihilation, which use the sexual violence suffered by dissidents as a metaphor, are also expressed in dreams of escape that promise survival. Attempting to avoid the systems of moral indoctrination, conversion therapies, and intimidation that threaten their psychological and even physical well-being, efforts to survive tend toward estrangement. Two models of estrangement complement and oppose one another; they overlap, diverge, and come back together in the imagining of homosexuality. On the one hand, internal exile, which feeds off the contrasts of the homosexual experience, that clandestinity, the code languages that actively seek the decoding of their *open secret*.[23] And on the other, external exile—the various forms of wandering, geographic drift, that personal deviation from the norm so eloquently described by Sylvia Molloy. But before that, others had thought of the journey as a form of penitence.

"Yo he pasado lo que llaman una vida errante que consiste en no vegetar en una sola de las dependencias de esta posesión nuestra que viene a ser el mundo" [I have lived what they call a wandering life, which means refusing to stagnate in place in this possession of ours that becomes the world] (*El hermano* 220), writes the impenitent traveler Augusto D'Halmar (Augusto Goemine Thomson, who not only left Chile but also fled his original name). Not only is wandering a state of perpetually abandoning, but it also indicates a search—the wanderer leaves a place in an effort to reach a better one. In his chronicle *El hermano errante*, quoted above, D'Halmar says, "No tenía ni una madriguera que pudiera llamar hogar, ni un simple agujero que me sirviese de patria, yo a quien no esperaba nadie en ninguna parte

---

[23] José Quiroga uses this oxymoron. The community, he says, "know[s] exactly what to read, while the writers go on with their social affairs" (25). These decrypting techniques for the initiated are also an aesthetic and political strategy, maneuvers that function as a mask that in concealing the true face also reveals the very act of concealment.

y que no poseía sino todo el mundo y toda la vida, el pabellón unitario de los cielos y la desolada libertad de ser un hombre de doquiera, deseé limitarme, recluirme en algún sitio que me fuese propicio" [I had no lair to call my own, not even a simple hole in the ground as my homeland, and no one waiting for me anywhere. Possessing nothing more than the whole world and my whole life, the vast pavilion of the heavens and the desolate freedom of being a man from anywhere, I wanted to limit myself, to shut myself away in some place that was to my liking] (222). Here, he uses the verb *recluir* [to lock up or shut away], imagines his arrival in *algún sitio* [some place] that remains as yet unidentified. Half a century later, Reinaldo Arenas would echo D'Halmar's longing: "Un homosexual es un ser aéreo, desasido, sin sitio fijo o propio, que anhela de alguna manera retornar a no se sabe exactamente qué lugar" [A homosexual is an aerial, untethered being, with no fixed place, no place to call his own, who yearns to return to . . . —but, my friends, he knows not where] (*El color* 403; *The Color* 358). The homosexual's departure was seen back then as an uncertain geographic displacement: abandoning home, migrating from countryside to city, journeying abroad in vagabondage or tourism or even the painful permanence of exile. Travel would allow those wanderers to escape a closed space and enter another, and especially to enter into contact with others like them and create a shared fiction in which national origin was less determinant. It was as if those displacements—whether real or only imagined and fictionalized— were preparatory exercises for initiation into the mobile community that would form over the course of the following decades. Under the patronage of the new capitalist travel industry, that chronic anguish, that chronic unsatisfied desire, would become the community's capital: that energy would mobilize the transnational circulation of the fictions that preceded the epidemic and shaped the formation of a dissident identity, of a community of affinities that spanned national boundaries.

If we go back in time, we find that it was the operation of the free market itself that provided the way out of the disciplinary, armored, excluding nation toward a space that transcended borders, one in which the excluded could imagine another kind of community: the community beyond. But outside of what center? Out in the periphery? More than one historian of homosexuality has suggested that the diaspora has moved not toward the margins but instead gradually toward the most populous cities, toward the capitals. Already at the beginning of the twentieth century, the mechanisms of industrial production had produced a progressive weakening of the cohesive and watchful structure of the family (and of its subsistence economy) by causing people to leave their homes in the suburbs or countryside. The youngest members left in search of work in the cities. These displacements moved mostly within but occasionally outside national territory, and were evident in labor migration from country to city, from town to city, and eventually from poor countries to rich ones. They produced previously unimaginable contact between populations. In industrial cities, displaced people encountered others like them, discovering shared shameful desires and seeing themselves, perhaps for the first time, as part of a community of equals. The incipient mechanisms of identification caused associations that, though they were clandestine and marginal, gave rise to collectives that transcended (though without necessarily being in open opposition to) the nation, which continued, through political, legal, medical, and religious apparatuses, to repress these *deviations.*[24]

This process taking place within nations was also mirrored outside them in a series of desire-filled journeys that were never read as such.[25] These *wanderings* characterized a whole generation. The abovementioned D'Halmar, for example, was carried by the maritime transport industry to new destinations and offered experiences that were still unthinkable in his homeland. Ahead of his time, the Chilean had in 1904 helped found the Colonia Tolstoyana, where he strove, behind the protective facade of a literary and artistic coterie, to solidify an ambiguous relationship between himself and one of his writer friends. But a group of that sort did not provide favorable conditions. Taking advantage of his diplomatic post, D'Halmar then left in search of a community abroad. We see this undertaking

---

[24] In a now classic article, "Capitalism and Gay Identity," the historian John D'Emilio has explained this relationship. In addition, in *Médicos, maleantes y maricas* Jorge Salessi discusses a similar process in Argentina, describing the relationship between modernity, capitalist development, and the unwelcome visibility of the homosexual in Buenos Aires, which would often be punished. Under Peronism, for example, state support for the revival of tango came at least in part from a desire to rein in homosexuality and encourage a more heterosexual urban eroticism.

[25] The Orientalist French and Anglo-Saxon journeys examined by the postcolonial critic Joseph Boone are charged with homoeroticism; nevertheless, the libidinal energy that drove the travelers does not appear in the analysis of Edward Said, the theorist who coined the term. In *Orientalism* (1978), Said defines the term as a longstanding practice that generates idealized or simply distorted images of the Middle East and Asia that have served to justify colonial interventions. Yet in looking at the images constructed by travelers, Said fails to examine the component of desire and the presence of homosexual tourists; it is for precisely this omission that Boone criticizes him.

again and again: world travel becomes the biographical commonplace of early sexual dissidence, raising dissidents' awareness of a transnational group gradually being established in a number of cities across the globe. The historical trend indicates that although until the mid-twentieth century the possibility of finding and forming an eccentric community was hardly even imaginable, those strange solitary men, later aided by the amazing technologies of the capitalist system, were able to create concrete options not just in major metropolises but in the invented capitals of fiction.

This process would take a while. For a long time, the incipient formation of alternative communities took place behind the nation's back, sometimes outside the nation altogether. Yet the community also existed in its members' imaginations. Such is Benedict Anderson's claim, in the abstract but possible plane of theory: communities distinguish themselves from one another through how they imagine themselves, through the images they create of themselves in texts that circulate among their members. And we should therefore highlight an exception to the concealment generally found in continental fiction, a scene—one that I consider foundational to the dissident community—that appears in the Argentine novel by Polish writer Witold Gombrowicz, *Trans-Atlantyk* (1953), so titled after the ocean voyage that brought the writer to the southern capital, and especially because of his transoceanic, transcultural, transgressive aim: to reject the idea of the nation and instead form relationships based on sexual associations. The novel includes not just a diatribe against the fatherland's demands for sacrifice but also a vision of a community articulated by the eroticism of the young sons of that fatherland. The *filistria* (sonland) celebrated in the novel is conceived as a betrayal (the suspicion of betrayal is another commonplace in homosexual writing); its members, a carnivalesque combination of freaks of nature and seductive young men in pursuit of mutual pleasure, would be the new militants of a sect for which national origin was subordinated to desire. The novel is marked by the demands of origin: the old Poles are there to ensure that the young men exiled in Buenos Aires maintain their moral standing, sexual purity, mental health, and military loyalty, even thousands of kilometers away from home. It is against those assumptions of national belonging that the novel pushes. *Trans-Atlantyk* is itself a radically free text, but it is the tale of characters trapped by two simultaneous local forces: the Argentine nation and the Polish nation-in-exile. The author seems to suggest that a citizen cannot simply leave—not yet. The nation is dragged along to every new destination. And the gesture of resistance symbolically set out in the plot is the push to eliminate the nation—to shoot it down if necessary. In inventing a community in opposition to the national imperative, *Trans-Atlantyk* is a novel ahead of its time, and its central themes resonated with only a few readers. Judging by the silence narrated in subsequent texts, some time would have to pass before that fictional community could become reality.

So let's move ahead, skipping a few decades as we follow the sometimes inconstant trail from Gombrowiczian *filistria* to the communitarian fiction of Reinaldo Arenas, a late contemporary of the Pole who, in contrast to the other writer, presented himself more nakedly, shattering all taboos. Arenas, who died of AIDS in 1990, used his last years to directly question the homophobic assumptions that undergirded Castro's revolutionary project and to confirm, in a settling of scores that was never complete, ever recurrent in his writing, the power that the regime had over his work. His enormous novel *El color del verano o Nuevo jardín de las delicias* (1990; *The Color of Summer, or New Garden of Earthly Delights*), written or dictated while Arenas was also finishing his autobiography, follows the trials and tribulations of Cuban *pájaros* ["birds," a slang term for homosexuals], a multitude, a supposed nation that has no place within national borders—and perhaps not outside it, either. They are a people who live in the air because there, at least, there are no borders; a people, Arenas writes, who are always, even on land, ready to take flight in pursuit of pleasure.[26]

The *patria pájara* [nation of *pájaros*] that Arenas positions in opposition to Castro's unyielding male chauvinism (or, in the words of Zoé Valdés, another *gusana* like Arenas, his "*machismo-leninismo*" [chauvinist Leninism]) is radically mobile; in flight, it surpasses not only the expected spatial boundaries but also temporal ones. It is an imagined homeland, but one that exists at the wrong time, or despite

---

[26] Reinaldo Arenas appropriates the pernicious animal metaphors used for homosexuals, redefining and deactivating them by rehabilitating them as fundamentally liberating epithets. Similarly, it is important to note that these zoomorphic metaphors abound in the homosexual corpus as a way to resist certain stigmatizing discourses that, according to the sociologist Erwin Goffman, suggest that "the person with a stigma is not quite human" (5). For an exploration of the repeated use of these zoomorphic metaphors (especially flying creatures such as *pájaros* [birds], *palomas* [pigeons], *patos* [ducks], *gansos* [geese], *gallinas* [hens], *mariposas* [butterflies], *mariquitas* [ladybugs], *abejas reina* [queen bees], and *hadas* [fairies]) to refer to homosexuals of both sexes in different countries and cultural and linguistic contexts, see the exhaustive lexicographical, literary, and media analysis of La Fountain-Stokes (2007).

time, or outside time because it includes dissidents from every era. His writing brings together the political heroes of yesteryear and the intellectuals and writers of the global canon; Arenas, wise exegete of the "language of implications" (Quiroga), includes Gombrowicz among them. Each member of this winged country exhibits a double affiliation: they are, as noted above, existential exiles who continue to inhabit national coordinates, bearing, in their transcendent flight, the indelible marks of their own culture in a foreign place. Without ridding itself of that baggage entirely, but lightening the load, this mobile community understands origin as something that makes its members part of but also *separates* them from the national community, allowing them and other homelandless to see exile as a reality that became a possibility in the 1980s.

Migrations to the Gay Ghetto

Taken together, the biography and writing of Reinaldo Arenas allow us to examine the before and after of the community at the turning point of the epidemic. The work of this compulsive storyteller contains both a Cuban time that imagines itself to be immune to the virus and another, later American time—the AIDS era. Arenas has unwittingly[27] gone into exile in the heart of the epidemic. He takes the Mariel boatlift to Miami in 1980 a few months before the mysterious *pink plague* lands in New York, when the illness begins to spread, both in real life and in the discourse. In his paradoxical flight from Cuba, Arenas travels toward a culturally determined end, as a member of that "estirpe condenada que lleva en su cuerpo la marca de una eliminación prometida" [doomed bloodline that bears on its body the mark of a promised elimination] (Giorgi, *Sueños* 23). This anti-Castro ambassador of Latin American AIDS arrives in a city that still remembered the confrontations in the Stonewall bar[28] at the

---

[27] As the author tells it in *Antes que anochezca* (*Before Night Falls*), leaving seemed an impossibility: Arenas was on the government's blacklist. It was only by chance that a single letter—a skinny *e* that he crowned with a dot, disguising it as an *i*—threw off the official inspecting his papers and got him out of the country as Reinaldo *Arinas*.

[28] The Stonewall bar was a meeting point for a New York's diverse gay community. On June 28, 1969, the police carried out a raid that sparked a series of violent, drawn-out riots as a spontaneous reaction from the dissident community not just against the police force but also against the United States' homophobic legal system. The diverse and dispersed community came together in the following weeks and organized forces to put an end to arrests of homosexuals. This event also made possible the subsequent formation of activist collectives in the United States.

end of the 1970s, which marked a watershed moment for American dissident cultures: for the first time, the gay community was fending off police attacks, denouncing homophobia, and demonstrating the power it had attained. It was during this period that certain laws were changed and less discriminatory policies put in place, allowing a sort of mainstreaming of dissidence in the international public arena. The author reflects briefly on these events in *Antes que anochezca* (*Before Night Falls*), one of his last books. In it, there is an ongoing battle to demedicalize homosexuality, to do away with secrecy, with illegitimacy, with homosexuals' reputation as being somehow abnormal. There is also a sexual liberation—the utopia of an emancipation achieved—that is magnetic, pulling Arenas into the celebration of freedom upon his arrival. According to Perlongher, another insightful observer of the period, in *El fantasma del sida* (1988; The ghost of AIDS), the new "territorialización de las poblaciones homosexuales norteamericanas, que con tanto frenesí habían salido de los roperos del ocultamiento" [territorialization of the American homosexual populations, which had so eagerly come out of the closets where they'd been hiding] (58) became a model for other dissidents and their fledgling movements:

> Hubo verdaderas migraciones hacia los grandes guetos gay (barrios enteros habitados solo por homosexuales) de Nueva York y California. La ciudad de San Francisco, centro cultural de beatniks y hippies, se convertiría en la capital del mundo homosexual: mundo de círculos cerrados donde un gay se relaciona solo con otro gay…, pero también verdaderos laboratorios de experimentación sexual. (58–59)
> [There were migrations to the large gay ghettos (entire neighborhoods inhabited exclusively by homosexuals) of New York and California. The city of San Francisco, cultural center for beatniks and hippies, became the capital of the homosexual world: a world of closed circles in which gays interacted only with other gays…, but also true laboratories of sexual experimentation.]

This opening up seemed to coincide with an expansion of the unstable threshold of permissibility for openly transgressive behaviors and the unrestrained consumption of sex in clubs, bars, bathhouses, and other commercial establishments of the lifestyle. All of these developments moved in concert with influential American gay organizations, with a way of thinking that was beginning to prevail in certain spaces.

But the celebration of freedom would not last long enough in the festive, sleepless city, as seen in the story of two Puerto Rican writers who settled in Manhattan: the celebrated writer Manuel Ramos Otero, who died in 1990, the same year that Arenas died and also the year that Alberto Sandoval was diagnosed with the disease that would leave him blind in one eye. In his description of the frenzied period he survived, Sandoval recalls an entire "generation of Latino gay men that in a self-imposed sexile migrated to the United States from the Caribbean and Latin America in search of independence and sex, satisfaction and love" (311). Sandoval puts exact dates on this period of the gay liberation "party":

> [It] started with the Stonewall riots in 1969 [and] was over by 1982 with the intrusion of AIDS. We all witnessed when Thanatos killed Eros with the mirrored disco ball on the dance floor. Gone with it were the beams of light that penetrated every single heart to the beat of Donna Summer's erotic cadence of "love to love you baby." Gone were the dancing bodies covered in sweat, smelling sex, desiring an orgasm that would be fatal attraction. *Uno tras otro*, one after the other they succumbed to AIDS: Enrique from Cuba, Hernán from Colombia, Conrado from Puerto Rico, Orlando from Venezuela, Manuel from El Salvador, José from México, Luis from Panama. (311)

Arenas, from Holguín, Cuba, was an astute reader of the cultural tea leaves and also an extraordinary fabulist. Watching the slaughter, he developed a conspiracy theory inspired by a number of rumors, according to which the army of cosmopolitan fags, as Arenas calls it in *El color de verano*,[29] that had sought shelter from Latin American homophobia on the streets and in the parks of New York City was now the target of an attack by an alliance between reactionary powers that had put aside their ideological disagreements and granted Fidel Castro a dominant role in the assault, dropping a viral bomb that would destroy them all. In Arenas's HIV-positive work, the virus became a device manufactured for political ends, a biological weapon aimed at the cosmopolitan community. It was from there that the disease would spread as a virus, splintering out across the planet. Arenas thus inverts the official route of infection, placing its center in

---

[29] In his novel, Arenas refers to "ejércitos clandestinos, silenciosos y siempre en peligro inminente pero que no estaban dispuestos, de ninguna manera, a renunciar a la vida, esto es, a hacer gozar a los demás" [clandestine, silent armies, always in imminent danger of defeat but utterly unwilling to renounce life, which is defined by giving pleasure to others] (*El color* 401; *The Color* 356). He later discusses the "ejércitos del placer" [armies of pleasure] (*El color* 404; *The Color* 358).

the developed world. He also turns the blame back on the capitalist north, which he saw as being as reactionary as the socialist south. An analysis of the circumstances nevertheless makes it clear that the process of the liberation and organization of nonnormative sexualities had a much more turbulent and inauspicious beginning in Latin America than in the United States. Their difficulties are many and varied—and sometimes contradictory. The nascent emancipation movements were first violently repressed by the right-wing military dictatorships (which controlled most of the continent by the 1970s), but homosexuals suffered just as much under the left-wing revolutionary regimes, which considered them a bourgeois aberration that must be extirpated. The community in each country had a rocky road toward liberation, and each tells a story of slowly finding the pulse of freedom.

But here I must pause for a moment on the paradigmatic case of Chilean sexual dissidence, where a harsh Left and a repressive, pragmatic Right joined forces. The liberation movement had begun in the pro-Allende demonstrations of 1972, marches that were not entirely welcome. After the coup the following year, the more visible homosexuals became collateral victims of the repression that came down on the Left and on any citizen suspected of political dissidence (Robles, "History in the Making" 36). But after a long, repressive wait, the military regime's capitalist convictions would paradoxically liberate the homosexual community. In importing the American economic model, the Chilean "Chicago boys"[30] facilitated the loosening of restrictions on sexual exchange with prostitutes and transvestites, as dictated by neoliberal market theory. In the laboratory of Chilean capitalism, sexual consumption—which came along with certain tourist elements—was another niche market to be exploited. The dictatorship was thus forced to juggle a liberalized economy and the rigid morality the military had promised to the upper classes. It was a delicate maneuver: allowing the existence of dives that facilitated sexual transactions, interfering with these alternative spaces only sporadically and temporarily, while also reassuring the traditional sectors. The scene is described in the accounts of transvestite writer Pedro Lemebel and confirmed by Jorge Marchant Lazcano, his compatriot and contemporary, in the novel *Sangre como la mía* (2006; Blood like

---

[30] The Chicago boys, a group formed by Milton Friedman and Arnold Harberger at the University of Chicago, also included economists from Mexico, Costa Rica, Argentina, and Uruguay who would be influential in the neoliberal economic restructuring of their respective countries during this period.

mine): there were gay bars under the dictatorship, a few nightclubs, countless young men in a park in downtown Santiago after curfew. Rather than actively pursuing them, the police showed up from time to time and selected a few individuals to be punished and quell conservative anxieties for a while. Another political extravagance: keeping sodomy illegal but turning a blind eye to it.[31] The homosexual body was neither a preferred target for extermination nor a primary object of violence (although there was ridicule and abuse, disappearance and death) because in the perverse military mind it acquired the seductive gleam of profit.

But the relief that the international economic model offered to these minority populations was, predictably enough, a double-edged sword. And Pedro Lemebel gestured toward this danger throughout his prolific career, arguing that the free market had only temporarily spared Chilean homosexuals: the opening of economic borders had introduced to Chile not only the neoliberal logic of the market and its capitals but also foreign ideas that would transform sexual behaviors and destroy the uniqueness of the transvestite communities. From his local vantage point, the so-called globalization of sexualities looked like a deceptive liberation. The arrival of American gay ideology threatened to wipe out the unacceptable *loca* [transvestite] in favor of the virile and viral homosexual. Indeed, if, as the Mexican writer Carlos Monsiváis claims, "el gay latinoamericano *es* el travesti" [the Latin American gay *is* the transvestite] and "sólo hay un tipo de homosexual: el afeminado" [there is only one type of homosexual: the effeminate male],[32] then all dissidence on the southern continent would end up disappearing, suffocated by a homosexuality (rebranded *gay*) that had been co-opted by the market and reproduced relationships of domination. HIV became, in Lemebel's acid commentaries, a metaphor for the ideological extermination of the local *loca* under American empire.[33] Lemebel expressed his wariness quite clearly in

---

[31] Sodomy remained a crime between consenting adults until 1999, when consensual sex between men was decriminalized. The age of consent for homosexual male sex, however, was set at 18, even though the age of consent for heterosexual and lesbian sex is 14.

[32] Quoted in Molloy and McKee (30).

[33] Years later, this opposition to neocolonialism would be repeated in an article on Spanish singer Miguel Bosé. Regarding Bosé's public stance on his sexual orientation, Lemebel would write, "Ese cuento de la bisexualidad de los famosos siempre me ha sonado a negocio" [That old story that celebrities tell about how they're bisexual has always sounded like marketing to me] (*Adiós* 182).

a visit to Manhattan for a gay pride parade in 1994, in which he participated dressed as a haloed Christ with a crown of "thorns" (syringes full of infected blood) and carrying a suggestive poster, written in English: "Chile returns AIDS." Not only was Lemebel symbolically and peformatively carrying AIDS back to its supposed point of origin, but he was also declaring—or, rather, restating—his notion of a community split between the pathetic feminine queen and the ideal of the masculine gay, who could never belong to the same community. Along these lines, he recounts a visit to the historic Stonewall bar, where he perceives that the American gays consider him inferior:

> Y como te van a ver si uno es tan re fea y arrastra por el mundo su desnutrición de loca tercermundista. Como te van a dar pelota si uno lleva esta cara chilena asombrada frente a este Olimpo de homosexuales potentes y bien comidos que te miran con asco, como diciéndote: Te hacemos el favor de traerte, indiecita, a la catedral del orgullo gay.[34]
>
> [And how else are they going to see you, when you're so damn ugly and haul your malnourished Third-World queerness around? They couldn't give a rat's ass about you, with your Chilean face all agape at this pantheon of powerful, well-fed homosexuals, who eye you with disgust, as if to say, "We're doing you a favor by bringing you here, little Indian girl, to the temple of gay pride."]

Describing this same trip in an interview upon his return, Lemebel says, "En Nueva York no vi locas. Daba miedo encontrarse con ese Olimpo macho, con los cueros, los músculos. Rechazo esta construcción ideológica y me pregunto hasta qué punto los homos han sido también *cogidos* por el sistema" [I did not see *locas* in New York. It unnerved me to come across this Olympian man, with his leathers, his muscles. I reject this ideological construction, and I ask myself to what extent homos have been co-opted by the system].[35] Lemebel shared this anguish with other archetypal queens—Arenas's *pájaros*, Perlongher's inverts, Joaquín Hurtado's gaudy transvestites, the materialistic *pato* of Ángel Lozada who has gone broke ringing up

---

[34] The quotation comes from a piece later incorporated into the Spanish edition of *Loco afán* published in 2000 (70).

[35] Interview quoted in Palaversich (104). Lemebel chooses the verb *coger*, not typically used in Chilean sexual slang, to emphasize its double meaning. The quotation could thus also read "to what extent homos have been *screwed* by the system."

charges on his various American credit cards.[36] Arenas himself came to perceive, from his box seat in New York shared with so many other Latin American dissidents, an expanding wave of a masculinized sexuality and the possible extinction of sexual practices that were more their own, more Mediterranean, more—why not?—*Latin American* at the time. Like Lemebel, Arenas understood that feminine behavior had no place in the north, where, instead of having defined roles, "todo el mundo hace de todo" [everybody does everything] (*Antes* 132; *Before* 106). How could that bring satisfaction, he wondered, when "precisamente uno lo que busca es su contrario" [what we are really looking for is our opposite] (*Antes* 132; *Before* 106)? Arenas even admitted that equality, understood as homogeneity of sexual practice, as the elimination of difference, did not interest him in the slightest.

The ambivalence provoked by the confrontation between two allied yet opposite logics is evident. Looking back from the late stages of his illness, Arenas's answer was to romanticize his sexual past, even claiming that the sex had been better, wilder, under the socialist dictatorship. On the other side of the viral vertigo, in Chile's rightwing dictatorship, Lemebel highlighted the close link between sexual freedom and the free market, stating, in a cheeky twist on Marxist thought, that all these new freedoms contained the seeds of their own destruction. This was the crucial moment at which globalization was considered from a gender-based perspective: as a system in which the northern gay presence would be imposed on and eliminate that of the south and in which masculinity would eradicate any element of femininity, including, as we will see, women's very bodies. The gist of some of these texts makes it clear that the warning was not an exaggerated one. But in the view of American queer thinkers, that resistance to globalization would be—repetition intended—resisted, within a questionable rhetoric of difference: "Globalization does not abolish difference as much as it redistributes it, so that certain styles and consumer fashions are internationalized" while others are not (Altman,

---

[36] Lozada first wrote *La patografía* (1998; Patography), a novel in which the homosexual Puerto Rican *pato* undergoes a Kafkaesque transformation into a duck (*pato*) and is devoured by the national community. In his second novel, *No quiero quedarme sola y vacía* (2006; I don't want to end up empty and alone), written in the Latino/ New York context, an explicit connection is drawn between the protagonist's infection and the uninhibited consumption of all sorts of things, including sex.

"Globalization" 560). What is not examined in this statement is precisely which styles, fashions, models of sexuality are removed from or
fall out of the circuit. And we should add another question, too: What
has happened to these styles and fashions in their local contexts? After
all, I would suggest, that disappearance is not accidental. There was
a gradual recognition of the public presence of the American-style
homosexual, a masculine, moneyed gay who normalized a particular manner of being different—and, in appearance, not so different.
The economic gap between the discreet homosexual and the other,
whom Arenas called *escandaloso* (flamboyant), is shaped by the global
dynamic of privilege and privation, highlighting a distancing from
and the eventual abandonment of community spirit. Some may refute
this thesis, which I have borrowed from others; I may be warned (as
an outsider to this crisis) that portraying the gay community as a
particularly economically privileged and well-traveled group carries
the risk of reinforcing homophobia (Binnie 102). Yet accommodating this correction made from the north would require ignoring the
incredible heterogeneity of the dissident community, the undeniable fact that although these dissimilar groups came together in the
struggle against the epidemic, they remained divided regarding the
commodification of sexual models that are more acceptable among
the dominant classes. The community's agenda includes a range of
political, economic, and racial interests. To note these differences is
not merely to succumb to the "fetishization of the local" described
by Jon Binnie. It is to rescue from comfortable oblivion the dual epidemic assault suffered by effeminate or transvestite homosexuals: one
viral, and the other global. Because those who were once the *only*
dissidents—that is, the only ones who were *visible*—were at risk of
also becoming the only ones to disappear altogether.

From the Cryptic to the Explicit

There is more to say about disappearances. At the peak of the deaths—
both in this corpus and in this crisis—we see a battle against extinction break out that is also a struggle against silence. To the extent
they can, the activists raised their voices and encouraged the fearful
to join the marches—many had hesitated to come out of the closet,
but the epidemic pushed them out. The high-heeled queens made
their demands more loudly. Feminists and some infected women
did their thing, holding up signs on the sidewalks. It was always an
unequal and perhaps untimely struggle, one that played out between
certain minorities that remained undecided and others determined

to see a change. This battle for representation slowly wore down the silence entrenched in the culture. It perhaps seems strange now that the silence of prudish Latin American society was to some extent shared by a contingent of sexual dissidents who were reluctant—and not without reason—to display what had historically been a source of stigma and resisted the politicization of private life that could end up regimenting difference. This complexity divided a number of groups for a long time. Entering into political negotiations with the nation required cleaning up the public image, renouncing the more transgressive elements of the community. And putting the community in the hands of science meant taking a step back, accepting the medicalization of sexual behaviors.

On another, theoretical level, accepting Latin American difference implied marginalizing it as the experience of an *other*, but eliminating all difference implied accepting the universalist paradigm of identity discourses created in the United States.[37] Profoundly skeptical arguments appeared. Statements from many authors—the big guns of homosexual writing—referred to their wariness about identity politics, which they saw as a foreign import, and about the possibility of ending up in a ghetto of difference. French-style, some narrators attempted to deconstruct categories, not defend them, not participate in the theater of confessions (as Michel Foucault did, and was then judged harshly by many of his admirers). Equally convinced that defining himself was a bad strategy even during the epidemic, Manuel Puig, who in his novels had explored the tension between desire and political beliefs and who used a number of illnesses as a narrative device,[38] insisted up until his death (of AIDS, rumor has it, though his family denies it) that identity is not linked to sexuality. He even denied the existence of differences in sexual orientation: "Lo que hay," he said, encompassing all sexual behavior, "son *actos* heterosexuales u homosexuales" [What we have are heterosexual or homosexual *acts*] (Gillio 15). The same notion prevails in the statements of Severo Sarduy, diagnosed in 1991: "¿La homosexualidad? Si no hablo de eso con frecuencia es porque, para mí,

---

[37] For a critical analysis of identity politics in Latin America, see *Tropics of Desire*, in which José Quiroga recognizes the crucial gains produced by said political practices in certain historical contexts but also criticizes their dogmatic approach to identity, their "sexual conservatism" (3).

[38] Puig never wrote about AIDS, but he did write about other diseases: tuberculosis in *Boquitas pintadas* (1969; *Heartbreak Tango*), cancer in *Pubis angelical* (1979; *Pubis Angelical*), and diabetes in *Maldición eterna a quien lea estas páginas* (1980; *Eternal Curse on the Reader of These Pages*).

es un asunto, estrictamente, de gusto personal. No le otorgo ninguna connotación, ningún valor, ni positivo ni negativo. No creo que represente una subversión, ni una virtud. Es como ser diabético o filatélico. Algo que no merece ni el menor comentario" [Homosexuality? I don't talk about this often because for me it's strictly a matter of personal taste. I don't think it's a sort of subversion, or a virtue. It's like being diabetic or a philatelist. Something not worth mentioning] ("Para una biografía" 25). Separating the private from the political, considering sexual desire to be a matter of personal taste—the comparison drawn here between homosexuality, the chronic condition of diabetes, and stamp collecting is fascinating—bears no discussion, in his view. At least that's what he writes here, but Sarduy later contradicts himself. He suddenly remembers the political aspect of that *personal taste*, the need and even the responsibility to condemn abuses committed against dissidence (abuses not experienced by other sick people or by hobbyists): "Considero, demás está decirlo, que la persecución de homosexuales que hubo en Cuba—espero que se haya terminado—fue una verdadera ignominia [que] hubiera querido denunciar públicamente, como lo hice por escrito en el libro de Néstor Almendros" [Obviously, I think that the persecution of homosexuals that took place in Cuba—I hope it's over by now—was a real disgrace that I would have liked to denounce publicly, the way I did in Néstor Almendros's book] (25).[39] Reinaldo Arenas, who was included both in that book and in the famous documentary *Conducta impropia* (1984; *Improper Conduct*) also referred to the issue, though in somewhat ambivalent terms. In exile in New York, he stated, "La militancia homosexual ha dado derechos que son formidables para los homosexuales del mundo libre, pero también ha atrofiado el encanto maravilloso de encontrarse…con un hombre que sienta el deseo de poseer a otro hombre y que no tenga que ser poseído a la vez" [Homosexual militancy has gained considerable rights for free-world gays. But what has been lost is the wonderful feeling of meeting…men who would get pleasure from possessing another man and who would not, in turn, have to be possessed] (*Antes* 133; *Before* 108). But though Arenas was critical, he never opted for silence. Puig, on the other hand, set up shop there. And Sarduy, when diagnosed with HIV, shifted from concealment to condemnation. It is as if, forced to choose between the fear of being disciplined for his sexuality or the horror of accepting alien categories, and the anguish of doing absolutely nothing, not even *screaming* (as Arenas suggested), Sarduy

---

[39] He was referring to the book *Conducta impropia* (1984; *Improper conduct*), which includes all of the interviews conducted for the controversial documentary of the same name that explores the persecution of sexual dissidents in Cuba.

chose in the end to abandon his cryptic approach and to knock over a viral inkpot on his pages.

Severo Sarduy's writing on the epidemic is an indication of what would later happen both in reality and in the translation of reality into literature. AIDS gradually became a cultural fissure, a sort of "textual intervention." If we had to rely on what we find in literature immediately after the announcement of the epidemic—testimonies produced in tiny print runs or written in code, poems read aloud to an inner circle or at gatherings of the affected, books published abroad or badly distributed—if we had to rely on the *open secret* to which only a few had access, or on the critical reception of the texts, which ignored their HIV-positive aspect, we would likely not notice the virus's presence in the consciousness of those early years.[40] A few references were scattered here and there throughout the texts, but at first you had to dig to find them. According to the data, the epidemic only began to appear in Latin America in 1983 (two years after its global diagnosis); it was in that year that the epidemic began to show up in medical records. But they were still isolated cases; no narrative of the threat formed in the discourse. The infections were cordoned off by an imaginary hygienic barrier; society thought itself protected from the risk of contagion. The local writers held off, waiting cautiously for the evidence to be narrated before they set out to document it or use it as a starting point in their fiction (literature is always slow to respond; it is a more elaborate and meandering discourse).

It is no surprise, then, that HIV-positive literary production on the continent only began (and I say this carefully, after a lengthy review of the corpus) in a 1984 novel written by Severo Sarduy in exile in Paris, where the situation was dire.[41] But the virus appears only in a fleeting cameo in *Colibrí* (Hummingbird). The reader comes across a brief

---

[40] In a story by the Paraguayan writer Jorge Canese, "Eminente peluquero visita nuestro país, ¡chake sida!" (1987; Prominent hairdresser is visiting our country—Watch out for AIDS!), the author offers a detailed staging of the *open secret*. Despite all the clues provided (a foreign hairdresser who seems not so much exhausted as very ill), the homosexual passes undetected as such. His mysterious illness and the ambiguity of his sexual proclivities are read as being correlated to the cryptic warning parenthetically attached to the title: "¡chake sida!"—that is, "Watch out for AIDS!" The exclamation is written in Guaraní, a language understood only by locals, and thus goes unnoticed. The hairdresser is pestered for sex by both men and women; afraid of contracting the virus that, as the text suggests, he already carries, they eventually drive him to "abandonar[se] blandamente en los brazos de la fortuna" [let himself sink softly into the arms of fortune] (103), represented by the wife of another prominent local hairdresser.

[41] In 1983 came the death of Michel Foucault, one of the great French intellectuals and a known sexual radical whom Severo Sarduy visited often. Foucault never spoke publicly of his illness, and even managed to call it into doubt.

account of a small boat that might remind him of the celebrated ship of fools and of the old motif of the *traveling plague*. Straight out of the fifteenth-century imagination—the anachronism here is intentional—the boat is transporting a group of men marked by sarcoma, gnawed by a leprosy that eats away at their faces; men with pustules, buboes, glass (notes Sarduy) in their bronchial tubes. In this wretched way, the infected pass through the novel, with no sense of morality or any apparent direction. A few lines later, alongside this purulent aimlessness, we find a typically Sarduyian neobaroque maneuver that immediately reveals to the initiated—and perhaps only to them—the fundamental contemporaneity of the grim image.[42] Sarduy carefully shifts the scene into the present, producing, in the dialogue that follows, two acrostics that read SI DA (in French or Spanish) and AI DS (in English). The acrostics have what is certainly a triple meaning: in them, the disease is duplicated; in them, we find the three languages that Sarduy spoke and the two (French and English) in which the virus was being studied at the time;[43] in them, we have the first HIV-positive texts, seeking, in their way, to make the crisis visible on the surface of society.

Sarduy's strategy of partial concealment, which correlated with social stigma, did change over time. Following those cryptic narratives in 1984, he wrote the short vignettes of *El cristo de la rue Jacob* (1987; *Christ on the Rue Jacob*) in which AIDS is identified by name; soon afterward, though already posthumously, his explicit final novel, *Pájaros de la playa* (1993; *Beach Birds*), appeared. This gradual unveiling also included aphoristic essays, a "plague diary," and interviews published in the mass media after his death. There is no doubt that the illness itself, diagnosed at the end of the 1980s, transformed the literary language of the last of the Latin American neobaroque writers. After spending "meses sin poder escribir" [months without being able to write] ("Diario" 33), the novelist took up his pen again, feeling the need for a less linguistically elaborate (and less metaphorical) text that would allow him to strip himself bare, using autobiography to

---

[42] Sarduy sprinkles in some even less telling traces, even more encrypted clues, toward the end of the book. For a detailed look at his literary exploration of the disease, see Ulloa (1994) and Ingenschay (2005).

[43] The first investigations resulted in a fierce competition between French and American scientists. Robert Gallo in the United States and Luc Montagnier in France isolated the virus in 1983, calling it HTLV-III and LAV, respectively. The coincidence in timing provoked a heated dispute about which researcher was entitled to claim the discovery. The dispute was resolved, after a fashion, by the Swedish Academy, which gave Montagnier a Nobel Prize in physiology or medicine for the achievement in 2008.

levy his condemnation: "Yo me enfermé, estuve dos veces en un hospital, cada vez durante tres semanas. Eso cambió mi escritura....Ese Yo hospitalizado es la imagen de la enfermedad y *cambió mi escritura*. Ese Yo es el Yo de mi cuerpo, con todas sus cicatrices" [I got sick; I was in the hospital twice, for three weeks each time. That changed my writing....That hospitalized self is the image of illness, and *it changed my writing*. That self is the self of my body, with all its scars] (qtd. in Klengel 41). His language had become, for therapeutic as much as for community-minded motives, "quizá más legible" [perhaps more legible] (40).[44] Sarduy, who had once formed an avant-garde of language, at the end of the 1980s would join another avant-garde: that of HIV-positive Latin American literature. The year 1993, when *Pájaros de la playa* was published, marked a turning point, an awakening of lettered consciousness that led to the proliferation of Latin American AIDS writing. The sudden appearance of texts, whether locally distributed or with massive international circulation, panned or praised, helped build a corpus of reading for the beleaguered community. It bolstered the militant brotherhood of homosexuals in those writings, identifying them, representing them, offering them the knowledge of a shared existence within and beyond national borders. However tragic those symbolic formulations were, they created a space in which the community could come together, sharing through reading.

Conservative Fear Returns to the World

Reading this HIV-positive corpus as a unit, it is less difficult to get an idea of the crisis's early impact than it is to understand the slowness of the pace at which it reached every level of society. The surprising denial of the crisis found at its epicenter in the United States was matched by a corresponding attitude in Latin America. If we look back to the 1980s, we will find that a great deal of misinformation and narratives that surpassed understanding were circulating between the lines. Society created metaphors that took familiar concepts and combined them with this new phenomenon: the *peste rosa* [pink plague], *gay cancer* (cancer by association with sarcoma,

---

[44] During a conference on Sarduy's work in the city of Colorado (1990), the author, who was present, "hizo referencia a un cierto cambio de actitud hacia su escritura, porque si antes pasaba muchísimo tiempo seleccionando el adjetivo, ahora se interesa más en otros asuntos que le atañen" [referred to a certain change in his attitude toward writing: although he used to spend a lot of time choosing the right adjective, now he is more interested in other issues that concern him] (Ulloa 278).

gay by association with the community that was most affected), the *síndrome marica* [fag syndrome]. These and other configurations of the discursive epidemic (Treichler) came to reaffirm a solid rhetorical and ideological link between the disease and the stigma of moral and mental degradation that had been attributed to sexual dissidence since time immemorial. Society's structural homophobia caused a general—indeed, global—reluctance to address the crisis. It can be argued (as others have already) that the citizenry shielded itself from the virus, secure in their conviction that homosexuals had this *plague* coming, that they (a *they* that was conveniently constructed and then reinforced by public discourses) were "una estirpe condenada que lleva en su cuerpo la marca de una eliminacion prometida" [a doomed bloodline that bears on its body the mark of a promised elimination] (Giorgi, *Sueños* 23). It was practically inhuman, but, to paraphrase the ironic epigraph of a chilling novel of the epidemic, any inhumanity can, with time, become human (Bellatin, *Salón*). Again, the epidemic ended up catapulting the community back in time: back toward social hygiene policies, the creation of new, exportable pathologizing categories, and traditional family values defended by a conservatism that stood in opposition to what it saw as a general loosening of morals. Homophobia became a political practice that was legitimated and cloaked in scientific and political discourse about the defense of the populace. The government of Ronald Reagan, great liberator of markets and slasher of social welfare systems, argued that the sick should be left to their fate; this policy was not an exception but a rule followed around the globe.

But that refusal to act, the lethal silence that American activists read as discrimination's calling card (they even made it into a protest slogan, "Silence = Death"), would not last long: cases soon appeared beyond the borders of the gay ghetto, the primary *at-risk population*.[45] It became clear that it was too late to contain the virus: its origin was indeterminable, its spread undetectable, its mechanisms of transmission unknown, at least at first—and its latency period could last an entire decade. These cases, which mounted day by day (Randy Shilts's documentary on the topic refers to 13,000 cases in 1985), broke only with an extraordinary piece of news: the actor Rock Hudson, an iconic figure of traditional family values but actually, as

[45] This term, a euphemism for homosexuals, heroin addicts, Haitians, and hemophiliacs (also known as the four *h*'s of infection), is not only inappropriate but also discriminatory; it would later be reformulated as "risk behaviors," a term that is itself not entirely satisfactory.

Cindy Patton asserts, a "closet gay / screen heterosexual personality" (*Inventing* 127), confirmed the rumors that he had AIDS.[46] It was 1985, and a retaining wall had just tumbled down: Western masculinity was under threat. Because if Hudson was sick, anyone could be; if Hudson was gay, anyone could be—and even if they weren't, carrying the virus would end up *homosexualizing* them. Terror spread through Latin America, too, when it became clear that the disease did not just attack homosexuals and that, what's more, men who had sex with other men were not always plainly identifiable. It was a tricky category: in many places *homosexuality* referred only to effeminate or feminine, supposedly passive men—but what about those who were still in the closet, penetrators, married men, the plainly macho, bisexuals, all those men who did not fit into that category, who did not identify with homosexuality and perhaps did not perceive danger to themselves or others in their own sex lives? Like Rock Hudson, the *virile* or *undercover* gay personified the terror of a *fluid* sexuality; the categories of epidemiological risk were supposed to contain this fluid sexuality but, especially in Latin America, were unable to do so.

The actor's confession of his illness and his eventual death in October 1985 dramatically shortened the distances between heterosexuals and homosexuals, making the boundaries that separated them porous. These events also shortened the distance between the apparent epicenter of the virus and the rest of the world. The news of both spread around the globe like another epidemic: indeed, it was through the news that AIDS first arrived in Latin America.[47] One symptom of the panic produced by the story's media coverage was the frequency with which the death of the iconic Hollywood figure was invoked as a significant event in the infection and as the start of real public awareness on the continent. "La primera vez [que escuché hablar de esta enfermedad] fue cuando murió Hudson," said one unnamed gay man from Antioquia. "Recuerdo que entonces se

---

[46] Rock Hudson was the first popular figure to put a face on the crisis. The actor said at first that he had end-stage liver cancer, but in July 1985 he announced that he was HIV-positive and attributed his infection to blood transfusions received during a coronary bypass. Hudson never publicly admitted that he was homosexual.

[47] A comparative study on press coverage of the epidemic in the United States (*New York Times*), France (*Le Monde*), and Spain (*El País* and *La Vanguardia*) shows that between the death of Michel Foucault in 1983 and that of ballet dancer Rudolf Nureyev in 1993, the death from AIDS that received the most publicity and attention was that of Rock Hudson—and by a mile. *El País*, perhaps the most widely read foreign newspaper in Latin America, nearly matched the amount of coverage provided in the *New York Times*. See Tuñón (1994).

escribió mucho y los artistas se reunieron para colectar dinero a favor de la lucha contra el sida" [The first time (I heard of the disease) was when Hudson died. I remember that at the time there was a lot written about it and artists were getting together to raise money to fight AIDS] (Sonia Gómez 135). "El temor al sida ha llegado, debido a los medios de comunicación, hasta los rincones más apartados" [Through the mass media, the fear of AIDS has spread to the farthest reaches of the earth], said a Colombian nurse (77).[48] And it was not until the media started talking about that emblematic death that the protagonist of an Argentine AIDS novel let go of "el prejuicio estúpido de que [la epidemia] solo iba a ocurrir en Estados Unidos" [the foolish notion that (the epidemic) was only going to happen in the United States] (Zeiger, *Adiós* 29).[49]

Once that initial moment of disbelief had passed, the news from the north altered the way the infection was read: unlike the American interpretation that the epidemic had originated in Africa and come to the United States through immigrants from the Caribbean, in Latin America the direction was reversed and transformed into a multiple inoculation: viral, media, and ideological, the perfect reflection of postcolonial influence, of the importation of a new logic into free, virgin territories. In 1987 a prostitute in Haiti explained to a writer for *Life* magazine that the virus was an imperialist invention: "It is a false disease invented by the American government to take advantage of the poor countries. The American President [Reagan] hates poor people, so now he makes up AIDS to take away the little we have" (qtd. in Treichler, "AIDS and HIV Infection" 382). The notion of the fabrication of the disease as a political maneuver contains previously noted echoes of neocolonialism, but it also indicates, first, the mobility and multidirectionality of the rhetoric about the virus's origins in a context of such uncertainty, and second, the existence of tense conspiracy theories that reflect the

---

[48] The same would be said of a television program broadcast in his country: "Vimos *Hombres de blanco* y nos dimos cuenta de que los profesionales de la salud de los Estados Unidos estaban sufriendo las mismas angustias que nosotros a tantos kilómetros de distancia" [We watched *Men in White* and realized that health-care professionals in the United States were grappling with the same problems that we were, all those kilometers away] (Sonia Gómez 70).

[49] Hudson appears as a glamorous image of death in *Crónica sero* (Sero chronicle) by the Mexican writer Joaquín Hurtado (53) and as a figure of redemption in a Chilean story in which the protagonist, dying of AIDS, refuses to accept society's blame, saying, "Nadie se ha buscado nada.... Los artistas famosos no se lo buscan. Rock Hudson no se lo buscó ni tampoco yo" [Nobody asked for any of this.... Famous artists don't ask for it. Rock Hudson didn't ask for it, and neither did I] (Sutherland 83).

paranoid production of an infectious *other*. Moreover, it underscores the profound impact of a person's geographic and political position on his or her reading of the origin: in the first decade of the crisis, it was thought that identifying the distant place of origin and finding the first carriers of the virus would somehow allow the world to close off the infected territories, prevent the sick from crossing national boundaries, and finally put an end to the spreading infection.

ORIGINS OF THE CALAMITY

If we delve into the past for a moment, we will find the same scene repeated again and again throughout the course of history: the search for an infection's origin. Halting the spread of an infectious disease, conceived of as foreign from the beginning,[50] would require going back in time, at least in the imagination, tracing the disease's route back to its starting point. That was—inevitably—the main question in the early years of this contemporary calamity. Though fingers were pointed at fixed territories—on one side of the world, the target was Africa, and on the other, the United States, personified in its president—those cartographic distinctions soon proved useless. They took the most conspicuous examples of movement in the global era—mass labor migration, mass tourism—and, by extension, examined the individuals who move between territories instead of remaining in them. The metonymic drift between the origin of the virus and the traveler who carried it was one of the most powerful themes in the discursive representation of the epidemic. Both the virus and the syndrome would be identified and even confused with travelers—masculine, intelligent, difficult to impede,[51] linked to the various contemporary modes of transport: foreign exiles and undocumented workers (Haitians as a bridge from the exotic latitudes of Africa),[52] people accused of prostitution, nomads and vagabonds, sex tourists as a bridge from the developed world to

[50] In its Greek formulation, an epidemic is something that occurs among or upon (*epi*) the people (*demos*), suggesting, by extension, the advent of *something*—or *somebody*, notes Julia Epstein—that mysteriously appears and sets up shop *among the people*.

[51] In the short story "En ti confío" (I trust you) by Chilean writer Juan Pablo Sutherland, the idea is expressed thus: "Dicen que es muy inteligente [el virus], por eso no lo pueden detener" [They say (the virus) is very intelligent, and that's why they can't stop it] (83). Here, man and virus are one and the same thing.

[52] Large groups of Haitian immigrants have legally and illegally entered the United States—seen as a land of opportunity—since the 1950s, fleeing political repression and economic hardship.

another, more vulnerable world. Always men of *dubious inclinations*, until the epidemic was already very far along.

Even before the startling news of Rock Hudson's illness, real panic was setting in about those suspect men—women remained invisible until much later—and focused on the figure of the quintessential traveler: the male flight attendant. (The flight attendant as an aerial traveler, Hudson as a media traveler.) In repeating a journey that connected infinite points on the planet, in the multidirectionality of their constant—yet circular—movement, flight attendants combined labor migration (travel as a means of supporting work) with the movement of sex tourism. They were stigmatized as global representatives of an infection that defied the traditional containment logic of quarantine. But the emergence of this figure was no accident: one of the most persistent social endeavors, a veritable shared obsession, was to retrospectively determine the *routes of transmission*. Examining the mutations of the virus offered only a few dubious clues, but the scientific community clung to them. Fervently emphasizing prevention as their excuse in interviews and in tests, they constructed the guilty traveler par excellence, the epidemic's *patient zero*. Gaëtan Dugas was a Quebecois head flight attendant for Air Canada who worked routes to Los Angeles, San Francisco, New York, and Paris: the world's most visibly affected cities. Deemed responsible for the global infection, the man who had brought the disease from Africa, Dugas soon became the notorious archetype of an insidious globalization, the carrier for the world's ills. He was an *un-American* traveler, a *promiscuous* young man who refused, like many sexual dissidents of the time, to believe in the existence of a *pink plague* and who, in the last stages of his illness, proudly claimed to have had anal intercourse with more than 2,000 men (3,000 fewer than Reinaldo had claimed at 25, but we will return to Arenas later). Dugas was accused of having *deliberately* spread the virus throughout the world, and the press immediately made him the "plague rat of AIDS," possibly referring to the plague rat that turns up dead in the opening pages of Albert Camus's *The Plague* (1947) as a sign of the lethal epidemic that is about to unfold in that novel.

Though the theory was a dubious one—and has since been debunked—it would be taken as fact in a meticulous journalistic investigation that was read as documentary fiction. In *And the Band Played On* (1987), California journalist Randy Shilts, who would die of AIDS in 1994, not only decries the indifference of the political establishment and the US Centers for Disease Control and Prevention during at least the first five years of the epidemic but also, believing in the objectivity of the scientific accusations, immortalizes the

Canadian flight attendant as a sociopathic pervert. Shilts's bulky tome was a contradictory mix of skepticism and gullibility, both a diatribe against policy and a mimetic translation of the official discourse, replicating the official homophobia it simultaneously defied. Shilts's work was soon discredited by critics in the gay community who accused him of not being dissident at all and of replicating straight thinking about the epidemic. Heeding Douglas Crimp's call for *cultural activism*, James Miller called for what he termed the hypothetical Novel of Cultural Activism (266), which should push to subvert the negative representation of the disease and of men who had contracted it, promoting a questionable version of official "truths" that simplified the complexity of politics and of all writing, including AIDS writing.[53]

The theme of the flight attendant's sexual nomadism, the equivalence between his geographic movement in pursuit of sex and the contagious mobility of his story, was not restricted to the northern hemisphere: the flight attendant as a contemptible figure would find an exact counterpart in Latin America. In 1984—the year of the infamous Dugas's death, the year in which he was declared *patient zero*, and the year previous to Hudson's death—another flight attendant appeared in Medellín who was identified as the first HIV-positive Colombian. In a sinister calque of Dugas, the flight attendant was accused of bringing the virus from Africa and promiscuously spreading it through the local homosexual community.[54] According to the testimony of Marta Arroyave, a nurse at the San Vicente de Paul Hospital in Medellín, that first patient even physically resembled

[53] Examples of a *cultural activism* that reduced complexity. The critic Paul Reed denounced Shilts for having produced a "gay male AIDS melodrama" that instead of questioning stereotypes confirmed them. At the same time, Miller set out to expose and undermine the homophobic metaphors and prescriptively detailed the "tasks" of the activist novel. These included writing about HIV-positive people who were actively engaged (rather than passively waiting), using as a protagonist a cultural activist who resisted the fatalism of government leaders and fundamentalist conservatives, giving voice to the infected rather than reinforcing calls for safe sex, and pointing out that heterosexuals' sexual practices and cultural privileges did not make them immune to the disease. Were they to be read through that lens, many Latin American AIDS texts would have to be condemned rather than read in their interesting and often *improper* complexity.

[54] In her informative book *Sida en Colombia* (1988; AIDS in Colombia), Sonia Gómez corrects the report of this "first" Colombian case, identifying another diagnosed just a few months earlier in Cali. The patient was a 23-year-old Cali prostitute who claimed to have contracted the disease from an unknown sailor, "del cual nunca volvió a saberse" [of whom nothing more was ever discovered] (65). As this version involved a sex worker, not only is it impossible to verify, but it also fits very well with the narratives of mystery and uncertainty of a foreign contagion.

Dugas: "Rubio, apuesto, empleado de una aerolínea que cubría rutas africanas, [y que le hacía] evocar la historia de ese otro auxiliar de vuelo de la aerolínea Air Canada" [Blond, handsome, employed by an airline who covered African routes, (and) reminiscent of the story of that other flight attendant from Air Canada] (Sonia Gómez 65). But in Colombia, land of *magical* excesses, there was not just one flight attendant but two. The nurse claimed that months later another flight attendant had come to the hospital; this one worked "la misma ruta a Zaíre [y sería] diagnosticado con los mismos síntomas del hombre anterior, muerto seis meses antes" [the same route to Zaire (and would be) diagnosed with the same symptoms as the previous man, who had died six months earlier] (66). The two Colombians had been companions both in the skies and in bed. Reiterating the dogma of the traveling epidemic, however, the nurse soon concluded that although her compatriots were suffering from the *same* AIDS, it must be "un sida importado" [an imported AIDS] (67) that had entered the country aboard their bodies.

The constructions of the traveler and of the foreigner, which were combined and crystallized in the person of the suspect flight attendant who crossed oceans and continents, spreading infection everywhere he went, took on other incarnations. In one common version of the epidemic journey, the virus moved the way its potential carriers do, from the rich passenger to the poor traveler of the global era. Whether a celebrity, a flight attendant, a first-class tourist, or a last-class immigrant, those travelers were the living image of a globalizing world that, having previously celebrated total movement and absolute freedom, was now, with the crisis, on high alert. The world began to yearn for the now impossible possibility of containment. HIV, as the "icon of the global age, moving on rather than settling in" (Sennett 2), as the "first great cosmopolitan…, respects neither geographical, cultural, sexual, class, or racial barriers" (Haver 7). It crosses borders to hide from the systems of power, it "continually escapes the boundaries placed on it by positivist medical science, and its meanings mutate on a parallel with the virus itself" (Treichler, "AIDS and HIV Infection" 391). All these ideas were ineluctably present in the statement of Francisco Casas, a poet from the southern end of the continent, who saw AIDS as "la mitificación del viajante, él que trafica, va o viene, o sea, *el portador* que cruza la frontera-cuerpo, penetra los límites anales, intravenosos, con un desconocido *polizón* en su estructura" [the mythification of the traveler, of him who traffics, comes or goes—that is, the *carrier* who crosses the border/

body, penetrating anal or intravenous boundaries, with an unknown stowaway in his interstices].[55]

THE LOCAL AS AN OMINOUS HOME

In Latin America, the rhetoric of origin referred back both to a historical tension between the two continents and to their historical relationship of economic and political intervention. As Casas, Lemebel, and other authors who offered a perspective influenced by postcolonial theory noted, the virus arrived in the south like a destructive imperialist stowaway. But however *foreign* the disease, once it had moved within the national borders of Latin American countries, it provoked a number of changes in how the illness and sexual dissidence were perceived and dealt with at a local level. Reality hit Latin American dissident communities particularly hard, dividing them in terms of strategy. While in some places AIDS caused them to return to secrecy to avoid greater dangers—such as obligatory tests and forced internment in Cuban AIDS camps[56]—in other countries, where the governments ignored the crisis, dissident movements formed or were strengthened. Because of the epidemic, many people, especially men, who had not previously experienced either the desire or the political need to express their sexuality came out of the closet.

The threat of death compelled affected communities not only to organize at the global and local levels but also to work to raise public awareness and demand that national governments end the rhetoric of humiliation, recognizing them as citizens with a legitimate right to policies that would provide prevention and assistance. Through this little-recognized but historic gesture, local activism was able, perhaps for the first time, to transform its relationship with the nation, claiming—even demanding—recognition by and inclusion in the national community, which had traditionally excluded it. My intention

---

[55] See Casas (18). The exact reference in this article is unclear: the old photocopy lists no date but only the author, journal, and page number.

[56] Cuba is unique in this approach. After the news of the death of "el señor Hudson," notes the prologue of one anthology, the media attention provoked a controversial response: Castro declared it a patriotic duty to test everyone for AIDS and impose mandatory confinement on all those found to carry the disease. The only people exempt were diplomats and tourists; resident foreigners would also have to be tested, and if they had the virus, they were deported. For details on this situation, see Leiner (117–48).

is not to idealize a tumultuous moment that was still largely characterized by state indifference, citizen hostility, public opposition, and disagreement among the various affected groups,[57] but to underscore how, paradoxically, the crisis caused many dissidents, in order to survive, to insist that they, too, were part of the nation, and to call for an end to the intolerance that had driven them either to leave or to disguise themselves. With the decline of the failed cosmopolitan utopia, coming out of the closet was a symbolic return home, a demand that the *homeland* act like one and take them in. This demand for inclusion, which I would argue was a psychological mechanism of return, was clearly expressed in literature. The proximity of death caused a reverse migration in fiction that took a number of different forms. In Arenas, that return implied the reinvention of a past in which the homeland, unlike exile, allowed the community most affected, rejected, or injured to enjoy at least its own life and others' bodies. In other authors, the return was a more polemical and political act. Heading back in time became a motif in certain narratives of the sexual diaspora, with "jóvenes viejos" [old-young men], as Sarduy suggests throughout his novel, or "living dead young men who…went to their homeland to die" (312), as Sandoval put it.

What these different return journeys shared was that the young men who had once celebrated capitalism's promises of freedom no longer believed in them. Instead, paradoxically, their HIV-positive narratives confirmed that, both within the homeland and beyond its borders, to be different or dissident, but above all to be sick, was to make visible an ancient stigma. Or worse, that the intensification of the movement in the postnational age also meant the intensification of that negative mark. In the deadliest decade, the epidemic provoked the fictional return to a home cum *hospice*, not *hospital*, home cum inescapable tomb: allegorical but always inconclusive representations of the nation. The "moribund young men" of fiction were going not *home* to repatriate but to twilight homes before moving on to the cemetery, to the finality of death. Copi (Raul Damonte), an Argentine playwright in Paris, sends his fictionalized self to a Buenos Aires hospital, where he is visited inopportunely by a feminized, or perhaps transvestite, death figure who is also a star of the stage. She tries to seduce him, to carry him far away, but the protagonist is only willing to die theatrically, on stage. Severo Sarduy, too, sends

[57] For a detailed account of the epidemic in Brazil, Chile, Costa Rica, Guatemala, Mexico, Peru, and Trinidad and Tobago, as well as of the various strategies of activists in those countries, see Frasca (2005).

his fictionalized self from Paris to a sanatorium on an island entirely isolated from the modern world—it could well be a rewritten Cuba or an exaggerated representation of the concentration camps for AIDS patients established there by Fidel Castro starting in 1986. From exile, these authors portrayed the nationalization of AIDS on the page, creating a more sinister, more radical image: in Mario Bellatin's *Salón de belleza* (1994; *Beauty Salon*), the nation becomes an allegorical concentration camp in which the state has abandoned its caretaking functions and left its citizens at the mercy of whomever wishes to aid or to destroy them. The altruistic hairstylist who turns his salon into a place of refuge is gradually swayed by a logic of genocidal alienation and ends up carrying out inhuman acts, unleashing an awful transformation that evokes the community's past to warn that there is no possible escape from the epidemic: the state is allegorized, posited as a death camp for dissidents.[58]

The Ambiguity of Global Aid

Literature translates and rewrites reality at will; the AIDS corpus is haunted by death. In the HIV-positive imaginary of the first decade, we find a depiction of the disappearance of spaces in which life is possible, the destruction of any future territory for the community, either at home or abroad. The vast scale of the epidemic meant that,

---

[58] The idea of planned genocide and the comparison of the epidemic with the Jewish Holocaust appears again and again in the HIV-positive corpus. Arenas implies it when he accuses the world powers of planning the death of sexual dissidents; Sarduy says it more openly, musing in an essay on the crisis, "Todo adquiere la gravedad de una amenaza. Los judíos, parece ser, conocen muy bien esta sensación" [Everything gathers the weight of a threat. The Jews, it seems, know this feeling well] (*El Cristo* 28; *Christ* 34). The logic of Bellatin's death camp also contains this suggestion. In *Vivir afuera* (1998; Living out), a Fogwill novel not discussed in this book, the protagonist is a terminally ill homosexual and a wandering Jew: "Un cuerpo paradigmático de la máquina biopolítica moderna en el que se conectan las persecuciones antiguas y las contemporáneas" [A body that is paradigmatic for the modern biopolitical machine, combining ancient and contemporary persecutions] (Giorgi, "Historias" 174). Giorgi alludes to the way Jews were blamed for the Black Death and draws a connection with the protagonist's HIV-positive status. The association is not just a literary one. The Holocaust was a powerful metaphor in the community's playbook. In 1990 a spokesperson for the American activist collective ACT UP stated in a public hearing before the Maryland AIDS Commission that "Schaefer [the Governor] is Hitler, AIDS is the holocaust, Maryland is Auschwitz. This is a conscious genocide and can only be seen as the Governor's desire to wipe out this population" (Martin 366). (See notes 120 and 189.)

far from becoming less relevant, the state became all the more necessary. The exponential spread of the disease in a wide range of sectors of the population and the increasing opportunistic infections meant that, despite their homophobia, despite the dictates of their moralist churches, despite their budget shortfalls and the imposition of neoliberal measures to reduce public spending, governments were forced to respond to public alarm over the crisis to avoid coming to be seen as illegitimate by their terrified citizens. The United States, in the grip of Ronald Reagan's social conservatism, only responded once the epidemic was fairly far along and no other option remained: in 1986 (immediately after Hudson's death), Congress announced the allocation of special funds for developing medicines to treat the virus and providing humanitarian aid to those regions of Africa and the Caribbean that were most affected.

The weak economies of many of the most afflicted countries limited their response capabilities. Systems of international cooperation were thus needed to reinforce, through aid, the idea of global citizenship (Altman, "Globalization" 559). At the same time, the US State Department and the World Health Organization organized the first International AIDS Conference. Public campaigns were launched. More resources were given to global—that is, American and European—organizations whose purpose was to help the rest of the world with the crisis. The relationship between these organizations and other affected governments, regional NGOs, local gay rights associations, and women's groups would be strengthened, though there was little sensitivity to the stark cultural differences between the various communities and groups; they operated, in other words, against a backdrop of ideas that verged on the improbable. In the north, some queer globalization theorists argued that thinking about AIDS as a global problem could be positive, to the extent that it generated resources, strategies, and policies to grapple with the crisis (Binnie 113), but the result was more ambiguous and less equitable than predicted. In the United States, a program of global cooperation had been envisioned that disregarded the cultural complexity of each region. Funds flowed into the affected areas, but they were accompanied by a preventionist rhetoric based on dubious—if not flatly erroneous and moralistic—assumptions. The instruments of aid, which had been developed to address other realities, other circumstances, and used abstractions about sex that lacked any ethnographic foundation, did little to alleviate the crisis. One paradigmatic example of the obtuse application of these instruments was the survey on sexuality used in Latin America during the first decade of the epidemic. The survey assumed synonymy between a *homosexual* and a *man who has sex with men*; but in many places people used the former term only for effeminate men—the accepted *passive* partner in the relationship.[59] Many men who had sex with men were not counted in these statistics because they did not identify with the category: the *Mediterranean* quality of certain Latin American sexualities thus eluded the prevention campaigns.[60] The dissident community was not a homogenous group with a singular self-definition. The issue went beyond that of nomenclature: at bottom, the problem was that the production of epidemiological knowledge was taking place in centers of production of discursive knowledge that were far away from or not involved with those most affected by the epidemic, a sort of antiethnography, motivated by a homophobic ideology, that refused to listen to the patients scattered around the world. Paula Treichler, author of a number of essential essays on the epidemic's discursive forms, has said that the "institutional forces and cultural precedents in the First World prevent us from hearing the story of AIDS in the Third World as a complex narrative" ("AIDS and HIV Infection" 400). She also notes that in that dialogue, which was more of an imposed monologue, the imperialist aspects of "a strategy that valorizes itself as universal rather than culturally produced" (395) held sway.

Foreign aid was thus shown to function as a foundation for ideological intervention. Economic assistance and low-interest loans to resolve the crisis created relationships of subordination with neocolonial overtones, retracing a well-worn path of intervention. National governments were exempted from their responsibility to care for their citizens through a scrupulously neocapitalist logic that has led to those governments' total decline, eliciting bitter musings from one of the main figures in the Mexican corpus: "Al gobierno le conviene que se mueran pronto los pacientes, mantenerlos vivos resulta muy costoso"

---

[59] In many places the *active* partner still does not identify with the category, but this difference still is not understood in the United States, as is apparent in the sarcastic tone of an article that appeared in the *New York Times* during an international conference held in Mexico in 2008. An HIV-positive Mexican man interviewed in it explains, "I have never felt that I am homosexual because I have never let them make love to me.... It's the opposite. I penetrate" (Lacey). (See notes 12, 22, and 104.)

[60] In the 1990s survey questions were changed to use the more inclusive term *MSM* (men who have sex with men). But this more inclusive category has recently been called into question because it tends to erase the homosexual identity of those who culturally identify with that term. MSM, argue its critics, would eliminate an entire vision of a community and reduce certain social networks to a mere sexual act. For a history of this debate, see Young and Meyer (2005).

[It's in the government's interest that the patients die quickly; keeping them alive is very expensive] (Cacho 76). This statement by feminist writer Lydia Cacho forcefully argues for both the impossibility of the state and the need for foreign aid, thus reinforcing the hierarchies already existing between the north and Latin America. The two complemented each other in constructing an asymmetrical relationship between global and local spaces that would also find its correlate in the imagination of Pedro Lemebel. The Chilean writer translated that relationship into the text of a fictional letter to the great benefactor of the moment, the glamorous star who established the American Foundation for AIDS Research: Elizabeth Taylor. The poor *loca* from the southern end of the world begs Rock Hudson's dear friend for one of her emeralds so he can resell it (as the letter puts it) and buy the AZT that might be able to save him (*Loco afán* [1996] 56). Like Cacho, Lemebel notes the cost of AZT, a highly toxic drug that at the time extended life only six months[61] and was offered at astronomical prices by US labs that refused to relinquish their patents. It cost an emerald that neither the community nor national governments could afford. The problem of access sparked a Darwinian competition among groups that had initially collaborated in pursuit of the shared objective of demanding attention and aid from the state.[62] The struggle for foreign funds splintered unity and distracted the dissident groups from a central element of their traditional agenda: the political right to sexual freedom. Seeking international protection against the virus meant abandoning the pursuit of this freedom and submitting to the positivist mechanism of abstinence and vigilance, of constant confession of private behavior and permanent redefinition of identity in survey vocabulary; it meant submitting to a series of tests, to dubious experimental treatments shaped by scientific discourses that delegitimized all other approaches. In this invasive situation, living life as a free agent was forbidden. Everyday life was now a routine in which pleasure had come under threat. But resistance to such unpleasant

---

[61] AZT, created in 1964 by Jerome Horwitz for the treatment of cancer, was so toxic that it was not tested on human beings until 1987, the year that it was approved by the US Food and Drug Administration for the treatment of AIDS. The drug became ineffective after six months of use as the virus became resistant. In addition, it came with awful side effects.

[62] Foreign aid was distributed to shoestring organizations attempting, amid the chaos and despite the obstruction of local governments, to prevent further infection in the population and help those already affected grapple with the situation. For details on the relationship between international bodies and local organizations, see Frasca (2005).

conditions would produce responses that were unimaginable to the rigid, prudish mind of science; it broke molds that had never been a good match for spontaneous actions.

LIVING LIFE, REIMAGINING COMMUNITY

A turning point in the epidemic came in 1996, when the XI International AIDS Conference in Vancouver announced that the new combination therapy, or tritherapy (which included AZT, ddI or ddC, and a protease inhibitor), if taken as prescribed, was able to reduce the viral load of HIV-positive individuals to the point that it was undetectable.[63] The announcement that the lethal disease might become a chronic condition was at first a relief to the scientists, patients, family members, and doctors meeting to discuss the ever-worsening crisis. By 1996, an estimated 8,000 people were infected each year, and the total number of cases of HIV infection was estimated to be 20 million (a decade and a half later, it would be nearly double that). The antiviral cocktail, which was highly effective at prolonging and improving the quality of life, offered an important palliative against the development of the disease, but not a cure, not a solution. The viral load might diminish, but HIV still lay in wait, lurking in the lymph nodes or the brain or some other corner of the body, and could become resistant to the cocktail if the medication was not taken regularly. The virus might reappear in the bloodstream with renewed strength at the least provocation. It was also feared that the announcement would encourage some to stop taking the necessary precautions and be reinfected with the same virus or one of its mutations. Despite these limitations and the unpleasant side effects of the cocktail—"¿Lo llamarán coctel para volverlo atractivo?" [Do they call it a cocktail to make it sound appealing?], asked the Argentine poet Pablo Pérez in his diary (*Un año* 66)—a large HIV-positive population demanded immediate access to the benefits of combination therapy. The crucial element, according to a witness, the most quoted sentence during the Vancouver conference: "pegar fuerte y pegar temprano..., comenzando tan pronto sea posible despues de la infeccion [para] mantenerse siempre un paso por delante del virus" [strike hard

---

[63] In 1996 it was discovered that the combination was needed to attack the virus at different stages of its development, thus preventing it from becoming resistant. Nevertheless, the cocktail could become ineffective, so variations on those medications continued to be developed.

and strike early . . . , starting as soon as possible after infection (to) stay one step ahead of the virus at all times] (Davidovich).

Yet this ideal collided with a difficult reality. The heralded reformulation of AIDS as a chronic illness was a deceptive promise. Many people continued to die if they did not receive treatment in time, before opportunistic infections had set in. All too often, clinical diagnosis came after symptoms had already appeared, at which point the cocktail was not as effective. But perhaps the greatest impediment to successful deployment of the polytherapeutic formula was the high cost of the medications, which were even more expensive than AZT alone. In economic terms, the advent of the cocktail hardly constituted a happy hour for the heavily indebted and impoverished Latin American states, which were unable to meet the immediate overwhelming demand for the therapy. Nor were they able to manufacture their own medicine. The pharmacological technology in the neoliberal era of the virus was and continues to be controlled by an industry whose ultimate goal, despite its advertising campaigns' claims to the contrary, is not life but profit, protecting its patents rather than ensuring the survival of the most vulnerable citizens. The medicines increased the pressure on the national governments, which faced a dual crisis. The first element of that crisis was epidemiological, because although the number of deaths was decreasing, the number of infected individuals needing treatment and pushing for universal access to the expensive drugs was rising. In addition, by extension, governments faced a crisis of political legitimacy in managing a situation that clearly called for a solvent state that could take care of its citizens. There was also a third challenge: depending on foreign aid, accepting old formulations of international dependency.[64]

At bottom, the question to be resolved was this: Who is responsible for securing the cocktail, the state or the patient? This dilemma arises in a number of Argentine narratives of seropositivity, including the raw accounts published by Buenos Aires writer Marta Dillón in *Vivir con virus. Relatos de la vida cotidiana* (2004; Living with the virus: Stories of everyday life). Dillón, the only admitted carrier of the virus

---

[64] Brazil was a perfect example of this: in 2005, after rejecting the discounts offered by laboratories in the United States, its legislature passed a law to disregard patent law and produce its own generic medicines, allowing the state to provide free access to the cocktail without going broke. The policy produced a savings of some $50 million a year. In 2007, the Mercosur treaty allowed states who deemed it necessary to emulate that policy, accommodating exceptional circumstances that constituted a national emergency.

in the corpus, wrote her first column about the disease in 1995, a year after her diagnosis,[65] and used her personal experience as a foundation for describing obstacles that exemplify the way the personal is transformed into a radically political posture. We see her refusal of treatment with AZT, which has been shown to be ineffective, and her resistance to the antiviral cocktail until she has no other option. We also see various types of private and social upheaval described by an unflappable mind. With an astute, clinical eye, Dillón evaluates and questions the punitive rigidity of the pharmaceutical regimen. The strict schedule imposed for taking the various pills is aggressive and complicated, with many warnings and restrictions.[66] But perhaps the most delicate problem is the economic distress caused by the treatment and the political awareness it inspires: "En ese momento se necesitaba mucho dinero para acceder a él. Por suerte mi papá lo tenía" [At the time you needed a lot of money to get it. Luckily, my father had that] (90), Dillón says, confessing to a *privilege* (a word she uses often) that temporarily exempts her from the risk of physical decline. On this occasion, her father's economic solvency makes up for the insolvency of the nation and points to a fundamental problem, one that is not specific to Argentina but shared across Latin America: the nation's responsibility for the well-being of its citizens.

Dillón's body plays host to not one but two deaths that are parallel and suspended in time. Dillón carries dormant within her a lethal illness that the state refuses to take on; she also carries another's death, one that remains unacknowledged by the state. In her writings Dillón is the same age as her mother was when she was kidnapped and murdered by the dictatorship in 1976, and so the two deaths meld together in a single body. It is this citizen's (and by extension the entire Argentine citizenry's) unsettling relationship with the state that gives her and the others affected the strength to resist it. Indeed, HIV-positive Argentines accused successive democratic governments of violating human rights and of producing—though now through neglect rather than active malice—a new kind of disappearance. Local activists went through the courts to sue the government

---

[65] Dillón's columns appeared between October 1995 and the end of 2003 under the title "Convivir con virus" (Living with the virus) in the newspaper *Página/12*'s *Suplemento No*; they were later compiled and published in *Vivir con virus* (2004; Living with the virus).

[66] In the first years of combination therapy, patients had to take at least 20 pills a day, every 4 or 6 hours, some accompanied by food and some on an empty stomach. Later treatments involved fewer pills and fewer alimentary complications.

for contributing to these deaths. And in 1997 Argentina's Supreme Court ruled in favor of the plaintiffs. The state was compelled to provide universal access to treatment, which, Dillón writes in 1996, "queda muy bien en los papeles, pero el presupuesto [de salud] de este año fue menor en cinco millones de pesos al del año pasado" [looks great on paper, but the (health-care) budget this year was five million pesos less than last year's] (55). The drug was not always available at the distribution centers; people had to return again and again "a buscar algo para ir tirando" [looking for something to tide them over] (55). They had to share, to parcel the drugs out to those whose health was poorest amid the state's "total impunidad" [absolute impunity] (56).

Even though she receives the treatment for free, Dillón does not forgive the state for the economic crisis that not only threatens the public at large but also keeps the infected at constant risk of running out of medication. Though Dillón recognizes that she is constantly irresponsible with her own chronic illness, she sees the social irresponsibility of the negligent state (itself also chronically ill, though Dillón does not say it) as indefensible. The state *must* always ensure the life and survival of its citizens. "Puedo quedarme dormida de puro cansancio y olvidarme de las pastillas de la noche," she says. "Puedo simplemente olvidarme de tomar el bendito coctel sin ninguna excusa a mano. Pero una cosa es que me olvide yo y otra muy distinta es que te obliguen a interrumpir el tratamiento y que encima te traten de estúpida" [I can fall asleep from sheer exhaustion and forget to take my pills at night. I can just forget to take the damn pills without any excuse at all. But it's one thing for me to forget, and something else altogether for them to force you to interrupt your treatment, and treat you like an idiot on top of it] (197). Dillón then describes the bureaucratic labyrinth that requires that all HIV-positive individuals go first to the public hospital for a prescription, then to the health insurance agency to have the prescription authorized, and finally to the drug bank to pick up their three bottles of pills. But the prescriptions get lost and the drugs don't arrive on time:

Al cuarto día sin pastillas me resfrié, mal. Obviamente puedo tomarme las cosas con calma pero eso no evita la psicosis de pensar en todas las catástrofes que pueden suceder después de todas esas tomas omitidas. Al quinto día mi tono en el teléfono empezó a tornarse violento, y mi amigo amenazó con un cacerolazo en la sede del banco de drogas. Llegábamos al viernes, el sábado y el domingo amenazaban con las dependencias cerradas y yo sin pastillas. Intentando hacer un chiste negro les dije a mis compañeritas de escritorio, "si me muero, échenle la culpa a los burócratas." Pero no les causó mucha gracia. (198–99)

[On the fourth day without pills, I got really sick. Obviously I can take things in stride, but that doesn't mean I don't obsess about all the catastrophes that might occur as a result of all those skipped doses. On the fifth day, my tone of voice on the telephone began to get aggressive, and my friend threatened to organize a protest outside the drug bank. We made it to Friday; on Saturday and Sunday the offices were closed, and me without any pills. Trying for a bit of black humor, I told my coworkers, "If I die, blame the bureaucrats." But they weren't amused.]

In the absence of a state that fulfills its caretaking role, that can and indeed makes the effort to offer assistance to all of its citizens, the idea of traveling in search of protection beyond national borders reappears. Dillón describes how, again and again, people write her emails asking for information on HIV: "La necesita para solicitar asilo político en el gran país del norte" [They need it to apply for political asylum in the United States] (201). The reasons they cite: "La falta crónica de medicamentos, la entrega fraccionada—¿cuánto tiempo se puede perseguir un puñado de pastillas?—, la dudosa calidad de lo que te entregan, la falta de políticas públicas de prevención, la falta de insumos en el hospital público" [The chronic shortage of medicine, the only partial fillings of prescriptions—how long can a person keep chasing after a handful of pills?—the dubious quality of what they give you, the lack of public prevention policies, the lack of supplies in the public hospital] (202). On top of all that, there is labor discrimination and huge populations that, the essayist writes, receive no treatment at all because they don't even make it into the health system.[67] Yet seeking political asylum abroad was merely a reformulation of the old global pipe dream, as futile as trying to flee down a dead-end alley. The situation was no better in the north. It was even worse than in Latin America, if you consider that, in the world's greatest superpower, some 45 million people, one-third of them Latin Americans, were living without any sort of health coverage.[68] These figures rendered that utopia inoperative and offered a new answer to the distressing Darwinesque question posed toward the end of *Vivir con virus*: "¿Quiénes serán los más fuertes [para sobrevivir]?" [Who will be the strongest ones (in order to survive)?] (202). That question can be interpreted in economic terms: Who will have access to the capital that will allow them to survive? The answer necessarily went beyond mere northern versus southern

---

[67] In 2004 it was estimated that some 35,000 people needed antiretroviral medications, but according to government statistics, only 30,000 were receiving them.

[68] See Navas-Walt, Proctor, and Lee (2006).

positioning, because the rich North and the defenseless South were reproduced within each national community. The answer could no longer be based on the simple premise of global versus local, but had instead to employ a logic that subsumed and reclassified these distinctions in a more complex and nuanced way.

Other Argentine AIDS writing of the time posed the question of survival in terms that were less about community, though no less anguished. These texts employed a vocabulary that attempted not to condemn the political establishment but to redefine the dissident community in the post-cocktail era. Framed by the temporal turning point of 1996, the protagonists of these other narratives accept the limitations of the local but make up for them by remaining virtually or globally connected with others. They wonder about a possible return to sex and love, but in terms that are not so much necessarily physical but instead, at least in theory, more abstract and perhaps more protected against contact and contagion. But they are weighed down by an enormous contradiction between the desire to love, to live together, and the fear of being with others. Reading Guillermo Saccomanno's story "Deje su mensaje después de la señal" (1994; Leave a message after the beep) together with Pablo Pérez's autobiographical *Un año sin amor. Diario del sida* (1998; A year without love: AIDS diary), written and above all lived during the "año bisagra" [watershed year] of 1996,[69] as well as his next book from 2001 and Daniel Link's 2004 novel *La ansiedad* (Anxiety), one might expect that the characters would suffer from irremediable melancholy or, quite the opposite, that they would celebrate survival. But in the radical presentness of these narratives, the psychological power of elegy and of euphoria has been lost. We see the squeamishness of the survivor who does not trust medicine and who faces the daily challenge of existing in complete solitude or in the company of strangers. The dissident community is alive, active, scattered across the entire planet; though the group makes its presence felt, it loses connections just as fast as it forms them. Fear pulses within this "mundo virtual del 'entre nosotros', provisional y permanente, real y ficticio...en el que las fronteras se diluyen, en el cual el cuerpo se esfuma" [virtual world of "between us," provisional and permanent, real and fictional...in which borders dissolve, in which the body disappears] (Le Breton 191).

[69] I take this insightful formulation from Roberto Jacoby, the iconic musician and lyricist from the now-defunct Argentine New Wave group Virus, and who is currently nurturing artistic projects on the Internet. In the prologue to Pérez's diary, Jacoby refers to 1996 as the year in which the AIDS situation changed (*Un año* 10).

Fear again—fear always—and anguish prowling nearby. Death still so close, death still possible but in a latent state, is visible in the subject's fear and giddiness about the return to coitus (so absent from the texts of the virus's lethal period), and in his anxieties about love. That torment permeated the HIV-positive corpus from the beginning: Sarduy describes the feeling in a 1987 essay that tells of an encounter in which he and another man masturbated "lamiéndose apenas los sexos, sin duda por miedo al sida" [lick(ing) each other's penis only very lightly—no doubt for fear of AIDS] (*El Cristo* 55; *Christ* 69). But that essay and the bulk of the corpus on the Latin American epidemic precede the celebrated medical achievements, while the contemporary texts mentioned above speak from the posttritherapy era. If we think of these three final, deeply dissimilar narratives as documents of daily life, we will likely conclude that pharmacological technology did not help prevent either the virus or fear from spreading through the community: the cocktail was no longer seen as a risky relief from the illness. On this topic Saccomanno, Pérez, and Link are rigorously realistic: medication was not a definitive cure; the vaccine was a promise deferred. It is no wonder, then, that fear continued to be so emphasized. What is surprising is that fear, rather than bringing them together, deactivated the old utopia of being with others, of thinking and especially feeling, and of living together. It was at this point that a clear difference from the 1970s generation of dreamers, who traveled literally or literarily in order to be part of a shared community, became apparent. There was also some distance from the texts of the *terminal* generation of the 1980s, which was activated and politically united by the crisis until death ended up breaking the bond (although in some cases, not even death separated the lovers, as their ghosts remained like indissoluble traces of memory).[70] Especially in the narratives of

---

[70] The trope of the ominous presence haunts all HIV-positive narratives. Néstor Perlongher's essay *El fantasma del sida* (The ghost of AIDS) suggests a relationship between the psychological energy of the dead person who is reluctant to depart and the Derridean notion of socialism as a specter that haunts the present era. In addition, in fiction we find ghosts that refuse to leave and relatives who refuse to let them go. These bodies-in-absence travel with their lovers. For example, Venezuelan playwright Isaac Chocrón's *Escrito y sellado* (1993; Written and sealed) portrays a trip to the American South to mourn and forget a dead lover, but the lover follows, refusing to be relegated to oblivion. The scene itself is also ghostly: everything appears in black and white, as if the dead man as a *negative* of life had marked the entire space. In *Melodrama* (2006; Melodrama), a novel by the Colombian writer Jorge Franco, the protagonist who gets sick in Paris is already dead: he is a ghost narrator. Fernando Vallejo sets up his fictional self in *El desbarrancadero* (2001; The precipice) as a soul in pain, fated to provide a final testimony of someone else's death that is also symbolically his own. (See note 109.)

the HIV-positive present, or, to be more exact, in Pérez and in Link, the *we* remains in agonizing suspense. They grapple with the slow dissolution of a possibility: that of meeting and sharing *something* in the same place, in the same moment—the *being together* discussed by Roland Barthes. It is apparent that communication technologies offer, if only in part, a way out of feelings that cannot be soothed. Not having to deal with another's body but also not being faced with being completely alone.

Far from diminishing in the cocktail era, fear of infection but also of loneliness gradually intensified in these writings, while at the same time the dissolution of concrete reality through technology became more and more evident. In Guillermo Saccomanno's story, set at the end of the uncertain AZT era, a woman who is afraid she is infected (we never learn whether she is or not) refuses to answer repeated phone calls from her bisexual lover, who has just found out he is a carrier. Determined to be alone but without renouncing pleasure (nor abstaining from listening to each new message from her lover), the protagonist spends the afternoon watching porn. The only form of safe sex that appears to remain to her is sex mediated by video technology in which she comes together with simulated lovers who accede to her every desire; the reencounter with the body or voice of her lover, meanwhile, never happens. The diaries of Pablo Pérez, written not much later, contain another frenzied quest for companionship through two communication apparatuses: a telephone that keeps ringing and recording messages, and a computer with Internet access that also facilitates future encounters. These *encounters* always take place in the same form—as imagined or fleeting sex with strangers, acts ritualized by sadomasochistic practice that replaces the love relationship and because of which Pérez titles his diary *Un año sin amor*. A desolate ferment also drives the plot of Daniel Link's novel: the protagonist constantly refers to his anxiety about being alone but at the same time rejects the possible stability of coupledom with a foreigner who moves to Buenos Aires for love. The narrator is not ready to give up the innumerable virtual temptations offered by the screen. He is as devoted a user of new communication technologies as he is disciplined in taking his medication.

An involuntary apostle of the late-capitalist system, evangelizing the gospel of impatience that governs that system, the restless protagonist of *La ansiedad* appears to be one of those ideal subjects of capitalism described by Richard Sennett and mentioned at the beginning of this essay: men seriously prepared to take on risk, consumers who keep the markets alive. As in *Un año sin amor*, the protagonist of *La ansiedad* is one of those insatiable figures celebrated by the new global capitalism. His way of thinking about consumption—of goods, bodies, even emotions—is no longer guided, as the previous system was, by the need for stability or accumulation. These men pursue not the permanent possession of the other but the ephemeral enjoyment of another person's body, whether physical or virtual. Their relationships are read as transactions of desire that last only as long as their consummation. In them, the desire for the permanency of possession is eliminated, made fungible and fleeting. That man still surrounded by fear now believes in the freedom of desiring nothing; he tries to convince himself that rejecting the other is not a loss but an opportunity for the stimulus of new consumption: "Surrender of an object is not experienced as loss. Rather abandonment fits into the process of finding new stimulations" (Sennett 150). Not being a slave to desire is thought of as a form of freedom. But the sociologist warns us that "these changes [in the new culture of capitalism] have not set people free" (13). Interestingly, in literature, Pérez's and Link's protagonists experience Sennett's claim as a certainty: they are angels fallen into the disgrace of anguish.

Anxiety saturates these stories, but they contain not just anxiety and despair about loneliness but also a paradoxical faith that communication technology, which in these narratives is at its peak, will allow them to avoid (or at least think they can avoid) the bond of present-ness that creates intimacy between individuals. Yet these characters think about the *need* to be with a man as being analogous to *communicating* with him. Both texts are dominated by scenes in which the protagonists write, seeking an interlocutor who does not always answer (who is not always identified, who sometimes disappears mid-conversation), and the faster the technology, the more hollow the messages. The fragmentation of the text, which parallels the splintering of personal bonds, plays out on the page. Indeed, *La ansiedad* contains a combination of writing modes that point to the existence of a reader. Reproduced on the page appear fragments of essays that reflect on the old genre of the love letter; there are emails, text messages, and endless chat conversations. In all these writings, dialogue is forever interrupted—we read only the sender's part—or, rather, the dialogue is suspended, indicating the interruption or perhaps even the inexistence of the relationship. Yet that situation triggers endless new texts that spread through the world "como una epidemia viral (y al mismo tiempo que las epidemias virales)" [like a viral epidemic (and at the same time as the viral epidemics)][71] looking for someone to receive the message, for someone to respond. Sociology sometimes returned to the subject: Richard Sennett and Zygmunt Bauman expressed their skepticism, and David Le Breton noted the paradoxes of what he called *adiós al cuerpo* (goodbye to the body), presenting evidence that real encounters had not lost meaning but were instead subject to the strange paradox of being cut off from the discursive processes, subject to the power of the text. But there is no need to turn to the descriptive accounts of the social sciences: literature documents—in a way that is both eloquent and perceptive, and certainly more complete and complex—how as contact within the community becomes virtualized, relationships become a purely verbal mechanism; the contact in these texts is mediated by incorporeal words. The writing, like its writers, has refused to commit to a single reader/interlocutor, becoming promiscuous itself. Thus, in the novel there is compulsive contact that is both textual (citations of other essays and novels) and sexual (with concrete or virtual bodies). Lots of *loveless*—and even, at times, *bodiless*—sex. And, of course, there is pleasure in the sexual transaction, but there is no talk of eroticism, as if removing the erotic would mean the negation of the physical body that seeks contact, if only in the imagination.

I point out the unease produced by this situation not, then, simply to condemn the virtual forms of contemporary cohabitation in a conservative critique that makes no room for today's virtual sexualities. That unease is apparent in texts written by dissident authors who use technology in daily life; anxiety and lovelessness are precisely the public calling card they've chosen. In their writing, we witness the construction of a virtual topography in which the local loses its power and experience is confirmed to be global. But the relationships that form in the virtual space, in contrast to what might be expected, to what the protagonists themselves expect, do not satisfy, or at least not entirely. The idea of a community that is connected—that can be activated, that is available and accessible despite its anonymity—serves only as a prophylactic effect of the screen. Being together can be made manifest, while living together is seen as a potential reality that never takes shape. These relationships and perhaps even affections are everywhere at once but at the same time corporally absent. This is neither

---

[71] Quotation taken from the website of Daniel Link, who in addition to being an academic and novelist is an active blogger: <linkillo.blogspot.com>. Entry dated January 20, 2005.

a displaced group nor necessarily a peripatetic one, as in texts from earlier periods. Nor is it the spectral host of the dead, ghosts whose psychological and emotional energy lingers on the scene. This virtually imagined community demands that we reconsider in the present whether the texts have predicted the end of the face-to-face, body-to-body encounter, whether they point to the certain impossibility of being together for the community.

Absent Communities

In this overview of the global crisis, a complex and even inscrutable issue remains to be discussed: the exclusionary politics evident in this body of HIV-positive texts. Perhaps there is no need to note that they are largely written by homosexuals, many of them carriers of the virus, who valiantly strove to document the epidemic, making writing a political tool or thinking of disease as an aesthetic device. Perhaps the overwhelming response, not only in mainstream cultural activism but also in the most radical and least polite literary texts, symbolized a taking possession of the crisis on the part of the most affected community. Taking on the crisis as a symbol was risky because the social image of the epidemic was at the time exclusively homosexual, and that subversive gesture reinforced, with sinister coherence, the entrenched negative association between the dissident community and the disease, between those groups and a fate of death that had historically been invoked by the nation. Appropriating the epidemic and its stigma was not a naive or wrongheaded approach. Nor was it new. Groups of dissident men had taken on the nomenclature of stigma to limit it, redefine it, invert it. The words *gay* and *queer*, insults at the end of the nineteenth century, had been rewritten positively a century later, and the same thing happened in the Latin American context with the word *marica*, with the words *pájaro* and *loca* (even, in some sectors, with the word *homosexual*).

The gesture of making AIDS their own, saturating the field of representation, can thus be understood as a necessary way to operate in language and politics in a critical moment. Homosexualizing the disease was urgently needed but a delicate operation, burdened by setbacks and accusations from excluded communities. Looking back on it now, it's no surprise that this response produced tensions. There was no critical distance, it's true: instead, there was the imminence of extinction and desperate responses to it. There were other infected people in just as much turmoil, but the most affected and most organized community closed ranks and took absolute possession of the

AIDS calamity. Its writers refused to share the tragic situation, to take what might have been a more subversive or literary approach and imagine the whole nation as being infected. Across a range of writing, we find a shared lack of interest in offering other affected communities the possibility of participating in the crisis as martyrs. That role—victimhood—became a disputed trophy in the battle for social figuration. It did not take long for it to become the source of a schism between the various groups seeking more active intervention on the part of the state.

Desperation and an urgent need to be seen constitute one possible explanation, but perhaps a different understanding of the homosexual communities' isolationist response is possible—perhaps it merely reflected a factual reality. One might say, as some critics have, that hemophiliacs, a small community that rarely appeared in the media, did not become part of the Latin American HIV-positive narrative because the corpus only began to form after the blood banks had already changed their protocols and taken precautions.[72] One might even argue that the near total absence of heroin addicts and other intravenous drug users was because they were not a major part of the epidemic in real life and were only visible in the crisis in Argentina, where the consumption of injected drugs was a mark of distinction for intellectuals returning from exile. This was such common knowledge that "the average Argentine often assumed that anyone with HIV had been a drug user" (Frasca, *AIDS* 165). But this unique circumstance rarely appears in that country's literature. A review of the texts reveals only one HIV-positive needle user in Buenos Aires: a minor character in Claudio Zeiger's novel *Adiós a la calle* (2004; Farewell to the street), a young man who is certainly not an intellectual. In the most unexpected place, however, we find (in literature and in real life) a number of young men who inject themselves with infected blood to gain entrance to the well-supplied Cuban AIDS sanatoriums. At least two Cuban narratives refer to voluntary intravenous infection, both based on a well-publicized case on the island at the beginning of the 1990s. Amid the desperate economic crisis of the Período Especial (Special Period),[73] the young protagonists of

---

[72] There is only one mention found in Joaquín Hurtado's *Crónica sero*, in which a hemophiliac woman is declared HIV-positive but not her husband (37).

[73] Período Especial is the name of a lengthy period of economic crisis experienced in Cuba starting in 1991 as a result of the collapse of the Soviet Union and the end of its financial support of the island. This led to the implementation of major economic reforms and harsh rationing efforts.

"La moneda, la bóveda, yo solo trato de alcanzar" (Money, the vault, that's all I'm after) choose to inject themselves with HIV to enjoy, in Castro's new anti-AIDS *prisons*, benefits that healthy Cubans cannot access: color television, air conditioning, income, and especially food. The story, by Ronaldo Menéndez, who later went into exile in Spain, is just one version of what happened in reality, but it also appears, if obliquely, in Ricardo Arrieta's "Recuerdos obligatorios del olvido" (Obligatory memories of oblivion).[74] In the latter story, the protagonist notes that "algunos de los enfermos que conocía [del sanatorio] se habían inoculado el virus. Los motivos eran varios pero la consecuencia era única. No existía ninguna vía más segura de contagio que la transfusión sanguínea" [some of the patients (he) knew in the sanatorium had given themselves the virus. They all had different reasons, but the result was the same. There was no surer way to become infected than through a blood transfusion] (170). These two texts on infection through blood, in a country where the incidence of this kind of infection was in fact less common, refutes any possible quantitative argument. Numbers cannot explain how a social issue is interpreted symbolically. They are of some limited use: to reflect the low numbers of intravenous drug users, for example, or the absence of hemophiliacs and children in the literature of the epidemic as the development of new medical technologies made those populations less vulnerable.[75] But they fail utterly at representing mothers and infected women, whose numbers were growing.

THE IMAGINED IMMUNITY OF WOMEN

HIV-positive women were left in the shadows: from the beginning, AIDS was thought of as a masculine disease and strategically appropriated by the communities of dissident men. Women remained dangerously marginalized. I have no intention of mythologizing women as particularly victimized or of succumbing to the easy binaries that have done so much damage over the course of the epidemic. I am interested rather in exploring the exclusion of female bodies

---

[74] Both stories were collected in an anthology on Cuban AIDS, *Toda esa gente solitaria* (1997; All the lonely people), edited by Lourdes Zayón Jomolca and José Ramón Fajardo Atanes.

[75] The use of techniques such as sperm washing (in which the virus is separated from the sperm before insemination), standard testing of pregnant women, and, more recently, new medicines that prevent transmission between mother and child have significantly reduced the incidence of AIDS in newborns.

as a symptom of a tension between genders, a tension exacerbated by the growing presence of women in the public sphere, but also as an indication of a new masculinization of the social imaginary that attempts to reject any element of the feminine in the culture: the bodies both of women and of transvestites, who seek to em*body* a particular femininity.

For a little context, I will start by noting that the relative absence of textual representations of female carriers is perplexing if considered purely in statistical terms. Unlike the other excluded groups, which gradually became a smaller proportion of the infected population, the number of infected women grew consistently around the world.[76] In Africa there were never significant gender differences—contagion was heterosexual—but this data point was largely ignored because it did not coincide with the prevailing narrative of a homosexual virus. In the United States, symptoms of the syndrome were detected in women only a year after the official identification of the epidemic, but these were *buried* (as Paula Treichler funereally puts it) by the statistics on the disease for many years. Only in 1993 were the figures alarming *enough* to shatter the complacent social assumptions about female immunity. Similarly, in Latin America women rapidly reached the tragic infection rates of their masculine counterparts. In the 1990s, the number of women (and of the poor) had grown significantly, and rates of infection were no longer asymmetrical. The economy and demography of the infection had changed. After years of feminist efforts to refute the notion that AIDS in women was a "male disease in female bodies" (qtd. in Charlesworth 60), at last discussions emerged of the feminization of the syndrome—a common headline both in periodicals with a sensationalist bent and in forums for sober reflection.

Surprisingly, the idea that women were *more* immune than men persisted for a long time. And that powerful illusion seems to have resulted in the low number of women authors who decided to take on the task of narrating their own gender's situation in the crisis. HIV is largely absent from the works of female authors but makes frequent appearances in those of male authors, a difference that is inexplicable

---

[76] Currently some 60 percent of HIV-positive individuals around the world are women. Unlike in Africa, where the epidemic affects women and men equally (1:1), in Latin America the proportions have varied: at first they were very unequal (1:10), but that asymmetry has lessened in the last decade (1:3) in countries such as Chile, Mexico, Argentina, and Peru. For up-to-date information, see the site <www.who.int/gender/hiv_aids/en/>.

in comparison to the literature of disease as a whole, which is historically written by men but populated by women suffering from real diseases or metaphorical punishments that doctors must treat or purge from body and soul.[77] And even more inexplicable if we recall that female writers in recent decades capitalized on the body as the preferred object of their work. Yet in the direst period of the epidemic, every time the syndrome is mentioned (which does not happen often), these female authors, repeating a long-established and difficult-to-eradicate pattern, confirm it as unequivocally male.

Though there is little available evidence, this is not mere idle speculation. In *Diario del dolor* (2004; Pain diary), the Mexican author María Luisa Puga personifies her rheumatoid arthritis in these terms: "Es que por un lado está su aspecto tan...(lo voy a decir en voz baja, no se me vaya a enojar mas): huesudo, amarillo, si no supiera que es él [diría]: allá va otra víctima del sida" [On the one hand, he looks so...(I'll say it quietly so he doesn't flare up again): bony, yellow, if I didn't know it was him (I would say): there goes another AIDS victim] (44). Pain in Puga is related to AIDS and is an active subject that causes its victim constant suffering. This situation recurs in a number of variations: the virus is embodied by a male subject while the female characters think of themselves as having subordinate or service roles in the narrative of infection. They are the mothers and lovers, the sisters or cousins, the friends, the nurses, all of them taking care of the carrier, all stoic and self-sacrificing, sometimes hypochondriac and even paranoid, but never violating—indeed, bizarrely perpetuating—an established image. In other cases, such as in *La vera historia de Purificación* (1989; The true history of Purification), the Paraguayan novelist Raquel Saguier refers early on and quite in passing, as if unintentionally, to AIDS as marking a new era that seems alien to the narrative's main character, an older married woman who remained on the sidelines of sexual liberation and who is astonished by

---

[77] It is not difficult to find texts that allow the comparison of literary representations of other illnesses: in narratives about tuberculosis and cancer, women appear as frequently as men. Classics such as Abraham Valdelomar's *La ciudad de los tísicos* (1911; The city of consumptives) or Juan Carlos Onetti's *Los adioses* (1954; The goodbyes) are emblematic but not isolated examples in which the illness affects both sexes. Significantly, it is women who most frequently suffer cancer in Latin American literature: see Juan Carlos Onetti's *La vida breve* (1950; *A Brief Life*), Manuel Puig's *Pubis angelical* (1979; *Pubis Angelical*), José Donoso's *Lagartija sin cola* (2007; *The Lizard's Tale*), Marta Blanco's *Maradentro* (1997; Out to sea), or Margo Glantz's "Palabras para una fábula" (2005; Words for a fable).

the present: "¿Era realmente verdad que hubo una vez un tiempo en que nadie se moría de sida y los tranvías eran a caballo y de noche había necesidad de escupidera?" [Was it really true that there had been a time when nobody died of AIDS and the streetcars were pulled by horses and you needed a chamberpot at night?] (37). It also appears as a menacing but male presence in *Maradentro* (1997; Out to sea) by the Chilean author Marta Blanco. The familiar plot interweaves two diseases, both of them lethal and even linked in the popular imaginary of the epidemic: the cancer of the mother and the *mysterious* secret illness of her son who lies dying in a San Francisco hospital, surrounded by friends. It is the elderly mother who survives to keep her tragically young son company in his difficult final days. In the daring tale "Dueños de la arena" (2006; Masters of the sand) by Bolivian writer Giovanna Rivero, we find again the familiar presence of male AIDS and the sacrificial figure of the female protagonist, who, incestuous and suicidal, or perhaps feeling young and immortal, has sex with her cousin; but he is the one who carries the virus, while for her what remains uncertain is whether she has been infected. (This uncertainty, saturated with terror, is also seen in the story by Guillermo Saccomanno: the protagonist has just been given his diagnosis, and his lover refuses to answer his calls, as if just touching the telephone would confirm her infection.) Paranoia gradually sets in, an unmoored or unreal fear. In "Enfermedad mortal" (2006; Fatal illness), by Chilean writer Andrea Maturana, the story ambiguously explores the possibility of infection, considering whether VHL, a genetic autosomal condition secretly afflicting the protagonist's husband, is HIV. When the woman finally understands that it is not AIDS, that in fact her husband's night sweats and shivering could be related to cancer, she decides to ignore the whole thing as if it did not exist, constructing a mental state of immunity.

This paranoia and deep denial appear again in a recent tale by Margo Glantz: in "Tres personas distintas. ¿Alguna verdadera?" (2009; Three different people—any of them real?), the virus is already undeniably a threat to women. Terror soon sets in.[78] The text employs

---

[78] An earlier scene of female paranoia appears in the story "Todo tipo de médicos" (1988; All kinds of doctors) by the Mexican writer Luis Zapata, a late contemporary and compatriot of Glantz. From the point of view of its mocking male narrator, the female protagonist's fear is only manipulation or hysteria: she complains, "que tenía los ganglios muy inflamados...y que seguramente había pescado por allá [los Estados Unidos] una infección o un virus raro, que aquí [México] no le podían detectar" [that her lymph nodes were really swollen...and that when she was there (in the United States) she must have caught an infection or strange virus that here (in Mexico) they were unable to detect] (33).

at least three different but overlapping Nora Garcías, all of them victims of invasive medical interventions and hemmed in by various fears of infection. Nora the obsessive secretary of a pathologist and Nora the hypochondriac novelist in the endodontist's chair are joined by Nora the high-strung radio announcer who takes on the mission of reciting AIDS statistics for her listeners. Yet radio Nora refers not to the local epidemic but to the dismal situation in Africa, which she transfers, in a paranoid fit of imagination, to Mexico City:

> Un estudio [en una universidad sudafricana] ha determinado ahora [2008] que casi una de cuatro mujeres de entre veinte y veinticuatro años está infectada. El nivel de infección es mucho menor entre los hombres de la misma edad (me da susto, en el salón de belleza la manicurista me cortó la cutícula y me hizo sangrar, los instrumentos de manicure no parecían estar esterilizados) (¡quién me manda ir a salones de pacotilla!). (310)
>
> [A study (in a South African university) has now (2008) shown that nearly one in four women between the ages of twenty and twenty-four is infected. The infection levels are much lower in men of the same age (it scares me: in the beauty salon the manicurist cut my cuticle and made me bleed, and the manicure tools did not appear to be sterilized) (what am I doing in dodgy salons?!).]

Nora expresses her fright at the possibility of contracting a globalized virus that seems to have her surrounded, but, again, that possibility never comes to pass in the story. The statistics remind Nora only of the death of Michel Foucault in Paris: an old image of AIDS that once more associates the disease with a man, a homosexual who is distant from the protagonist both in space and especially in time. Read in conjunction, these stories portray an HIV that establishes itself in the male body, its transference to the female body being only a potentiality. It is as if the literary representations of the disease created by the few female writers of Latin American AIDS fiction, even current ones, were trying to alert women to the risk but also asserting a certain degree of safety, a discreet distance. The epidemic as they recount it, when they do at all, still has a defined identity: men carry the virus, and women remain largely immune to its impact.[79]

---

[79] Worth mentioning here is *La nada cotidiana* (1995; The daily nothing) by Cuban writer Zoé Valdés, the only author in the corpus who talks about the possibility of infection between women; her work is discussed in the second part of this study.

Teaching HIV-Positive Women a Lesson

Women with AIDS may have appeared only infrequently and intermittently, but they were subject to a startlingly consistent negative critique: the initial gender imbalance that seemed to explain female invisibility or the illusion of female immunity was followed by a stereotyped, even moralistic take on gender and AIDS. When it became socially convenient to emphasize female infection to reinforce a conservative gender politics, the female carrier reappeared, divided into two archetypal figures. One was the image of excessive, roaming sexuality, synthesized in the blameworthy prostitute. The second was constructed in contrast to the first: the domesticated woman who is made ill by her partner's uncontrolled sexuality. The submissive woman becomes the victim of an alien illness; she is sacrificed to and even sanctified by the epidemic, which also underscores the link between illness and guilt. Though they might seem it, the docile victim and the victimizing prostitute are not opposing figures but two inverse aspects of infection in which a moralizing social discourse converges. All too often, the discussion revolved around the "risk they [wives and prostitutes] posed to men rather than the risk the virus posed for them" (Hammonds 233).

Yet the order of their appearance was the inverse. Among women, it was prostitutes who first entered the infectious current of the pandemic and were identified as the supposed source of heterosexual contagion. We can date that moment to 1987, when the discussion of the epidemic began to include mentions of women who engaged in sex work. It was Sander Gilman who said (and he was not alone in making this claim) that when the virus began to spread to groups that were not considered marginal, the source of infection was immediately linked to that nineteenth-century image of women secretly nurtured to keep the institution of bourgeois marriage running smoothly. Although it was not the first time they'd been accused of threatening society,[80] the emergence of AIDS meant that prostitutes were immediately included among the socially *aberrant* groups, along with other sexual dissidents. According to a

---

[80] The prostitute was also a figure of infection in the modernization processes of the Latin American city. Sylvia Saitta (2006) examines the textual representation of the poor little seamstress who brings illness to Buenos Aires at the beginning of the twentieth century: moving to the capital in search of a better life, she catches tuberculosis and also infects others with the disease.

constructed perception, they were homosexuals' doubles, a mirror image of transvestites, made equivalent by their *excessive* femininity and the apparent similarity of their sexual transactions. Not only was prostitution, both female and male, the object of social stigma, but it also occupied a place in the new economic logic; especially at the end of the twentieth century, prostitution signified an intervention of the market in the national space symmetrical to that of the sex worker. Prostitution is, Georg Simmel claims, "the sign of the impact of the laws of exchange on the most intimate or private zones of modern life" (122). Prostitution, he writes, is not a social anomaly but a model for human relationships within the capitalist system. It was precisely this model that went into crisis with the appearance of AIDS. Sexuality as an object of consumption became risky. And in the crucial moment, as the transvestite died, representing the eradication of homosexuality, the prostitute became the gravest threat to the heterosexual world. She menaced the nation's most beloved figure: the patriarch who was both the foundation of the national community and the apex of power. It is no surprise, then, that the character of the prostitute became an object of attention. She was the official subject of interviews in many nonfiction texts, and in some works of fiction replaced homosexuals as the focus of the disease. It is significant that in at least half of the short stories included in the collection *Toda esa gente solitaria* (1997; All the lonely people), written by members of the literary workshop in the Cuban AIDS sanatorium Los Cocos (among whom not a single female name appears), prostitutes fulfill a singular role as infectors, while mothers and lovers fulfill a service role. The mercenary whore allows herself to be infected by foreigners and passes HIV on to the good Cuban citizen. The sexually liberated female tourist serves the same function: to introduce the virus as an agent of the capitalist world. She becomes the means of transmission for the disease, there in the very cradle of Latin American socialism, where the word *homosexual* can no longer even be uttered.

This negative characterization of the HIV-positive prostitute progressively expands to include women who do not sell their bodies, condemning those other carriers as faithless wives or bad mothers. Didactic texts resist this destructive image, attempting to repair prostitutes' reputation in society at large; in other words, rather than questioning the ideological substrate of the condemnation, these narratives repeat pedagogical discourses against sex and in doing so reinforce the condemnation of all women. Redemptive testimonies repeat, without any critical analysis, narratives of the female as an innocent victim, tacitly insinuating the possibility that somebody else is guilty. These are simplified stereotypes of resignation to AIDS, which becomes a reason to write: a personal diary, a tear-soaked confession, a survival notebook stripped of any political substance. Illness is confirmed as a rhetorical site for understanding what has happened, motivated by a desire for change that nevertheless precedes the acceptance of events—another veiled form of female sacrifice that appears in the theater of confession. The early precursor of this gesture is the aforementioned Colombian writer Sonia Gómez, whose book *Sida en Colombia: "Nunca me imaginé que podría infectarme"* (1988; AIDS in Colombia: "I never thought I could get sick") compiles testimonies from men and women who seize on their infection as an opportunity for personal growth. Next, perhaps, comes the Mexican Rosa Esquivel, in whose *Amor a la vida* (1995; Love for life) HIV-positive women exhibit a resignation that is both systematic and apolitical. "El destino así te tocó y pus ni modo" [It was fate; you didn't have any other option], confesses Amalia, while Sofía asserts, "Ahora me siento feliz, deveras" [Now I feel truly happy]. And there are still other models that are just as submissive: heroines who suffer but endure for the good of the family; mothers who sublimate the need for activism as they embrace a domestic role; women who hold themselves in check and are thus symbolically located within the metaphor of cancer, a disease associated, as already mentioned, with the repression of desire.

Despite the era's feminist aspects, beneath its gender-reaffirming shell lurked a conservative core. These discourses were promoted especially by journalists who thought of themselves as performing a public service, and repeated in texts that called themselves novels despite being mere mimesis bereft of symbolic density and contaminated with the language of prevention campaigns. Instead, these texts constituted a project of female consciousness-raising structured around the preventive model imposed by the search for a guilty party: the transvestite who *tempts* the man into the ambiguous territory of bisexuality, the prostitute or liberated woman who *induces* the married man into unprotected sex, the unfaithful individual who then takes the virus back home: infection as another form of domestic violence. In other versions, women are also responsible for not having protected themselves sexually. (In this heteronormative model, lesbians and the possibility that they might become infected do not exist.) AIDS is not shared like a social or familial circumstance; instead, it divides the protagonists, pits them against each other, assigning them fixed positions in the representation of a kind of *immorality*. One example of this model is found in the work of the journalist Edmée Pardo, in a text in which literary qualities had to be set aside to make way for medicine's informatory approach, a text that I highlight here because it reiterates a conservative program that urges married or adulterous women not to trust their sexual partners. María Luisa Puga employs a confessional mode to explore the motif of the masculine virus discussed above. Even in the original title, *El primo Javier* (1996; Cousin Javier),[81] the masculine is assigned blame. In fact, there is no cousin; Javier is the name given to the virus, confounding it with a male family member in a rhetorical maneuver that threatens to become part of an unfortunate convention. The adulterous female protagonist becomes a possible victim of a symbolically masculine assault: the patriarchal law that punishes her through her male lover and through a virus that is constructed as masculine. Her unfaithful affiliation with this man-virus harms love and confirms the masculine origin of the disease. The fear of infection—this fear of punishment produced by the violation of marriage vows—can only be shared with her female friends, although this instance of female solidarity is also an occasion for teaching the principles of prevention that every good woman should follow. This idea is reaffirmed from an apparently opposite perspective in another pedagogical novel that positions the submissive wife and perfect mother as the only innocent victim of AIDS. *Muérdele el corazón* (2006; Bite his heart),[82] by journalist and activist Lydia Cacho, recounts the narrator's discovery that she has been infected by her husband after his repeated infidelity in a love triangle. The adulterous act, but especially the revelation of her husband's bisexuality, is the great ordeal that allows the protagonist to gather her strength to pursue emancipation from the well-mannered conventions of female submissiveness, but her push toward freedom soon founders under society's disciplinary rigidity: she blames her husband for the sexual deviance that has made him HIV-positive, refuses to think of the situation from any other perspective, sees herself as a victim, and reaffirms her maternal role by finally forgiving the man because her children will remain with him.

---

[81] This book was republished as *Morir de amor* (Dying of love) in 2002.
[82] This novel was published in 2003 under the title *Las provincias del alma* (The provinces of the soul).

Among these texts, one brilliant work stands out, one that despite its pedagogical approach is also proactive and not at all rigid in its thinking. It is a political text, or rather a compilation of texts: the aforementioned anthology of Argentine accounts by Marta Dillón. Unlike any other narrator, this journalist chooses to publish a large number of familiar cases, variations on the complex development of the epidemic that allow us to move past the clichés and moralistic readings of the disease. The only female Latin American writer who has admitted to being HIV-positive, Dillón avoids a simplistic discourse of responsibility and punishment; she also, wisely, avoids the theme of heterosexual domestic violence that pits men against women, refuses to see women as either prostitutes or saints, and strips bare the innumerable contradictions of living with the virus, both privately and publicly. Her essays engage with the political aspects of that critical moment, examining the tensions between the biological body and the social body and calling upon men and women to share the experience of infection, to demand an acceptable and even enjoyable survival—one that reaffirms sex and rejects the imposition of double-edged discourses of health and morality.

EXILE OF THE FEMININE

The scanty representation of the feminine appears in three simultaneous but distinct ways: first, the apparent immunity of women to the disease and its complement, paranoia; second, the assignation to prostitutes of blame for infection; and third, the heroic victimization of the wife in certain AIDS dogmas. Yet another dubious and perhaps more radical model appears, if only occasionally,[83] in the writing of their male counterparts: a total exclusion of the female body from the narrative imaginary, as well as the virtual eradication of the transvestite body because it bears the sign of the feminine. In a surprising and dark turn, we witness the disappearance of a segment, the most *escandaloso* [flamboyant] segment, as Arenas put it, of the homosexual community. This suppression came out of an ideological

---

[83] This brings up a methodological issue: whereas because of their abundance many HIV-positive texts written by men have not been analyzed critically, all of the texts written by women (at least the ones that I found) have already been studied: it would otherwise have been impossible to make a comparison.

tendency that gradually grew more prevalent both in Latin American reality and in its literary canon, until there was eventually a systematic rejection of any element of the feminine, indicating a turn toward the masculine that was linked with the notion that arose during the epidemic of a return to a heteronormative ideology (in which men are dominant and women subjugated) as a sign of health. This idea echoed an early warning issued by Néstor Perlongher and Pedro Lemebel about the elimination of the transvestite in the neocolonial evolution of capitalist culture at the end of the twentieth century. In his essays, Lemebel foresaw a grim future for the transvestite thanks to the emergence of a homogenizing global gay culture that compelled the *loca* to either submit or go extinct. Lemebel's ominous prediction, which was echoed throughout Latin American AIDS writing, applied not only to the transvestite but also to the symbolic elision of the feminine.

Few texts from the HIV-positive corpus better reflect this feminine loss—the exclusion of women, the elimination of transvestites—than Bellatin's *Salón de belleza* and controversial Colombian Fernando Vallejo's *El desbarrancadero* (2001; The precipice). Both novels return to sexist models at the peak of the epidemic and reaffirm the value of masculinity as a sign of health. When the crisis begins, the beauty salon, which previously functioned in alliance with women—a mutually beneficial arrangement in which the transvestite provided style and the woman served as a model—changes its objectives. It closes its door to women and to the mission of offering them beauty and opens them exclusively to the sick, with morbid intentions. The transition from salon to death house marks a shift in identity both in the space and in the narrator, who ceases to be the *queen* of the place and becomes a regent who manages, with sinister efficiency, the suppression of the weakened patients. In the transvestite's push to eliminate, he burns all of his feminine garments before disappearing himself. It is a gradual shutting down of everything that heteronormative conventions cast as feminine: women, transvestites, the submissive sick people at death's door. It is these bodies that the story whisks away. And when they are gone—an allegory for the disappearance of AIDS from the social imaginary—the space is available. The place is empty but open, ready to be occupied once more when the epidemic is over.

A similar mechanism is at work in Vallejo's *El desbarrancadero*, an HIV-positive novel that reasserts the theme of female exclusion. We see a definitive reterritorialization of the masculine values celebrated by the narrators in all of his novels. The old binary hierarchy that queer dissidence would like to see fall into disuse is reestablished, as vigorous as ever, and localized, even in this HIV-positive text, presented as civilization versus *Colombian* violence, as order versus urban chaos, as health versus the tragedy of the AIDS afflicting the protagonist's brother. These concepts are all translated, rewritten, even synthesized in an oppositional gender politics: between men as the favored subject and women as a device that reproduces violence, chaos, and disease. Women in Vallejo contribute to the general state of social decay and are always accused of causing the population increase and thus the crisis; yet in this novel, I would argue, woman—the mother of the characters—becomes the origin of death (and death, as a character, is also feminine). But it is to that place of death—the maternal home, the *pequeña Colombia* [little Colombia] referred to in the story—that the two brothers return: one to die and the other to lovingly oversee his death. The experience of death confirms the brothers as a loving, allegorical couple that excludes the mother (indeed, that must exclude her in order to be possible). But terminal illness also produces a gradual distancing between the younger brother, who is sick and weak, the shadow of a perhaps feminine dependence on medication, and the healthy firstborn, who takes on the role of scientist and doctor for his younger brother. The survivor, who occupies the symbolically powerful role of speaking, is the one who challenges the mother in decisions on caring for the dying brother, demanding control of the mother's house. This demand for power is justified by the unhealthy home run by the mother, whom the narrator calls, suggestively, *la loca* [madwoman, but also, as we have seen, slang for a drag queen]. The mother and all that her sex represents must be conjured, as if femaleness were a disease, as if survival required her corporal and cultural exile and the formation of a new alliance, a healthy, vigorous, revitalized alliance with a healthy masculinity.

My review of this global survey of the epidemic and its discourses suggests that *Salón de belleza* and *El desbarrancadero* express an idea powerfully inscribed in the social imaginary of this capitalist era: the idea that survival is not a cooperative effort but is instead achieved through binary models of competition and profit in which illness and the ill are stigmatized for showing their neediness, for requiring inputs without generating outputs. For not being part of the promised progress. The disease is punished for signaling resistance to the new global capitalism. The unsettling reaffirmation of this mandate, set in motion as a self-destructive impulse by the narrative imaginary, demands a permanently watchful gaze, one that recognizes not only the shining moments but also the contradictions that plague the extended HIV-positive community of the present.

PART II

Viral Voyagers

Itinerant Infirmity

The motif of wandering appears with relentless frequency in twentieth-century Latin American dissident narratives. Long before the epidemic began, writers and their peregrinating protagonists traveled, whether in reality or in the imagination, in search of others with the same difference, or in flight from the stigma of moral and sexual illness ascribed to them. The persecution of homosexuals as pathological subjects who threaten to corrupt the nation has long-standing precedent in religion, and it continued in the medical and legal sciences that gradually imposed upon the certainty of faith the truths of science. Religion had tried to punish deviance, and now medicine would try to cure it. Curing homosexuals, making their desires conform to normality, was the objective, and only geographic escape could fend it off for a time. This escape was at first a gesture of resistance to the rigid expectations set out by the nation. These movements never followed a fixed pattern: though the nation was the point of departure, the destination changed. But that itinerancy always led toward a foreign place whose norms were not imposed on the traveler. An analysis of the situation makes it clear that this impatience to leave was a result of "very concrete processes of social engineering and modernization" (Quiroga 12) that preceded the emergence of the homosexual as a category imported from the old continent.[84] Homosexuals arose as the modern incarnation of a diagnosable danger. The new nomenclature medicalized and criminalized an ancient sexual practice that was suddenly understood as a threat to the pure body of the nation still under construction, a body whose existence depends on defining its limits—inventing its *others*. Distinctions were drawn, and the word *homosexual*, which came from Europe, also suggested the practice of homosexuality as something *foreign*, the result

---

[84] For an explanation of the use of the term *homosexual* in this book, see note 12.

of cultural importation made possible through the mechanisms of capitalism, itself also foreign.

The paradox is striking. Capitalism in metamorphosis, which, according to some purists, opened the door to the destruction of traditions, was also the great ally of a crucial internal displacement that had a profound influence on the creation of homosexual identity—an identity understood as a way of thinking, identity constructed as it was reflected in others. The processes of modernization altered the structure of society and produced irreversible shifts in the economic function of the family. Industrialization stimulated its collapse. Many left the sheltered but repressive home environment and moved toward less guarded spaces: the incessant movement that began at the time was from the countryside to the city and from one continent to another. In this slow, intermittent, unequal movement in search of paid work, we find the seeds of an incipient sexual liberation. Some of those men—and possibly some of those women[85]—could find partners of the same sex with whom to share a mutual desire and, even more crucially, with whom to identify. To put it another way, homosexuality—like community-mindedness, like political consciousness, like militancy—arose in those initial encounters and in that possibility of sexual fulfillment. The urban space was important not only because it allowed the establishment of certain erotic practices and particular modes of enjoyment (desire has always found an opportunity and a place in which to be fulfilled, however adverse the circumstances), and not only because it produced the more or less explicit recognition of a shared subjectivity. What constituted the homosexual subject, historian John D'Amilio has said, was his consciousness of his identity and of a community with rights: political engagement, not just an affinity of tastes.

Yet we should note the varying velocities at which these changes took place. The formation of Latin American dissident groups was a

---

[85] The lesbian presence in Latin American literature remained hidden: it is surpassingly difficult to find in the Latin American literary corpus traces of desire transformed into lesbian behavior or even consciousness. In addition to the scarcity of women writers, there is also the historical repression of female sexuality. In one early exception from Brazil, Patrícia Galvão's *Parque industrial* (1933; *Industrial Park*), the avant-garde writer links female sexuality to capitalist exploitation: a rich woman's exploitation of a working-class woman who cannot refuse her. Lesbianism, then, does not lead to liberation. Thus, traveling female writers fit better with the rhetoric of freedom. Although veiled, there are references to that possibility in the work and letters of traveling writers Teresa de la Parra, Lydia Cabrera, and Gabriela Mistral. For more references, see Foster (1991) and Molloy (1995).

markedly slower process. All sorts of factors—cultural, social, historical, and even linguistic—caused detours in the journey, which did not move in a straight line in the rest of the world, either. Among these factors were the beliefs about sex in the different local ethnicities; the influence of a stubborn, castrating Catholicism; the migratory trends of different eras that took on new patterns and names; the omnipotent presence of the family that, when it collapsed, was replaced by a patronage that was eerily similar in its workings; and the continent's slow, intermittent process of industrialization and its ever-postponed modernization. But sooner or later that alternative community would emerge. It grew despite being in impossible tension with the nation's moral precepts. Excluded from the masculine pact that defines proper citizens (one that forbids sex between men, transferring that erotic tension to the virile negotiation of power), homosexuals exercised their desire behind the nation's back, though never completely separated from it. They were tormented, split between national expectations and individual desires that did not conform to the norms of the nation. They were aware of the rejection and stigma attached to dissident bodies as if they were carriers of a contagious disease, a situation that later fictions allegorized in various violent acts that always led to the death of those enigmatic characters.

One wonders who, exactly, that nation is. Or what it is, how it imposes repression so consistently. Here I respond in accordance with the view of the renowned Benedict Anderson: the nation is a type of community, one of many possible types. The nation constitutes itself dynamically, conceives of itself or, rather, imagines itself— without knowing itself yet, without ever having seen or heard of any others—through supposedly shared elements: some occasional readings; a literature that represents exclusive values; common norms within a single sovereign, limited, and conjectured territory.[86] The nation, to legitimately exist, must think of itself as a brotherhood of men governed by a profoundly egalitarian camaraderie, the parameters of whose actions have been agreed upon among all included. Of course, that association between *equal* men is not, in fact, equal, nor is it, as we know, exclusively male and heterosexual. What is essential is that it conceive of itself that way in order to draw a line, to be able to

---

[86] In its abstract conceptualization, the essential character of the nation comes precisely from the act of imagining it, of producing a mental image through the reading of the press and of literature (and possibly, in the contemporary era, through images from television and cinema). Anderson does not limit the definition: in being *imagined*, that community can be transnational, global, or even virtual in nature.

exclude subjects who visibly do not conform to those imaginings. The nation justifies itself in the fiction of opposites, and homosexuals fulfill that necessary function. Their particular introduction into society at the beginning of the twentieth century must be understood strategically. In its beginnings it was limited to personal contact within a *secret* community: one community within another or, seen from another perspective, one that imagined itself simultaneously within and outside of the nation. From that ambivalent position, from those contradictory affiliations, the secret community articulated its own code, legible only to those who understood its grammar. They organized a parallel order in alternative spaces, with divided loyalties. The community's problematic coexistence with the nation (sometimes internalized, at others manifested in policies and practices of violence) sparked the dream of escape outside—beyond—immediate experience. There are no studies to confirm this, only isolated episodes in the texts of many authors of the time, tales of the displacement of strange, unsatisfied men, expressions of extraterritorial utopias that played out in the territories of desire.

It is key that the fledgling homosexual community of the diaspora, just like the national community, imagined itself as a brotherhood of equals (though it wasn't one, really, and never could be, thanks to the profound class and race differences among its members). Nevertheless, in order to be articulated, the sexual community *must* conceive of itself as being united by affinities and by a series of shared texts, a literature that circulated in secret, moving between and along with the members of this traveling caste. Yet the utopia of the wandering community that began to be established in the first half of the twentieth century was seen not as *no place* (*outopia*) nor merely as a *good place* (*eutopia*), but as the demarcation of spaces of specific sexual actions and interactions, places where those men made dates and practiced what Néstor Perlongher called *nomadismo erótico* [erotic nomadism]. Those spaces were seen as heterotopias, territories or counterterritories within society: a sort of utopia positioned in a particular space to represent, impugn, and invert or undiscipline (Foucault would say) all of society's real, fixed spaces.[87] Heterotopias

---

[87] Agreeing with other contemporary queer thinkers, Sylvia Molloy notes that these heterotopias are not enough to articulate alternative systems and suggests that perhaps they should not attempt to do so: "Cabe preguntarse hasta donde es deseable articular esos sistemas alternativos, so riesgo de disciplinarlos" [It is worth wondering to what degree it is desirable to articulate those alternative systems, at the risk of regimenting them] ("La cuestión" 819).

exist at the margins—which are not the same as the periphery—of legitimate spaces. These spaces of *others* that appear on Foucault's list are the insane asylum, the jail, and the circus, while Argentine critic Sylvia Molloy's queer list includes others: islands, for example. Islands are preferential locations for utopias, says Molloy, as they are spaces where "pequeñas comunidades idílicas" [small idyllic communities] are established behind the world's back ("La cuestión" 816). Domingo Faustino Sarmiento encountered some strange American castaways living on the island of Más Afuera (Farther Seaward)[88] in 1845 and was unable to persuade them to return to civilization: they'd gone far beyond *farther*, notes Molloy. Also included on that list of utopian alternatives to normative spaces are, of course, groups of disciples, guilds, cultural centers, and communes such as the short-lived Colonia Tolstoyana, founded in 1904 in a remote area of southern Chile by the nomadic writer—the *wandering brother*—of Chilean literature. Augusto D'Halmar was the most conspicuous figure to travel to East Asia and Europe, continents where he encountered travel companions and experiences that he later incorporated into his novels: his Egyptian lover was quite possibly transformed into the young man Aceitunita in *Pasión y muerte del cura Deusto*. D'Halmar's roving was the precursor to the journeys of a dissident community that sought to flee its sexual namelessness. This flight was apparent in the decades that followed, when the search for a place of their own was repeated in varying ways.

More recent and even more famous is the case of Federico García Lorca, whose geographic movements were more contradictory and less *communitarian* than those of D'Halmar. Lorca was forced out of Spain against his will. His father, worried by his son's nonchalance, arranged and funded his departure for New York to extract him from an unacceptable relationship, to cure him of that *illness* that was beginning to become public knowledge in 1930s Madrid (Lorca had had to leave southern Spain for the capital city to meet up with his lover and a small group of associates). That trip to the United States was a form of exile; remaining in Spain, even in the capital, was dangerous, and it was impossible for him to practice his homosexuality openly there. And yet New York allowed him to see ways of being with others, to discover a world that he had barely dreamed of in Madrid. Although Lorca made no mention in his poetry of the relationships he formed

[88] The island, now known as Alejandro Selkirk Island, is part of the Juan Fernández Islands, a Chilean archipelago.

in Manhattan (in *Poeta en Nueva York* [*Poet in New York*], like most avant-garde poets, he portrayed the great capitalist city as a dehumanized environment), his letters to his family reveal that it was a time of freedom and great friendships. It is no surprise that Lorca omitted from his letters any description of the great flourishing of gay theater taking place in the city at the time (Smith), and it can be assumed that nothing of the romantic aspects of his experiences in New York, Buenos Aires, or Cuba was ever put down in writing. Those spaces remained hidden, were kept secret: they depended on secrecy to avoid failure or a normative intervention that might destroy them.

Allow me to point out one additional case: that of the eccentric modernist writer Salvador Novo, founder of a homointellectual group that soon dissolved, the influential Mexican movement known as Los Contemporáneos (The Contemporaries). Novo, a personal friend of Lorca's from the time they met in Buenos Aires in 1933, was another homosexual who found in exile a way to negotiate local oppression. As he describes in "Continente vacío" (1934; Empty continent), written upon his return from New York and South America, the Mexican writer felt "en casa" [at home] when he disembarked in Rio de Janeiro. That feeling of being at home can be read as the projection of his own mental state onto the whole city. How else can we explain his choice of words, the "embriagadora avidez" [intoxicating eagerness] provoked in him by that "tierra lujuriosa" [lustful land] where the passengers, or perhaps just he alone, descended into the city, "ávidos de huir de sí mismos por 24 horas" [eager to flee from themselves for 24 hours] (746). Although Novo had to remain in Mexico, where he was known and accepted—he had become skilled at somehow saying everything but revealing nothing—he recognized in Brazil the inverse of Mexico, where he, had he been able to choose, "tendría que haber nacido" [should have been born] (748).

These movements are marked by a cartographic idealization: Lorca left Granada for Madrid and traveled from there to the Americas; D'Halmar began his journey from Chile to southern Spain and East Asia, passing through a number of Latin American port cities; Novo visited these same great cities; and later the Cuban writer Virgilio Piñera went to Buenos Aires, where he met and became friends with another mysterious European in exile, the Polish writer Witold Gombrowicz. What is striking is not the places they chose but that they were always far-flung capital cities where the traveler would be a foreigner—that is, someone who by definition does not belong and of whom nothing can be required. Removed from their origins, these men symbolically cut their ties with the past and were able to reinvent it. Only outside their homelands was it possible to create a homoerotic refuge with some guarantee—or at least the illusion—of safety.

A One-Way Trip from *Patria* to *Filistria*

Wandering is a one-way path. It is triggered by the experience of rejection and a need to seek out others. Once the journey has begun—the fevered rovings of Witold Gombrowicz—there seems to be no way to turn back. But how to keep going? That question is the most difficult to answer and demanded, in Gombrowicz's era, an uninhibited literary imagination like his. Let's follow the path he blazed. The Polish writer dared to set out a course for the mobile community, a community that could travel together and yet stay in one place—as he himself did, for many years, in Argentina. We'll start by going back to 1939, when Gombrowicz disembarked in Buenos Aires, an emblem of the modern city governed by the vast bureaucracies of social capitalism. At the time Buenos Aires was a thriving, cosmopolitan city, the destination for an endless wave of immigration from different backgrounds, itself difficult to distinguish from that other, sexual migration that was also slipping into the city and was identified, with increasing alarm, as something dangerous, a social ill—or illness. Gombrowicz fictionalized his arrival in the capital and his surprising decision to remain there in his first Argentine novel,[89] published 15 years after his arrival. Originally written in Polish and suggestively titled *Trans-Atlantyk* (1953), the plot is more than a simple tale of voluntary exile: the beginning of the Second World War and the German invasion of the author's native Poland that would have forced him back into the army, symbol of national heroism. Going back would have meant going to war, voluntarily dying for the limited imaginations of the homeland described by Anderson. Refusing to make that sacrifice,

---

[89] It is considered not only one of the author's masterpieces but one of the great Argentine novels of the twentieth century. Both Ricardo Piglia and Juan José Saer agree that the novel's Argentine identity comes from the profoundly *foreign* character of that country's novelistic tradition. Since its origins, "buena parte de nuestra literatura...ha sido escrita por extranjeros en idiomas extranjeros: alemán, inglés, francés, italiano" [a good portion of our literature...has been written by foreigners in foreign languages: German, English, French, Italian] and "Gombrowicz se inscribe en un lugar destacado de esa tradición" [Gombrowicz holds a distinguished place in that tradition] (Saer 20–21). This assessment, it seems to me, is plagued by the two nationalisms that Gombrowicz himself always criticized.

Gombrowicz opted instead to remain in the south, even though his desertion cost him: he was marked by that act of betrayal, bearing forevermore the suspect mark of foreignness.[90] Having made his decision, Gombrowicz began to formulate a brutal critique of Poland's policies of blood sacrifice. That critique is at the foundation of his Argentine novel, as he himself noted in his 1957 prologue.[91] In the prologue, Gombrowicz demands—and we should question this prescriptive approach—a restricted reading from his readers: "Debo [exigirlo] porque...se trata de una obra que tiene que ver con la Nación" [I must (demand it) because...this work is one that has to do with the Nation] (*Trans-Atlántico* 7). Further down, the nation is abstracted and universalized, transformed into a universal dilemma: "El problema se refiere no tanto a la relación entre un polaco y Polonia, sino entre un individuo y la nación a la que pertenece" [The problem has to do not so much with the relationship between a Pole and Poland as that between an individual and the nation to which he belongs] (9). Perhaps we should be surprised that this author, who was so adamantly opposed to essentialisms, would *demand* a single reading and reject all others, that he would completely censor the explicit homoerotic content of his autobiographical fiction. This is not just any questioning of the nation's mandates. The plot is unique because it contrasts two ways of thinking about community: a nation of paternal elders versus one of young men, nonprodigal sons, freed from moldering institutions or in open sexual rebellion. It is a risky narrative endeavor, which explains why Gombrowicz tries to distract our attention. Like many men of letters of the period, Gombrowicz knew that homosexuality could only be whispered, never stated aloud. It was

---

[90] Gombrowicz did not go back to live in Poland. After decades in Argentina, he went to France, where he recalled the discomfort of exile. Severo Sarduy discussed the subject with the author in about 1987: "Le digo un día, creo que en Royaumont, en todo caso bajo un árbol: 'Estoy perdido y solo, escribo en español, y más bien en cubano, en un país que no se interesa en nada que no sea su propia cultura, sus tradiciones...es como si no existiera.' // Con su habitual dejo de ironía, su sonrisa discreta pero burlona y ese jadeo asmático que entrecortaba sus frases, me responde cortante: ¿Y qué dirías, Nene, de un polaco en Buenos Aires?" [I tell him one day, I think in Royaumont, but under a tree in any event: "I'm lost and alone, I write in Spanish—worse, in Cuban—in a country that's only interested in its own culture and traditions....It's as if I didn't exist." // With his customary ironic tone, his discreet but mocking smile, and that asthmatic panting that punctuated his sentences, he responded curtly, "And what would you say, kid, of a Pole in Buenos Aires?"] ("El estampido" 37).

[91] *Translator's note*: This prologue is unfortunately not included in the published English-language translation of *Trans-Atlántico*. All translations from it are my own.

not yet time. Accepting that his book dealt with the tense relationship between the homosexual and the nation would have required acknowledging before the prudish society of the time that the figure of the writer Gombrowicz and that of the protagonist of his novel (an alter ego of ambiguous proclivities called "Gombrowicz" or "Señor Witold") *might* be the same. Gombrowicz the author does not seem ready to acknowledge the link that he himself creates by using his own name. Yet he returned to the topic again and again in other texts: "A quienes se interesan en el punto," he notes in his *Diario argentino*, "debo aclararles que jamás, aparte de ciertas experiencias esporádicas en mi temprana juventud, he sido homosexual" [For those interested in the matter, I should clarify that I have never, apart from a few isolated experiences in my early youth, been homosexual] (41).[92] Next, in the contradictory rhetoric that characterizes his style, the author explains that he goes at night to Retiro—an area of male prostitution, where "Gombrowicz" *withdraws* from conventions, where he establishes, at book's end, a community of sexual dissidents, perhaps the most explicit one of the period.

But it was not because of its explicitness that the novel was lauded in Latin American fiction. Novelists writing as critics, such as Juan José Saer and Ricardo Piglia, who both admired the book, did not seem to notice the sexual dissidence that Gombrowicz implies. The author collaborated in normalizing the reading, separating himself from his book and insisting, in his *Diario argentino*, that it was not erotic adventures that he was after in Retiro: "Aturdido, fuera de mí, *expatriado y descarrilado*, trabajado por ciegas pasiones que se encendieron al derrumbarse mi mundo y sentir mi destino en bancarrota...¿qué buscaba? La juventud...aquella juventud con uniforme de soldado o marinero, la juventud de aquellos ultra sencillos muchachos de Retiro" [Bewildered, beside myself, *exiled and derailed*, governed by blind passions that were kindled as my world collapsed and I saw my fate in tatters. What was I looking for? Youth....Youth dressed in a naval or army uniform, the youth of those simple boys from Retiro] (41, emphasis added). The apparent paradox? Here Gombrowicz idealizes the figure of the citizen soldier, the heroic and metonymic incarnation

---

[92] *Translator's note*: *Diario argentino* (Argentine diary) is a selection made from the writer's diaries by Gombrowicz himself and translated into Spanish by Sergio Pitol, who collaborated with Gombrowicz on a number of other translations. In accordance with Gombrowicz's wishes, the entries are undated, making the use of any published English-language translations of the diaries prohibitively difficult. All translations of the text are therefore my own.

of the limited, sovereign, fraternal nation as an exclusionary hetero-sexual masculine space. But in the author's view, these men embody virility off the battlefield, beyond the demands of the nation; they are young men who can be seduced, according to the metaphors provided in the novel, into a project that goes against national ideals.

A reader of the period would recall a recent event: the scandal of a few cadets discovered engaged in *inappropriate behavior*. That news, a still-fresh wound in Buenos Aires's normative heart, had revealed the existence of a large and vibrant dissident culture[93] and triggered legal sanctions against homosexuality in Argentina during the 1940s. The incident brought into public view that underground area of the city where the Gombrowicz of the diary makes his nighttime excursions. Aware of the reading that could be made of his wanderings in the underworld, the Pole hastens to clarify, "advertía que estaba aven-turándome en zonas peligrosas, y naturalmente, lo primero que se me ocurrió pensar fue que estaban trabajándose en el subconsciente tendencias homosexuales. Y por cierto, habría recibido con alivio tal hecho, que por lo menos me ubicaba en alguna realidad" [I realized that I was wandering into dangerous territories, and of course, my first thought was that I was operating out of subconscious homo-sexual tendencies. And I would have been relieved had that been the case, as it at least would have placed me in some kind of reality] (*Diario argentino* 42). Interestingly, the description of this descent into the dangerous underworld of Buenos Aires shares its language with that of Chilean critic Luis Oyarzún's account of his affairs in Santiago, included in his *Diario íntimo* (Personal diary, which, like Gombrowicz's, was written to be read—in the Chilean's case, out loud to his friends). Oyarzún only makes veiled mention to his par-ticular "diferencia—no la más superficial sino la más profunda" [dif-ference—not the most superficial but the most profound] (179). One entry from 1953 (the same year that *Trans-Atlantyk* was published) reflects on the freedom he experienced in the underworld:

> Me sentía desafiante, invadido por un soplo juvenil de aventura, per-fectamente libre y, además, invulnerable, por encima de todos los peli-gros. Ningún *cogotero* podía hacerme absolutamente nada. . . . Hoy, al despertar, he revivido con absoluta conciencia los peligros a los que

---

[93] In that area of the city there was permitted a sexual society that was not necessar-ily a group of men making a living from prostitution but a community of homosexuals from different social classes. There, sexual identity was more important than social class. This was particularly significant in a society like Argentina's, which was notable for its rigidly stratified social structure (Salessi, "The Argentine Dissemination").

me exponía tontamente, arrastrado por un deseo que ahora no podía aceptar sin repugnancia. Hoy rechazo libremente lo que libremente fui anoche, un poco borracho, medio delirante, pero instalado también, de un modo particular, en mi libertad. (195)
[I felt defiant, possessed by a youthful breath of adventure, perfectly free and also invulnerable, above all danger. No attacker could do anything to me.... Today, upon waking, I have relived with full awareness the dangers to which I foolishly exposed myself, dragged along by a desire that I could not now accept without revulsion. Today I freely reject what I freely was last night, a little drunk, half-mad, but also ensconced, in a way, in my freedom.]

Oyarzún and Gombrowicz seem to share a single experience: the nocturnal impulse is followed by a diurnal lucidity in which they *freely* reject what they had, in the darkness, also freely chosen.

Gombrowicz operates within that shadowy area of the discourse. In a long entry in his *Diario argentino* about "sinceridad insincera" [insincere sincerity] (17), which Gombrowicz uses to "fijar los límites de [sus] experiencias" [establish the limits of (his) experiences] (42) and give an official version, the writer contrasts his questionable nighttime walks in Retiro with a few satisfactory sexual (but not, he notes, emotional) relationships with women who, unlike the boys he mentions, remain utterly without identities, even disembodied, in the account. They are phantom lovers who lack narrative force compared to the clearly uniformed and identified presence of the boys. The author adds that his problem with those women is that they not only force him to take on the masculine role but also that of the adult male, thus helping to *kill* the boy in him and causing him, as a result, to try to regain his boyish self in new forays into the underworld (53). This return to the underground and to youthfulness would help restore something lost but not legitimate, given that the act of recovering it entailed a "juego encubierto" [masked game] that could not be confessed openly: "No podía decirlo todo. No podía hablar de ese lugar en mí, penetrado por la noche, que he llamado 'Retiro'" [I could not say everything. I could not talk about that place within me, penetrated by night, that I have called "Retiro"] (43).

Darkness sifts down over the definitions. The writer avoids them,[94] and it is not my intention to delve for biographical evidence.

---

[94] For Gombrowicz, writes José Quiroga, identity is a complex phenomenon: "Gombrowicz's struggle occurs on many levels—war, exile, ambivalent alliances, and even language—and to package all of these into one does a disservice to all the others" (102).

Nevertheless, if, as Molloy suggests, life can be read like any other text, retellings of life through writing can offer clues that are necessary for understanding the type of community established in Gombrowicz's work. Diary and novel share an attraction to youth in the abstract—and, more concretely, to the youths of Retiro. The autobiographical narrator identifies them as members of his chosen nation: "Al mirar las casitas donde algunos jóvenes sencillos se entregaban a sueños banales, pensaba que allí se había trasladado mi patria" [Looking at the little houses where humble youths were sunk in banal dreams, I thought that my homeland had moved to there] (*Diario argentino* 54). In a similar gesture, the narrator of the novel turns the youths into the protagonists of a national—or, rather, counternational—community. In *Trans-Atlantyk*, not only do those young men from different backgrounds desire each other carnally, but they also join in opposition to the fratricidal, sacrificial nation that heeds the orders of a militaristic tradition, a violent masculinity. This line of thinking follows the critical take of the European avant-garde: both in the novel and in his diary, Gombrowicz proposes dismantling that national "escuela de masculinidad" [school of masculinity] that only knows how to produce "machos convulsos" [spastic men]—that is, "monstruos" [monsters] ready to reject everything: desire, youth, even existence itself (*Trans-Atlántico* 67; *Trans-Atlantyk* 40). It is the idea mentioned earlier: the goal of "hacer saltar por los aires los sentimientos nacionalistas" [destroying nationalist sentiment], "aflojar esa relación que nos vuelve esclavos" [loosening that bond that makes us slaves], the bond that is a critical problem "entre todo individuo y la nación a la que pertenece" [between every individual and the nation he belongs to] (*Trans-Atlántico* 8–9).

In the novel, "Gombrowicz" decides to refuse his "civic duty" of returning and to defend his own integrity instead. Seeing the ocean liner *Chrobry* head off into the Atlantic, "Gombrowicz" hurls a page of imprecations at his countrymen: "¡Marchad a vuestra santísima y tal vez también maldita Nación! ¡Volved a ese Santo Monstruo Oscuro que está reventando desde hace siglos sin poder acabar de reventar!" [Sail to that holy Nation of yours haply Cursed! Sail to that St. Monster Dark, dying for ages yet unable to die!] (*Trans-Atlántico* 18; *Trans-Atlantyk* 6–7). He rebukes his national community with epithets normally used against the nation's *others*: *monstrous*, *dark*, and *holy* are adjectives that were attributed to the figure of the foreigner, the sick person, the homosexual. Other insults feminize that masculine entity: "La mentalidad [polaca], en el exilio o en la patria...continúa siendo deforme y hasta amanerada" [The Polish mentality, at home or in exile...remains deformed and even mincing] (*Trans-Atlántico* 7). The contortion here is complete: Why does returning to fight elicit such a negative response? How does the nation become synonymous with a mincing, deformed community? The terms are inverted. The text's parodic approach subverts meanings and makes it necessary to be wary of all definitions. Those characters who cling to categories, and especially those who are never gripped by doubt, provoke in "Gombrowicz" a profound sense of alienation. The protagonist's obsessive eye detects *strangenesses* in all men, but especially in those who boast of being Polish. Here are a few examples that emphasize this idea through repetition: "El Ministro [polaco] es uno de los hombres más *extraños* con los que he tropezado en la vida" [The (Polish) Minister (is) one of the strangest persons I've come upon in my life], he says (*Trans-Atlántico* 25; *Trans-Atlantyk* 12). "La *rareza* de aquellas personas (difícilmente hubiera podido encontrar gente más rara en toda mi vida), así como las riñas internas, me desalentaron mucho a entrar en contacto con ellos" [The strangeness of these people (and in all my Life it would be hard to search out stranger ones) and the brawl thay had been having amongst themselves greatly disinclined me from any contact with them], he says later (*Trans-Atlántico* 41; *Trans-Atlantyk* 21–22). About another compatriot, he adds, "Me había encontrado en muchos lugares y a personas aun más *extrañas* que tales lugares, pero aquellos lugares y aquellas personas no habían sido tan *extraños* como los que se presentaron en aquel momento de mi Vida" [In this whole life of mine many strange places and even stranger people I have beheld, but amidst those places and peoples naught so bizarre as the present episode of my Life] (*Trans-Atlántico* 44; *Trans-Atlantyk* 24). Of the Polish writer he faces off against in an absurd intellectual battle and whom he calls an "animal *raro*" [freak] (*Trans-Atlántico* 59; *Trans-Atlantyk* 34), he also says, "Aquel hombre (era la primera vez que veía a un individuo *tan raro*) era de lo más sofisticado" [That man (and haply so strange a man for the first time in my life I had seen) was uncommonly pampered and, what is more, was still Pampering himself] (*Trans-Atlántico* 55; *Trans-Atlantyk* 31). This *strangification* of the masculine universe in the novel was not neutral in Peronist Argentina, where the adjective was charged with homosexual implications and with state anxieties.[95] The carnivalesque device and the inversions of power that the plot sets

---

[95] As David William Foster has indicated, homophobia in Argentina can be traced in the cultural archive before the 1950s, as Jorge Salessi has done; however, it became increasingly explicit at the beginning of the second presidency of Juan Domingo Perón (1952–1955), precisely when this novel was being written ("Argentine Intellectuals" 443).

in motion must have been an affront, underscoring the theatrical excess or artificiality or even a certain dubiousness of the national *performance* of masculinity. But I detect another marker in the use of this word: the protagonist's hypertrophied sensitivity to strangeness can be read as a symptom of his own uncertainties: a forced reading, his reflection in the distorting mirror of his own mind. Because for the others, it is his own body that contains strangeness. In the exchange of glances around which the episode is organized, it does not take others long to detect a sign in the way he moves, in the hyperbolic "Walk, Walk, Walk"—just like that, repeated and capitalized[96]—through a room crammed with Polish exiles who have come to hear his reading. An "estupor general" [common amazement] is produced that leaves everyone "boquiabierto" [mouth agape] (*Trans-Atlántico* 60; *Trans-Atlantyk* 35). The grammar of this frenetic movement (an early novelistic form of contemporary cruising) *says* too much; although his aim is not to seduce, his unique way of walking is seen as a sign of disturbance and immediately deciphered by Gonzalo, another foreigner who is walking the same paths of eccentricity, of foreignness, of sexual deviancy, and who, as we soon discover, hopes to establish another sort of homeland in Buenos Aires. Gonzalo soon becomes a main character in the novel, and he pushes for them to walk together: "De pronto," notes the narrator, "vi que en un rincón…alguien más se había puesto a Caminar y Caminaba de tal modo que cuando yo Caminaba él también Caminaba" [And now I look and there by the Fireplace someone…someone likewise goes Walking, and Walks and Walks. And he so Walks and Walks that when I Walk he likewise Walks] (*Trans-Atlántico* 60–61; *Trans-Atlantyk* 35). Despite itself, that particular kind of walking expresses unity, establishes a common style, a joint movement that forms a bond between "Gombrowicz" and his new friend. In this scene of mutual recognition, not only has "Gombrowicz" been *seen* by Gonzalo, but also, reciprocally, "Gombrowicz" *has seen himself* as a sort of double of the foreigner who is imitating him. Like "Gombrowicz," Gonzalo is not South American, much less Argentine, as some critics have argued.[97] Instead, his

---

[96] All of the capital letters appear in the translations of the original and serve, I would argue, as markers of strangeness for the reader who knows how to read them.

[97] Piglia posits that the character is based on the Argentine writer Eduardo Mallea; others have seen in the character the author's dear friend during those years, the homosexual Cuban writer Virgilio Piñera, who was also the main force behind the remarkable Spanish-language translation of *Ferdydurke*, Gombrowicz's first novel. Setting aside the character's real-life referent, the novel presents him as a foreigner whose national origin is strategically hybrid.

national origin is unclear, shot through with a number of postcolonial divergences. Gonzalo, says "Gombrowicz," is "probablemente un Mestizo, un Portugués nacido en Libia, de madre persa o turca" [perchance Mestizo, Portuguese, of a Persian-Turkish mother in Libya born" (*Trans-Atlántico* 63; *Trans-Atlantyk* 37). In other words, Gonzalo embodies the Orientalist journeys: from his origins in the Middle East, that place where "the [homosexual] vice is said to flourish" (Boone 93), his forbears would have traveled to the African continent and thence to the Iberian Peninsula; after a time in Europe, Gonzalo arrives in Argentina. Significantly, his family history reproduces the movement of the homoerotic imaginary seen in the accounts of European travels of the period, such as that of D'Halmar, who in Egypt becomes an Arab man's lover.[98] Gonzalo's route is that of the wandering dissidents who arrive from various places in Latin America, as if Argentina were an Orient full of anonymous young men—disposable and at one's disposal—as if Buenos Aires could become a safe enclave in which to establish an extraterritorial community governed by its own interests. Throughout the novel, that is Gonzalo's desire: to use his money to surround himself with young men for sexual gratification. Gonzalo represents the foreign pederast that Jorge Salessi has identified as a prominent figure in the historical reconstruction of Argentina at the beginning of the twentieth century. Within the country's border, the homosexual pederast represents "the same infection and danger of epidemic" that consists of forming "secret international societies of young men" (Salessi, "The Argentine Dissemination" 353). In fiction, "Gombrowicz" recognizes Gonzalo's infectious potential; Gonzalo is, according to the nomenclature used, simultaneously an active proselytizer of sodomy, a passive effeminate homosexual—an invert—and perhaps a Uranian, a man with a feminine soul. Regardless of all these stereotypes, it is his radicalness that is instrumental in configuring a community that defies the national one.

The author's manifest desire had been to destroy the abominable carcass of masculinity. Gonzalo's is to carry out an enormously radical project that terrifies prudish "Gombrowicz." His Walking

---

[98] Joseph Boone attempts to correct Edward Said's erasure of the homosexual traveler in his celebrated book on orientalism. For Boone, the travelers omitted from Said's work form a crucial part of the postcolonial canon and of the sexualization of the notion of the Orient. Boone notes how in these European and American accounts, the Orient appears as the place of origin of the *homosexual vice*. From Asia the vice spreads to Africa and from the Middle East to Latin America. "As East spins back into West," says Boone, quoting a writer of that time, homosexuality spreads through European territory and its "modern capitals" (93).

companion has set out in pursuit of his desires: he is "un Hombre que siendo Hombre corre detrás de los Hombres y los Persigue como un obseso y a los Hombres adora, ay, y con los Hombres se excita, y a los Hombres desea, a los Hombres mira goloso, les coquetea, los galantea, los adula, [y] es llamado desdeñosamente por el pueblo de este país un *puto*" [(a) Man who, being a Man, fain would not be a Man but after Men chases, and after them Flies, admires, oh, Loves, Heats for them, Lusts for them, Hungers for them, makes up to them, simpers, adulates them, him folk hereabouts give the contemptuous name "puto"] (*Trans-Atlántico* 62; *Trans-Atlantyk* 36). That man betrays the definition of masculinity that "Gombrowicz" the character, like Gombrowicz the author of the novel, has not yet decided to reject. *Being a man* becomes even more complicated when Gonzalo introduces himself as Gonzala,[99] wearing women's makeup, acting like a woman, and then dressed in a skirt or dress. Stocky Gonzalo is not just feminized but gradually animalized in the scene. The text contests the system of binary oppositions, trying to define Gonzalo as She (versus He), as Cow (versus Bull), and as Mare (versus Stallion). "Ya no era ni lo uno ni lo otro," says the nervous narrator, "tenía el aspecto de una Criatura Extraña y no de un ser humano" [and now you wit not whether 'tis He or She...and perchance, being neither this nor that, he has the aspect of a Creature and not a human] (*Trans-Atlántico* 68; *Trans-Atlantyk* 40). He soon understands that some might think that he is "un Monstruo" [a Monster] (*Trans-Atlántico* 91; *Trans-Atlantyk* 56), anticipating the concept of the so-called crisis of categories (Garber) brought about by attempts to represent the effeminate homosexual and especially the transvestite. It is as if "Gombrowicz" were suddenly discovering, with the same anxiety experienced by governments when defining the social and cultural boundaries of nationhood at the beginning of the century, that the *truth* about gender is "a fantasy instituted and inscribed on the surface of bodies" (Butler, *Gender Trouble* 136). It is also as if he were presaging the division that would be established years later, during the AIDS era, between the *virile* homosexual and the transvestite; for the moment, that distinction is registered only in astonishment. The protagonists feel pressure to carry out the community-building project, and the alliance that forms between them is the first step toward establishing a community united by sexual

---

[99] The cross-dressed figure of Gonzalo predates by nearly 15 years the text that has been considered the first transvestite novel in Latin America: José Donoso's *El lugar sin límites* (1966).

affinity. The two characters are the foundational homosexual couple in Argentine fiction, a country founded, according to its intellectuals, by foreigners. "Gombrowicz" insists that because of "aquellos labios que a pesar de ser Masculinos sangraban *rouge* femenino… no pude tener la menor duda de que el destino me había unido con un Puto. Y con él había yo Caminado, habíamos Caminado juntos delante de todos como si para siempre me hubiera esposado con él" [those lips, the which although a Man's with Women's rouge bled, I could have no trace of doubt to have happened to me a Puto. It was he and I who before all Walked, as in a couple forever coupled!] (*Trans-Atlántico* 62; *Trans-Atlantyk* 36). That shared walk and that look of recognition clearly evoke marriage, promising eternal faithfulness between "Gombrowicz" and *Gonzala*; and the alliteration in their two names emphasizes the sameness between them, as if the two were one alone, even in their differences. The couple is the symbolic foundation of a new contract that upends the logic of the social/sexual compact of the nation. Replacing the female body with that of an effeminate male or transvestite destroys the premise presumed fundamental to the national community: the submissiveness of the woman or the ceding of her civil rights to her husband. In this couple, however, the one who moves forward is Gonzalo, while "Gombrowicz" retreats, gripped by intense panic—homosexual panic, Eve Kosofsky Sedgwick would no doubt tell us—that makes him turn despite himself to the Polish values that he once despised and satirically highlights the way the nation's defensive structure works against that form of dissidence. Despite his desires, this novel seems to suggest, the subject cannot free himself from those prescriptive social dictates on his own.

Again, the tension announced in the prologue of this Argentine book should be read as its opposite. Despite Gombrowicz's efforts to focus our reading, the novel sets out the struggle not just "between an individual and the nation to which he belongs" (as he noted in the prologue to *Trans-Atlántico*) but also between two kinds of relationships: one that is limited, sovereign, fraternal, and another that transcends all territorial and sexual limits, whose borders are marked by gender (women are absent) and age (older men are excluded). Whereas the *patria* is an old heterosexual formula dictated by the imagination of fathers and destined to disappear, the *filistria* (or son-land) proposed by Gonzalo—that is, by the novel itself—would be a new community of young men:

—¡Hay que librar a los Muchachos de la jaula paterna! [chilla Gonzalo en medio de un largo monólogo al que le sigue la respuesta de "Gombrowicz"].

—¡Calla! Cesa en tus instintos por corromperme. Es imposible que
yo me ponga contra el Padre y contra la Patria, en un momento como
este, por añadidura [retruca "Gombrowicz"].
    —¡Al Diablo con el Padre y con la Patria!– masculló [Gonzalo].
    —¡El Hijo! ¡El Hijo es lo único que interesa! ¿Para qué sirve la
Patria? ¿No es mejor la Filiatria? ¡Sustituye la Patria por la Filiatria y
verás lo que es bueno! (*Trans-Atlántico* 93)
    ["Oh, release Boys from the paternal cage!" (cries Gonzalo in the
middle of a long monologue, which is followed by "Gombrowicz's"
response).
    "Be still! Cease that Importuning of yours as 'tis impossible for me
to be against the Father and the land of our father, Pater and Patria,
and what's more, in a moment such as the present!"
    Mutters (Gonzalo): "To the Devil with Pater and Patria! The Son,
the Son's the thing, oh, indeed! But wherefore need you Patria? Is not
Filistria better? You exchange Patria for Filistria, and then you'll see!"]
(*Trans-Atlantyk* 57)[100]

That is the quandary: whether to respect the values of the father-
land/father allegorized in the figure of a Polish military veteran from
old Europe, or to opt for the *filistria* of the uprooted, marginalized sons of the young South American republic, that unemployed
army of sailors, soldiers, craftsmen, and apprentices and the many
servants of Gonzalo, but especially docile Ignacy, whose fate is to
be sent to die heroically for Polish independence. In a last twist of
the narrative, Ignacy becomes an object of desire for both Gonzalo
and "Gombrowicz," who attempt to save him and recruit him to the
filistria. The choice between *patria* and *filistria* is not at all simple.
Gombrowicz's ambivalent fictionalized self is skeptical of all affiliations and mistrusts the new configuration of loyalties. The idea of
recruiting or converting Ignacy becomes, "Gombrowicz" concedes,
"una astilla clavada en el cerebro" [a splinter in my head] (*Trans-
Atlántico* 97; *Trans-Atlantyk* 60) that illustrates the real difficulties
implied in the endeavor. Trying to make a decision, the narrator visits
Ignacy. Strictly speaking, he approaches in the darkness and watches
him as he sleeps, naked and uncovered, as if seeing "aquel pecho,

[100] It is interesting to note the dialectic of this conversation. The obsession with
youth and beauty and the disdain for certain nationalist obsessions expressed by
Gonzalo are very similar not just to some of the author's ideas presented in the prologue but to others found in his *Diario argentino*. This suggests that Gonzalo and
"Gombrowicz" represent two complementary and contradictory positions on an issue
that the author himself appears to still have been debating.

aquellos hombros, aquella cabeza y aquellas piernas" [his Chest so, his Shoulders so, head and legs so] (*Trans-Atlántico* 117; *Trans-Atlantyk* 73) were proof enough to convince him. Somewhere between panic and desire—or in the panic of desire—"Gombrowicz" moves through the plot as if along a tightrope that is perilously slack, setting off a series of entanglements and betrayals, even duels, that eliminate all of the characters in Gonzalo's eccentric palace. It is as if the text were trying to point the way outside the protected perimeter of Argentine Polishness and indicate the path to a *lugar sin límites* (place without limits) of any sort: Gonzalo's feud offers a parallel order in which men walk around naked or dressed as women, where even the boundaries between species are crossed.

The link between homosexuality and disease plays out powerfully in the text. Realizing that he himself has been *infected* by the logic of this new space, "Gombrowicz" warns Ignacy's father to flee from Gonzalo "como de la peste Bubónica" [as from Pestilence] (*Trans-Atlántico* 127; *Trans-Atlantyk* 79), because it is clear that only patricide will allow the young man to fornicate with whomever he desires, precisely when it is announced in the novel that old Poland has been defeated by the army of young German men.[101] Amid the horror and the false jubilation of the Polish defeat, "Gombrowicz" at last manages to accept that nothing matters to him: "nada me importaba, qué había que temer, por qué tenía que indignarme, es más, tenía deseos de que ocurriera lo que tenía que ocurrir, que todo se Quebrara, que se Rompiera, que se Abatiera y que surgiera la Filiatria, la Desconocida Filiatria" [naught, naught, may he, may he, what do I fear, what do I abhor, indeed, may what is to be, Become; may all Break, Burst, Fall apart, Fall apart, and oh, Filistria Becoming, Unknown Filistria!] (*Trans-Atlántico* 179–80; *Trans-Atlantyk* 115). The decision has been made. There we see the creation, even the acceptance, of this new community of youths within the young Argentine nation.

Trans-Atlantyk is thus a foundational text that was extremely radical for its time. It establishes the idea of a community of desire as a vision for the future: others took up the baton, imagining, in the present of their writings, a cosmopolitan alternative social bond, one

[101] The implications of this parallel are strange. Though presented as a moment of liberation, Nazism is an ideology linked to nationalism; thinking of Gombrowicz as offering a defense of Nazism is, in my view, inappropriate. Not just in political terms but also because in the terms of the novel itself, no young man should go to war. The young German soldiers are fighting for a nation that is just as rigid and heterosexist as Poland.

shaped by affinities of movement between territories (the nation, however violent, never appeared in the dissident imaginary) and by affinities of style and desire that began to be identified with a certain extraterritorial nomadism. The community, built upon the possibility of placelessness, was gradually aided by the burgeoning technologies of the capitalist system. From the bold *filistrian* dream of the 1950s on, not only was movement made possible, but also the first groups took definitive steps toward establishing themselves on the local and global levels: the sexual awakening of the 1960s was contagious, defying the repressive controls of all kinds of governments. Recalling this period, Reinaldo Arenas says in his autobiography, "Nunca se singó más en Cuba que en los años 60...precisamente cuando se promulgaron todas aquellas leyes en contra de los homosexuales, se desató la persecución contra ellos y se crearon los campos de concentración; precisamente cuando el acto sexual se convirtió en un tabú, se pregonaba al hombre nuevo y se exaltaba el machismo" [There was never more fucking going on than in those years, the decade of the sixties...precisely when all the new laws against homosexuals came into being, when the persecutions started and concentration camps were opened, when the sexual act became taboo while the "new man" was being proclaimed and masculinity exalted] (*Antes* 130–31; *Before* 105). Arenas adds, "Si una cosa desarrolló la represión sexual...fue, precisamente, la liberación sexual. Quizá como una protesta contra el régimen, las prácticas homosexuales comenzaron a proliferar cada vez con mayor desenfado" [I think that the sexual revolution in Cuba actually came about as a result of the existing sexual repression. Perhaps as a protest against the regime, homosexuality began to proliferate with ever-increasing defiance] (*Antes* 132; *Before* 107). Other protest groups managed, though not without difficulty, to survive the Latin American dictatorships of the following decades.[102] Although the process was different in each place, a certain continuity is apparent in the process of becoming self-aware as a community and expanding the imagination of the community, which was threatened in a crucial moment by the beginning of the AIDS epidemic. In other words: just as they became established, these communities were exposed to the possibility of their own definitive extinction. And the literary project therefore changed. Henceforth, the goal was

[102] Two other authors from the corpus agree with Arenas's view: despite the repression, the dictatorships were periods of heightened sexual activity. See Perlongher (1988) and Lemebel (1996).

not to imagine for a future that had not yet been conceived of, but to forge in the present a sexual community that could serve as a pleasurable alternative to the lethal masculinity of the antiquated European nation. The charge now was to document the existence of those incipient wandering communities and provide them with a destination. It was an ailing Reinaldo Arenas who, with the perspective offered by his exile in New York, devoted himself to narrating the situation of the marginalized community: his *patria pájara* standing in resistance to revolutionary repression.

PATRIA PÁJARA, OR THE ILLS OF EXILE

The theme of escape runs through the life and work of the irreverent Reinaldo Arenas. Severo Sarduy writes of Arenas's unquenchable thirst for freedom in one of the entries in his "Diario de la peste" (Diary of the epidemic), written only a few weeks after Arenas's death, in which he refers to the author's three rebellions: against the isolation of the countryside and the family in his hometown of Holguín; against a socialist revolution that persecuted homosexuals; and, from exile, against AIDS, which he saw as a final instance of repression. "Fue su última libertad," writes Sarduy. "Escoger su muerte. No dejarla en manos de nada. Ni de ese Nadie [Fidel Castro] que la decidió" [That was his ultimate freedom. To choose his own death. Not to leave it in anyone else's hands. Not even that Nobody (Fidel Castro) who decided it] ("Diario" 34). Different instances of that rebellion are seen in three successive journeys that were fundamental to Arenas's biography and writing: his migration from the countryside to the capital city, his 1980 escape to the United States (and the visits to other cities where he denounced the Cuban regime), and suicide as a final revolt in 1990. In all of these displacements, the author was driven by a need to ensure two inseparable freedoms: sexual and textual. For Arenas, "lo erótico y lo literario marchaban de la mano" [the erotic and the literary went hand in hand] (*Antes* 127; *Before* 101), but both spaces for expression had been denied him: first, in the oppressive rural area where he grew up, and then, as a result of a revolutionary doctrine that he had initially supported. Arenas understood that "school of masculinity" (Gombrowicz *dixit*) to be redefining the notion of national community, though not in terms that promised freedom but instead through the suppression of all dissidence.

The exclusion of dissidence happened quickly. While the political aspect of that history is well known, the sexual aspect is less so.

Under pressure from the United States in the middle of the Cold War,[103] Fidel Castro agreed to adopt the Soviet Union's Marxist-Leninist ideologies and hammered out political and trade agreements with the Soviets; but he also agreed as part of the treaty to accept a dogma of ideological purity that was intended to preserve the moral integrity of socialist citizens and to punish any who violated it. Committed to imported ideals, the revolutionary regime embarked on a dual crusade: against the bourgeoisie and against the members of the so-called three p's: Havana prostitutes, pimps, and pederasts who had benefited from the sexual tourism of the imperialist bourgeoisie under Batista (Epps 239). The *pájaros* got the worst of it when the Left became convinced that homosexuality (and the degenerate sensibility they claimed it fostered) was the product of a decadent capitalist society and decided to establish a national policy of homophobia. In Cuba, notions of political integrity merged with heterosexist norms defining certain sexual conduct as virile, and the effeminate men locally dubbed *pájaros* (a term also favored by Arenas) were considered counterrevolutionary subjects who must be exposed and threatened or sent to jail to do hard labor for their moral renewal and conversion into true Marxists.[104]

It is a remarkable paradox: the Revolution turned Arenas the socialist into a fierce counterrevolutionary. The efforts to persecute and prosecute him and the constant danger of imprisonment that he faced from the end of the 1960s,[105] along with the increased censorship and the confiscation and destruction of his *seditious* literary work, became a recurring and increasingly urgent issue.[106] Arenas was

---

[103] Just as in Gombrowicz, purist nationalism is exalted in the midst of military conflict.

[104] As indicated earlier, it is still very common in Latin America to identify homosexuality with effeminate behavior (the supposed *passive* or *penetrated* man), whereas the man whose behavior is virile (the *penetrator*) is not considered deviant. (See notes 12, 22, and 59.)

[105] The writer fictionalized his time in jail in *Arturo, la estrella más brillante* (1984; Arcturus, the brightest star) and later referred to these episodes in two posthumous texts: *Antes que anochezca* (181–248) and the third entry of *Viaje a La Habana* (93–153).

[106] Arenas explains: "Yo sufría, ya por entonces, en el año 69, una persecución constante de la Seguridad del Estado, y temía siempre por los manuscritos que, incesantemente, producía" [By the year 1969, I was already being subjected to persistent harassment by State Security, and feared for the manuscripts I was constantly producing] (*Antes* 139; *Before* 114). Given their systematic disappearance at the hands of state security forces, the stubborn task of memorizing and rewriting the texts was essential.

forced to emigrate to safeguard his most prized freedoms, but even before his exile, writing was the instrument of his emancipation, a means of resistance that was literally at hand. Arenas inherited this mandate from his mentor, the illustrious José Lezama Lima, who was condemned for not subscribing to socialist realism and because his masterpiece, *Paradiso* (1966; Paradise), celebrated conducts that had recently become the object of official censure.[107] Lezama Lima told him, "Recuerda que la única salvación que tenemos es por la palabra: escribe" [Remember that our only salvation lies in words: Write!] (Arenas, *Antes* 254; *Before* 230). And Arenas used literature to confront the Marxist moralism that waged an assault, as he saw it, on political, aesthetic, and sexual expression—an assault, Arenas claimed, on life itself: "Toda manifestación de vida es en sí un enemigo de cualquier régimen dogmático," he noted years later in his autobiography. "Era lógico que Fidel Castro nos persiguiera, no nos dejara fornicar y tratara de eliminar cualquier ostentación pública de vida" [All affirmations of life are diametrically opposed to dogmatic regimes. It was logical for Fidel Castro to persecute us, not to let us fuck, and to try to suppress any public display of the life force] (*Antes* 119; *Before* 93). I pause here on this point to underscore the echoes between Arenas's vitalist statements and those that appear in *Trans-Atlantyk*. Where Arenas says *life*, Gombrowicz says *youth*, but both words express a single idea: the free exercise of desire in opposition to the nation's oppressive ideals that would destroy it. Those words also say—practically shout—that it is necessary to go abroad to be able to exercise the freedoms restricted by Cuban society. Abroad, then, extends a promise. If we, as we should, read Gombrowicz's journey in detail, we find in his work a premonition that was later fulfilled in Arenas's journey. Abroad is only another of the utopias of the *free world* (as Arenas calls the capitalist world). In the viral age, the perverse logic within the nation is reproduced beyond its borders.

Reading chronologically, we can detect in the work of the prolific Cuban writer a need to find a way out, to expand a sphere of action that was ever more under threat. Through Arenas's physical displacement, we can examine the spatial philosophy that permeates

---

[107] Arenas called the publication of this novel under Castro "un acontecimiento heroico desde el punto de vista literario. Creo que nunca se llegó a publicar en Cuba una novela que fuera tan avasalladoramente homosexual" [(f)rom a literary standpoint…a truly heroic event. I do not think Cuba had ever witnessed the publication of a novel so explicitly homosexual] (*Antes* 110; *Before* 84).

his novelistic imaginary. In the early narratives, the sense of enclosure predominates, as does the urge to give voice to a dissident point of view in the erotic spaces or counterspaces of Havana society—movie theaters, buses, bathrooms, jails, barracks full of impatient recruits, universities overflowing with students. In the decade of his coming out, and toward the close of his life, the scene expands once more. In exile, from a distance, Arenas draws the map of the nation; upon that reconstructed cartography, he manages not only to *imagine himself* free but also to experience a certain liberation as a member of a growing cosmopolitan community. He appears to have seen his arrival in New York in 1981 as a moment of achieving a liberated utopia at last. A modern mechanical city, a city that never sleeps, a promise of infinite opportunities—Manhattan was all of that, and he found it all *extraordinario* (that is his adjective: the city and its inhabitants were extraordinary). The promise was quite apparent: after the Stonewall riots of 1969, many of the obstacles to the creation and reproduction of homosexual groups had fallen away. But that certainty, as we know, was only transitory, a promise that soon collapsed with the advent of the epidemic. Arenas arrived just in time to sample that *extraordinary* freedom, to take advantage of it, even to celebrate it. Even before his diagnosis in 1987, Arenas, who soon became the most famous HIV-positive Latin American abroad, was forced to accept that the flourishing extraterritorial community was entering a rapid extinction phase, which he once more felt compelled to document.

Between visits to the hospital, his last effort was to finish two books that he had outlined in Cuba, books that had suffered the dire fate of being disappeared by the state and that, according to the legend he built around himself, he wrote again from memory. In this rewriting, however, the impact of the crisis makes its mark. One of the works is his well-known autobiography, *Antes que anochezca*. The other is a massive novel titled *El color del verano o Nuevo jardín de las delicias*.[108] Written simultaneously and published posthumously in 1990, the two should be read as mirror versions of a single story: the main elements of the plot are identical. Yet whereas in the autobiography the text leans toward realist expression, in which the narrative self pretends to tell the whole truth (a truth one suspects is nevertheless

---

[108] Although the autobiography serves as a factual basis for the novel, which rewrites life "en forma imaginativa y desenfadada" [in a very imaginative, almost defiant manner] (*Antes* 14; *Before* xvi), and although both texts carry the disease in their pages, only the autobiography was read as an emblematic account of AIDS, while the other closely related but fictional text was ignored almost entirely.

exaggerated), in the novel, the contract with reality is definitively broken, defying the reader with a tangled, apocalyptic structure that might be summarized as follows. It is the year 1999—the twentieth century is coming to an end—and on the island the fortieth anniversary of Castro's revolution is being celebrated. In addition to the official festivities, the other community—the *patria pájara*, the homosexual world—organizes a large meeting at the same time to assert its existence and its struggles on the island. The *patria pájara* plans to take flight, following on the heels of some who have already done so—"Arenas," for example, and all of his alter egos. But the community is surrounded and flight seems impossible—at least for now. What they desire is mass escape, despite the careful vigilance of a dictator who represents the nation's most extreme values. Outside the nation's borders, the worst epidemic the world has ever seen intensifies, and Arenas's alter egos long to return, still unaware of the calamity that has also descended upon Cuba. *El color de verano* can be read as a story of a desire for the liberation of the alternative community against the menacing global backdrop of the virus.

Reinaldo Arenas saw the novel as a sort of structural cyclone. Reading it produces the impression of a manuscript tossed by the winds of freedom and hastily reassembled without any heed to chapter order. The prologue, for example, appears in the middle of the book, and the end could be anywhere except the usual place. Examining the novel closely, however, one must conclude that it has no possible order: the spiral contains various discursive forms (dramatic writing, pseudo-historical accounts, scientific/philosophical reflections, metanarrative texts, anguished letters, travel accounts, endless tongue twisters, parodies of a spelling book, classificatory lists, portraits, homages, and, again, displacements) and revolves around the carnival of the socialist revolution, the carnivalesque escape project, the inversions of meaning produced by the epidemic. Indeed, I would suggest that the textual disorder and the ruptures in the plot are simply another way to point to a critical process, the definitive splintering of the border between the nation and abroad, and, by extension, between the national community and the other, mysterious community, one that is felt or should be felt, even treated, as immoral, traitorous, bourgeois, foreign. What Arenas proposes, at bottom, is to reveal that, for better but especially for worse, AIDS knows no boundaries: there is no opposition, only continuity, between the two spaces. In this new scenario, the Cuban writer attempts to put his writing at the service of these reflections. He turns his gaze on the community using two complementary narrative resources: an extraterritorial self—mobile, bifurcated, and fictionalized—and the "we" of the Cubans still trapped within that territory, who are nevertheless considered a volatile community.

In an effort to integrate, like a subject adrift, the enormous community of fags, *bugarrones* (bisexuals), *locas*, and *pájaros*—terms that in the text serve as a joyous statement of group belonging—Arenas's narcissistic narrative self partially abdicates the excess that characterizes his work in order to examine the community, to reimagine it and give testimony of its insertion into a variety of spaces. The displaced, diseased "Arenas" of the final story is no longer a solitary self: he fractures, disperses, unfolds (depending on how we think of the process I have described), abandoning the supposed unity of authorial identity, letting himself be represented by three unstable and interchangeable characters who appeared in his earlier work: Gabriel, the peasant from Holguín, a *bugarrón* who is married with children; Reinaldo, the persecuted author of homosexual novels; and the hypersexual transvestite La Tétrica Mofeta (appearing in English translation as Skunk in a Funk), whom Arenas calls a *loca de atar* because of her uninhibited quality. It is as if these three characters—characters not fully recuperated from exile, carriers of the traveling bug—were trying to tell us that exile and illness are interchangeable signs: they both name a punishment, they both undermine capitalism's promises of freedom and turn the person suffering them into a ghost. Arenas says bitterly in his memoirs,

> Me doy cuenta de que para un desterrado no hay ningún sitio donde se pueda vivir; que no existe sitio, porque aquel donde soñamos, donde...tuvimos la primera aventura amorosa, sigue siendo el lugar soñado; en el exilio uno no es más que un fantasma, una sombra de alguien que nunca llega a alcanzar su completa realidad; yo no existo desde que llegué al exilio; desde entonces comencé a huir de mí mismo. (*Antes* 314)[109]
> [I realize that an exile has no place where he can live, because he is nowhere, because the place where we started to dream, where we...loved for the first time, is always the world of our dreams. In exile one is nothing but a ghost, the shadow of someone who never achieves full reality. I ceased to exist when I went into exile; I started to run away from myself.] (*Before* 293)

---

[109] Exile and sexile are two parallel modes of existence in a poem by Alberto Sandoval, a contemporary of Arenas: "It was not death but the phantom of death / opening the door / making me go around and around / in a revolving door that faced the emptiness: / exiled / there is no way back" (313). (See note 70.)

Here we find a pessimism reinforced by the reappearance, after the brief euphoria of liberation, of a policy of discrimination. Arenas complains bitterly about this personal circumstance in his memoirs, but in the novel he makes them a collective situation. There, each of his identities, from the most virile (Gabriel) to the most feminine (La Tétrica Mofeta), is a victim of these two contemporary forms of dystopia, that fictional society set in a near future and governed by absolute control, in which extermination under the cover of altruism is all too common. This is the world portrayed in the novel: no one, no matter where, can be saved, because *abroad* no longer exists.

The fusion between exile and illness, the realization that there is no escape, triggers the act of writing for Arenas's three characters, who are also allegories for the scattered community. But they do not write novels: strictly speaking, only "Arenas" could do that. Instead, their letters crisscross the globe. The author puts wandering to work through the mechanism of the epistolary travel account, tracing a conversation between various points and among members of the wandering community, which the writer represents by splitting himself into several fictionalized selves. Assuming the role of both senders and receivers, Gabriel, La Tétrica Mofeta, and "Arenas" send each other missives from the different cities through which the author traveled in the past, very purposely dated, like any dystopia, in the future: Paris 1993, New York 1996, Miami 1998, and a final farewell letter written by La Tétrica Mofeta from a future Havana 1999. In letters, Arenas diagrams a critical present and projects it various decades into the future to amplify the dispersal that is both cause and effect of the epidemic.

The letters talk about the impossibility of physically uniting all the parts of the community. Only literature calls them together, in writing, until they meet, if only briefly, in the library scene. It is no accident that they meet in person for the first and only time in the library, the place where the literary tradition demands to be read and where Reinaldo Arenas seeks to be included, through his gaggle of literary selves, as part of the canon—that is, as part of what the nation reads. Their meeting offers the only moment of wholeness for an expatriate community that longs to be reunited. It is a fleeting, phantasmal encounter in a novel not much given to stability, which soon begins to reproduce the dizzying, tragic effect of the disease: the text of each letter, like the letters themselves and the characters who write them, crosses space and time to communicate a desperate message.

But the most interesting epistolary exchange is also, of course, the most confusing: the writers all believe that the worst situation is visible from their vantage point. For the repressed homosexual still on the island (who always exchanges her identity with the others), the dream of a foreign utopia is extremely powerful. The characters already living abroad warn her that the situation is much more dire beyond Cuba's borders because the epidemic is worsening. The letter from Cuba insists that things can't be worse abroad: "No me vengan con lamentos, ni me digan que están solos ni me hablen de las plagas que los matan," warns La Tétrica Mofeta from the homeland of the other narrative selves now scattered around the world, "aquí también todos estamos solos y yo también tengo la plaga y además de no tener atención médica adecuada ni siquiera puedo soltar el menor lamento" [I'm really tired of all your moaning and carrying-on, and of hearing how alone you are, and about the plagues that are killing you. We're all alone here, too, and I have the plague, too, but I don't get the medical attention I need—there's *no way* for me to get it—and I can't make the slightest whimper] (*El color* 357; *The Color* 314).[110] La Tétrica Mofeta refutes the others, at the end of that last letter from 1999 that coincides with the anniversary of the revolution. She has decided to flee, even if it will cost her what life she has left. Even if abroad she will find only death.

This brings us back to the other side, to the hemmed-in nation that is still Cuba at century's end, the Cuba that Arenas never sees, no matter how much his writing insists that he does as he pushes us toward the future. "Arenas" in exile was multiplied to give a subjective account of the viral journey of those other selves, selves that were simultaneously personal and representative of the community as a whole. In Cuba, however, the story is dominated by a narrator with a broad vision who turns his incisive gaze inward and dedicates the bulk of the plot to the island. The novel revolves like a cyclone around the island, which is as dystopian as the rest of the novelistic universe. What compels the writer to recall his longed-for Cuba but place it ten years in the future? I offer this conjecture: Arenas, the dissident who made a relieved escape from Castro's Cuba; Arenas, the writer immersed in the city that is the ideological epicenter of the global discourse that he himself initially embraced; Arenas, who at the end of his life understands that he has been and will continue to be eternally a foreigner, doomed to

---

[110] The letter from La Tétrica Mofeta reiterates a fundamental idea from Arenas's autobiography: "En Cuba había soportado miles de calamidades porque siempre me alentó la posibilidad de la fuga....Ahora la única fuga que me queda es la muerte" [In Cuba I endured a thousand adversities because the hope of escaping...gave me strength. At this point, the only escape for me was death] (*Antes* 9; *Before* ix).

wander and die like the rest of his community, is compelled to look back and reflect, one last time—not without nostalgia, anguish, rage, or irony—on the historical contradictions of the homosexual community both within and outside the nation. His task is to retrieve, through a fictionalized documentation, the history of the community inside Cuba and its links to international homosexuality; it is to reflect, from the present, on how to liberate the oppressed sexual dissidents and other citizens resisting the onslaught of the puritanical revolution; and it is, finally, to ponder the dilemmas of the future community.

I will move slowly here, breaking the operation down, starting with an element that was not part of the heralded collapse but was nonetheless significant. Part of what this posthumous novel narrates is something that might now seem obvious but that at the time, for Spanish-language literature, was not: the affirmation of "la visión subterránea del mundo homosexual" [the underground vision of the homosexual world] (*El color* 262; *The Color* 228). A homosexual *world*, writes Arenas, not just a guild, a group, a community. He confers upon it a cosmopolitan, global status, a certain intrinsic universality even within Cuban borders. It is important to take this vision into account, the narrator suggests, because it "seguramente nunca aparecerá en ningún periódico del mundo y mucho menos en Cuba" [surely will never appear in any newspaper, and much less in Cuba] (*El color* 262; *The Color* 228). The homosexual world is now seen as being as embattled on the island as it is everywhere else. The author's approach—or feat—is to bring together the whole community during the commemorative festival organized by a megalomaniacal Fifo (Fidel Castro), to defend, in opposition to the system of national single-mindedness, the premises that define it both in its difference and in its normality. Emblematic figures from the past are summoned to that deliberately satirical carnival, as are representatives of Cubanness from throughout history (the temporal aspect is so flexible that it manages to encompass a complete historical time), their identities more or less masked. Authorities representing the virile values of the nation converge on the island: the political class, with Fifo as the headliner and Raúl Kastro [*sic*] as the opening act; the repressive state security forces, referred to as dwarves and sharks, that prevent the marine invasion; the religious class, represented by the Bishop No Condón [O'Condom], who dictates the heterosexist, monogamous, reproductive moral order and, of course, condemns homosexuality as deviant. Representatives of the people also appear, all sorts of antagonists, antiheroes, counterrevolutionaries, traitors, *pájaros*. What he calls, in still other words, "ejércitos clandestinos silenciosos y siempre en peligro inminente, pero que no estaban dispuestos, de ninguna manera, a renunciar a la vida, esto es, a dejar de hacer gozar a los demás" [clandestine, silent armies, always in imminent danger of defeat but utterly unwilling to renounce life, which is defined by giving pleasure to others] (*El color* 401; *The Color* 356). Not just a covert sexual guerrilla group but an organized army. (Here, by institutionalizing subversion in this key word of the nation's vocabulary, Arenas echoes Gombrowicz's proposal to reject the sacrificial protocols of the army but value its soldiers, desirous young men, as part of his personal homeland.) Arenas's secret army is composed of boys—armed with words and weapons—from all over the world and every time period. It is a valiant *transnational* and *transhistorical* saga that includes both those who in the present "siguen practicando, como sea y donde sea...el pecado nefando" [continue to practice, however and whenever they can...the sin against nature] (*El color* 402; *The Color* 356) and ancient Greek and Roman heroes, as well as, of course, Jesus Christ, "aquel joven de treinta y tres años que vagaba predicando el amor con doce mozalbetes" [that thirty-three-year-old man who wandered about the countryside preaching, and making love, to his twelve apostles] (*El color* 401; *The Color* 356). The more recent artists include prestigious writers, all of them men, from a community whose only possible nation was that of the arts: Shakespeare, Shelley, Byron, Michelangelo, Whitman, Tchaikovsky, Proust, Passolini, Gide, Mishima, Van Gogh, Wilde, Genet, Tennessee Williams, and, in Spanish-language literature, Lorca, Cortázar, Lezama Lima, Sarduy, Piñera, and Piñera's dear friend during his Argentine period, Witold Gombrowicz, whom Arenas claims as part of the community. Alongside all of these are also "otros mil nombres famosos" [a thousand other famous men] (*El color* 402; *The Color* 356).[111]

---

[111] This urge to list names and position oneself within a lettered community—one that is prestigious because of its culture and sophistication—is not Arenas's alone. Before him, in *The Normal Heart*, which premiered in New York in 1985, controversial American activist and writer Larry Kramer included a similar list of notable men whose sexual orientation had been silenced by history. It is quite possible that Kramer's play, attended by a large proportion of the cosmopolitan gay community of which Arenas was a part, inspired the Cuban author, especially as many of the names appear in both lists. Kramer wrote, "I belong to a culture that includes *Proust*, Henry James, *Tchaikovsky*, Cole Porter, Plato, Socrates, Aristotle, Alexander the Great, *Michelangelo*, Leonardo da Vinci, Christopher Marlowe, *Walt Whitman*, Herman Melville, *Tennessee Williams*, *Byron*, E. M. Forster, *Lorca*, Auden, Francis Bacon, James Baldwin, Harry Stack Sullivan, John Maynard Keynes, Dag Hammarskjold....These are not invisible men" (109; emphasis added to highlight the repeated names).

The narrative mechanism of the novel permits the coexistence of famous homosexuals who were still alive when it was written, such as Severo Sarduy (who appears as Zebro Sardoya), with distinguished deceased Cubans (including Julián del Casal, José María Heredia, and José Martí), all of them figures considered worthy representatives of the nation, and whose cultural capital, whose persistence in literary history, means that they remain more alive than dead—or, rather, both alive and dead—and above all that their sexual dilemmas are continually updated for those readers who can decode their message. The ability of this homoliterary community to be simultaneously on the earth and in the literary beyond, both on the island and in exile, both in the present and launched into the future, confirms a mobility that complements the ways that homosexuals conceived of themselves as a community.

In restoring this collective history, writers on the island (behind the disease's figurative back) boldly homosexualized all male bodies, doing away with heterosexuality as a norm. In his memoirs, Arenas describes a theory of universal homoerotic desire that he first saw in Cuba: "No era necesario ser homosexual para tener relaciones con un hombre, un hombre podía tener relaciones con otro como un acto normal" [you did not have to be homosexual to have a relationship with a man; a man could have intercourse with another man as an ordinary act] (*Antes* 133; *Before* 108). What's more, Arenas's autobiographical self states, perhaps hyperbolically (hyperbole is a strategic necessity in his work), that at 25 years old "unos complicados cálculos matemáticos [lo llevaron a] la convicción de que, por lo menos, había hecho el amor con unos cinco mil hombres" [(he) came to the conclusion, after complicated mathematical calculations, that (he'd) had sex with about five thousand men] (*Antes* 119; *Before* 93). The figure might seem outrageous, but the point here is not the accuracy of the numbers but the suggestion that erotic furor (as Arenas put it) between men is so frequent, incessant, recurrent, varied, and common that, by contrast, strangeness and perversion reside in the attempt of the whole world, not just Cuba, to repress it. Arenas's excess does carry the risk (though Arenas was an apologist for danger) of inadvertently confirming a powerful stereotype: that of loss of control, a promiscuity that leads to illness and therefore justifies the repressive intervention of the state to protect the confusingly so-called rest of society. Despite appearances, there is nothing involuntary in the rhetoric of numbers. This is not mere sexual exhibitionism (reminding us of the flight attendant Gaëtan Dugas, the so-called patient zero) but a whole policy that would reinstate sex between men as a habitual and completely healthy practice. Arenas, quintessential example of his own theory, presents those *complicated calculations*, that startling figure, to demonstrate, in the language of science itself, that if normality is defined by the frequency with which an act occurs, repeated lovemaking between men cannot be pathological.[112]

The plot follows the postulates of this radical theory of homoerotic desire both to flesh out its universal connections and especially to decry the heterosexist farce. During the parallel gathering organized by the homosexual *world* during the celebrations of the fortieth anniversary of the revolution, several speeches discuss the situation of the sexual dissident, which in Cuba is akin to being a political dissident. They explore the rules of the aforementioned lettered community that moves through space and time to become, in semisecret, part of the world canon. In addition, the members of the homosexual world are classified and distinguished according to their eventual mobility: from the placid *bugarrón* [bisexual] who only partly qualifies for membership in the community, to the *pájaro* who glories in his winged nickname, to the *loca suelta* (categories into which the Cuban writer's projections also fit: Gabriel, "Arenas," and La Tétrica Mofeta). The four main types of *bugarrones* travel only to engage in *ensartamiento* (as Arenas calls penetration); the four major categories of *locas*, however, are defined by their mobility. The *loca común* or *loca simple* (your basic model), the *loca tapada* (closeted, and probably married), and the *loca regia* (who has friends in high places) take wild trips to Varadero, to Bulgaria or Mongolia, and to the capitalist countries, respectively. The *loca de argolla* or *loca de atar*, so named because he is always getting caught, goes only to the forced labor camps; Reinaldo Arenas, the author, qualifies for this last definition, given that his behavior, which he himself calls flamboyant, has led him to be confined in the El Morro prison. What is not said openly at the convention, but is suggested in the rest of the text, is that all the other characters are suspected of not being completely heterosexual: the *locas* have witnessed sodomy committed by the sharks of the state security services, and even the homosexual practices of the dictator himself.

What we have here is an effort to create a community history both on and off the island, establishing categories that construct an ahistorical *patria pájara*. We also have an aborted celebration, the later

---

[112] Arenas seems to agree with the model proposed by Georges Canguilhem (1991), who notes that "a human characteristic is not normal because it is frequent but frequent because it is normal" (92).

denunciation of two dystopian systems—Castroist repression that is reproduced, with local or national variations, in the rest of the world. But is this novel also about the community that is brought down by AIDS? One might conclude so because, like the three characters, the community as a whole recognizes or condemns (the tone here becomes realist, resembling the language of the autobiography) the fact that there are no other options. Nothing seems to have changed: a homosexual continues to be "un ser aéreo, desasido, sin sitio fijo o propio, que anhela de alguna manera retornar a no se sabe exactamente qué lugar" [an aerial, untethered being, with no fixed place, no place to call his own, who yearns to return to . . . —but, my friends, he knows not where], as the participants say during the festivities. They continue,

> Estamos siempre buscando un sitio que aparentemente no existe. Estamos siempre como en el aire y atisbando. Nuestra condición de pájaro es perfecta, y está muy bien que así nos hayan calificado. Somos pájaros porque estamos siempre . . . en un aire que tampoco es nuestro, porque nuestro no es nada, pero que al menos no tiene frontera. Y aun cuando estemos en la tierra, como en estos momentos, estamos siempre como propensos a alzar el vuelo. (*El color* 403)
> [We are always seeking that apparently nonexistent place. We are always in the air, keeping our eyes peeled. Our aerial nature is perfect, and so it should not be strange that we have been called fairies. We are fairies because we are always . . . in an air that is not ours because it is unpossessable—though at least it is not bounded by the walls. And even when we're on terra firma, such as now, we are always somehow ready to take flight.] (*The Color* 358)

The idea is clearly stated here: the participants cannot imagine a place to go; they have no place to land.[113] Even the site of utopia is contaminated. It seems like an impossible dilemma. In the end, though, literature does not retreat, never gives up. Like the exploration of a boundary, like a reflection on the limits imposed by reality—because

---

[113] Coincidentally, in his autobiography, Arenas describes a dream he had in New York in the days before his diagnosis. In it, Arenas could fly—"privilegio imposible para un ser humano, aun cuando a los homosexuales nos digan pájaros" [a privilege not granted to humans, even though there we gays are called *pájaros* (birds)] (*Antes* 337; *Before* 313)—and returned to Cuba. In another dream—or a nightmare—Arenas recounts that he had to sleep in a bathroom full of excrement and "pájaros raros" [rare birds] that "le iban cerrando la posibilidad de escapatoria" [gradually closed all possibility of escape] (*Antes* 337; *Before* 313).

that, too, is *El color del verano*—the novel generates displacement to save the community. As if at the last minute Arenas were remembering Lezama Lima's statement ("our only salvation lies in words"), the dying writer finds a way out. Through writing, in a feat of the imagination, Arenas rescues the community from disaster. The *pájaros* of the island, the secret armies of pleasure that never lose hope or shrink or falter, leap into the water and, eluding the sharks of state security, eat away the base of the island until it comes loose from the continental shelf; they destroy, symbolically, the very foundation of Castroist homophobia, and the ideals of the old nation lose their base. In this narrativized act of vengeance, the whole community—*pájaros, locas, bugarrones*, and the other citizens—all of them now traitors to the nation, flee together, not *from* the imprisoning island but *on* it. It is a masterful moment: the island becomes a drifting ship aboard which the nation embarks, without compass or dictator, upon a collective wandering.

CHAPTER 2

The Comings and Goings of the Infectious Tourist

Again and again during the first decade of the crisis, a question arose, a nightmarish echo: What is AIDS? Where does it come from? Who carries it? Strictly speaking, this is not one but three different questions, but attempts to answer them always converged in an effort to identify a single origin. Solving this mystery was a society-wide obsession: behind the inquiries lurked a conviction that the origin of the crisis held the key to resolving it and that a precise answer could offer an equally precise solution. Establishing an origin became a highly contentious affair. Official statements in the West immediately assigned responsibility to *foreigners* of all stripes—economic immigrants, political exiles, homosexual tourists, and more than one flight attendant—but there were other versions of the story, too, scientific ones that, though they did not yet understand the syndrome, nevertheless obsessively strove to map its routes of contagion, tracing it back to the point of origin. The early theories were quickly refuted. HIV-positive writing would also devote ink to the problem, taking it on as a necessary challenge, sometimes confirming certain discourses but at others, in the most remarkable cases, subverting and complicating the map of the epidemic to transform established notions about the virus.

The key figure of Reinaldo Arenas appears once more in questioning the black legend of the plague. In 1990 the writer was at death's door, and as a sort of final meditation he wrote in the introduction to his autobiography,

> Veo que llego al final de esta presentación que es en realidad mi fin y no he hablado mucho del sida. No puedo hacerlo, no sé que es. Nadie lo sabe realmente. He visitado decenas de médicos y para todos es un enigma. Se atienden las enfermedades relativas al sida pero el sida

parece más bien un secreto de Estado. Sí puedo asegurar que, de ser una enfermedad, no es una enfermedad al estilo de todas las conocidas. Las enfermedades son producto de la naturaleza y, por lo tanto, como todo lo natural, no son perfectas, se pueden combatir y hasta minar. El sida es un mal perfecto porque está fuera de la naturaleza humana y su función es acabar con el ser humano de la manera más cruel y sistemática. Realmente jamás se ha conocido una calamidad tan invulnerable. Esta perfección diabólica es la que hace pensar a veces en la posibilidad de la mano del hombre. Los gobernantes del mundo entero, la clase reaccionaria siempre en el poder y los poderosos bajo cualquier sistema, tienen que sentirse muy contentos con el sida, pues gran parte de la población marginal... desaparecerá con esta calamidad. (*Antes* 15)[114]

[Now I see that I am almost coming to the end of this introduction, which is almost my end, and I have not said much about AIDS. I cannot. I do not know what it is. Nobody really knows. I have spoken with dozens of doctors and it is a puzzle to all of them. Illnesses related to AIDS are treated, but the actual nature of AIDS seems to be a state secret. I can attest, though, that as a disease it is different from all others. Diseases are natural phenomena and can somehow be fought and overcome. But AIDS is a perfect illness because it is so alien to human nature and has as its function to destroy life in the most cruel and systematic way. Never before has such a formidable calamity affected mankind. Such diabolic perfection makes one ponder the possibility that human beings may have had a hand in its creation.

Moreover, all the rulers of the world, the reactionary class always in power, and the powerful within any system, must feel grateful to AIDS because a good part of the marginal population... will be wiped out.] (*Before* xvi–xvii)

This declaration—this conspiracy theory—contains at least three complementary elements that signal an evolution in the argument: the illness as a puzzle, doubt about its natural origins, and the suggestion that AIDS is a biological weapon created to exterminate marginalized dissidents. Very much in keeping with representations of previous epidemics, Arenas begins by locating the origin of the deadly virus abroad: not only is it foreign to the human species, he claims,

---

[114] In her article on *Antes que anochezca*, Diana Davidson interprets this *not talking about AIDS because of not knowing what it is* as an epistemological, political, and personal difficulty for Arenas: "HIV/AIDS is an adversity that becomes a struggle in his writing rather than a problem that inspires writing" (54). As we will discuss, Arenas *uses* this *not knowing* strategically to suggest that the mystery arises out of the fact that the disease has been constructed by others as a perfect weapon of extermination.

but it transcends its victims' location. It is a "maldición" [curse], he says elsewhere (*Antes* 318; *Before* 297), that has fallen upon the city like the seven plagues of Egypt. Most interesting, though, is Arenas's insistence on the mysterious identity of the virus (*no sé qué es, nadie lo sabe*) when the scientific community was already offering an explanation. Since 1983, the official theory in the United States—which was widely accepted around the world (and persists even today)—argued for the *natural* origin of the illness through the proven existence of HIV, a retrovirus that was first thought (though the theory was later refuted) to have originated in an African species of monkey.[115] The natural origin hypothesis brought with it a specific demarcation on the map: AIDS was a disease that had come from Africa aboard the illegal bodies of Haitian immigrants. This theory, also known as the Africa hypothesis, was at first accepted and later challenged by the implicated governments, which, in a powerful rhetorical—if unscientific—counteroffensive, pointed an accusing finger at Western tourists, arguing that they, like the imperialist travelers before them, had facilitated the spread of AIDS in the dark continent. Setting aside the figure of the tourist, though, we see an effort to invert the course of the infection and examine the role of the United States in the epidemic. This inversion did not take place only in Africa. The socialist bloc also joined the postcolonial counterattack: the virus, it was argued within the ideological framework of the Cold War, could only be the product of a new period of aggression. The Soviet world already saw homosexuals as capitalist crusaders sent to undermine the virility of the new man, and now they became sort of roaming soldiers bearing an American biopolitical weapon *created* to dominate the world: the homosexual as a sexual suicide bomber *avant la lettre*. Agreeing with the version proposed by the still Soviet Russia and associated countries, the Cuban dictator, Fidel Castro, at first denied the existence of HIV—as if the island could be isolated from the disease—but later, pressed by circumstances, addressed his people in a 1988 speech that placed the blame on the United States: "Who brought AIDS to Latin America? Who was the great AIDS vector in the Third World? Why

---

[115] The retrovirus initially called HTLV-III and LAV was isolated simultaneously in 1983 in the United States and France. The theory of *natural origin* argued that HIV, harmless in the green monkeys of Central Africa, had jumped species and fatally injected itself into human beings. But this hypothesis of African origin, proposed by the American researcher Lawrence K. Altman in 1985 and accepted by other Western researchers during the first two decades of the epidemic, sparked a diplomatic dispute examined in Treichler ("AIDS and HIV Infection"). The theory was later discarded.

are there countries like the Dominican Republic, with 40,000 carriers of the virus, and Haiti, and other countries of South and Central America—high rates in Mexico, Brazil, and other countries? Who brought it? The United States did, that's a fact."[116]

The ideological reading did not fall on deaf ears. Some sectors of the American Left immediately began to evaluate those speculations about the manufactured origin of the virus.[117] Even before Castro's speech and Arenas's statement mentioned above, many scholars had begun to investigate the matter; they had developed at least five serious or, shall we say, scientific hypotheses that claimed to refute the official account of the disease.[118] These alternative theories examined the possible creation of a new vibrio, a mix of human and animal viruses, through genetic engineering in US Army laboratories; the hypothesis of the fusion and mutation of two viruses transmitted by mosquitoes; that of a virus carried by an African pig (not a monkey) and transmitted through food; one that identified nonmicrobial factors in the origin of the syndrome; and the idea of poisoning from the dioxides used in pesticides. None of these theories of the manufacture of AIDS, except perhaps the first one, achieved the weight of the official version. Yet all of them reflected

---

[116] Quoted in Leiner (131). Castro's strategy was ambiguous: he acknowledged the disease but then only allowed the release of infection figures that many claimed were questionable and laughably low. The official incidence rate in Cuba in 2005 was 0.05 percent, while the Latin American average was around 0.6 percent. Given that international verification was forbidden and that the Caribbean was the most affected region after sub-Saharan Africa, some considered the figure a dubious one. According to physician Antonio María de Gordon, eight cases of opportunistic infections in children had been documented in Cuba in 1977—that is, long before the diagnosis in the United States. And in blood stored since 1980 and later tested by foreign experts, "la tasa de seropositividad . . . era casi dos veces más alta que la tasa correspondiente de Nueva York" [the rate of HIV infection was nearly twice as high as the corresponding rate in New York] ("VIH-sida en Cuba"). These cases, invisible at the time, are now associated with the Cuban troops deployed to Angola beginning in 1975. Researchers such as Marvin Leiner, accepting the official Cuban claim of few cases of infection, suggest that the low rate was a result of the radical health policy of 1983 that prohibited the importation of blood and blood products from infected countries and later, in 1986, imposed the obligatory internment of all HIV-positive Cubans in special areas so they could be better cared for and to prevent the spread of the virus.

[117] As noted earlier in this book, the idea that AIDS was an imperialistic discursive fabrication was in circulation by the mid-1980s in Haiti and elsewhere.

[118] This information comes from a very detailed source: "Origin and Spread of AIDS: Is the West Responsible?" by American investigative journalist Robert Lederer, published in the New York gay magazine *CovertAction* in two parts (1987, 1988).

widespread suspicion about the possible *planning* of the extermina-tion on political, and not necessarily sexual, grounds. That sexual aspect would be emphasized by the dissident activists themselves. One of the articles published during the period in a well-known gay magazine in the United States begins with the rhetorical but inescapable question of the origin and spread of AIDS, inquiring whether Western institutions had any role in the creation of the epidemic: "Increasingly, that question is being asked by people worldwide as the death toll mounts. Particularly in Central Africa, Brazil, Haiti and in the gay and the Third World communities in western nations. In an era of supposed 'medical miracles,'" the article continues, "it is appropriate and urgent to ask why such a deadly new disease has surfaced....Given the historic oppression of Third World and gay people," the reporter adds, also pointing to the dissident community, "and the vicious western response to the current medical crisis, many people suspect AIDS is too conve-nient to be coincidental" (Lederer, "Is the West Responsible?" 43). Nor is it mere coincidence that Arenas replicated these arguments and carried them even further: the popular interpretations of every infection, as noted earlier, "often simply take the metaphors that occur in scientific writing a few paces further" (Martin 361). In this period of widespread misinformation and rampant speculation, not only did these alternative scientific hypotheses shape the preven-tion methods listed so authoritatively by Reinaldo Arenas at the beginning of *Antes que anochezca* and toward the end of *El color del verano*, but they also led to an unusual ideological interpretation of the subject. I have already discussed Arenas's claim in his memoirs that AIDS was a biological weapon created to destroy marginal-ized communities. In his fiction, he directly accused some institu-tions of being complicit in the extermination of homosexuals: "La ciencia, la política y la religión se han puesto al servicio de nuestra destrucción. Con la creación del virus del sida, fabricado especial-mente para aniquilarnos y aniquilar todo intento de aventura..., se quiere poner punto final a nuestra historia, historia que no puede tener fin porque es la historia de la vida misma en su manifestación más rebelde y auténtica" [Science, politics, and religion have taken up arms against us. The creation of the AIDS virus, manufactured with the clear intention of annihilating us and all those who, like us, seek after adventure...is but the most recent attempt to bring our history to an end—and yet ours is a history that cannot have an end, because it is the history of life itself in its most rebellious, authentic

manifestation] (*El color* 405; *The Color* 360).[119] By evoking the sinister deliberate manufacture of a genocidal virus,[120] Arenas exon-
erates homosexuals of the accusation that they produced, carried,
and spread the disease—that is, of being themselves, as always, metonymically, the disease. Through the same rhetorical gesture, he
assigns blame to the political class—"esa clase reaccionaria siempre
en el poder, bajo cualquier sistema" [that reactionary class always
in power, within any system]—whose hand, as visible as that of the
market, is the homophobic hand of global hegemony. Not only does
Arenas employ the whispered theory of a virus deliberately manufactured by Western power, but he also adds his own twist: a return
home, a *Cubanization*, of the disease. His version positions Fidel
Castro as the commander of a deadly operation. The writer claims
not only that the US Army is producing secret biological weapons,
that what he calls (in a happier section of his account) *el mundo libre*
[the free world] is directing these experiments, and that there is an
alliance among a group of homophobic leaders and their churches,
but also that, more perversely still, the powerful in every system
have shelved long-standing rivalries in solidarity against a common
enemy and under a single leader: Castro.[121] In a period marked by
the ideological confrontation of the Cold War, the island dictator is
accused of setting aside his communist ideals to collaborate with his
capitalist adversary in the joint destruction of their worst enemies.

These were not just the ravings of a dying man. In fact, the idea
has a precedent, one that Arenas revisited in his fiction to serve his
anti-Castro poetics. The veiled reference is to a prior, lesser-known
episode: during the Mariel boatlift, not only did Castro allow the asylum seekers in the Peruvian embassy to leave, but he also dispatched
to the United States the criminals, dissidents, and sick people that
the regime wanted to be rid of. Arenas tots it all up and realizes, in
outraged disbelief, that Castro did not free him and others but rather
got rid of them, sending them to meet their deaths in a world that
at first seems free but in the end proves just as hellish. The dictator
has extended the long reach of his power from the perfect prison of

[119] In the previous chapter, we clearly saw Arenas's effort not to repeat in fiction the
rhetoric of annihilation offered in the autobiography: in the novel, Arenas offers the
community a way out by detaching the island of Cuba from the continental shelf.

[120] The Jewish Holocaust was a recurring image in representations of AIDS policy,
material for another monograph. (See notes 58 and 189.)

[121] Fidel Castro appears again and again in Arenas's work, while Ronald Reagan,
the conservative president of the United States, is not mentioned once.

Cuba to the very heart of capitalism. And Arenas is trapped once more, and this time for good. True or not, this idea does not encourage any effort to separate out the facts from the fiction or reality of the metaphor; the emotional complexity with which certain episodes are recalled cannot be suppressed, nor can the literary rendering be anything but distorted and, in its distortion, revealing. Thus, in the brief "carta de despedida" [farewell letter] posthumously inserted as an epilogue to his autobiography,[122] Arenas portrays the tyrant as the only facilitator of his infection: "Solo hay un responsable: Fidel Castro. Los sufrimientos del exilio, las penas…, la soledad y las enfermedades que haya podido contraer en el destierro seguramente no las hubiera sufrido de haber vivido libre en mi país" [There is only one person I hold accountable: Fidel Castro. The sufferings of exile, the pain…, the loneliness, and the diseases contracted in exile would probably never have happened if I had been able to enjoy freedom in my country] (*Antes* 343; *Before* 317). But this is not the case, either. In his autobiography, Arenas is once more distorting a situation that he knows well and in fact alludes to in *El color del verano*: the elevated number of cases of HIV/AIDS in Cuba during that period. Fidel had instituted compulsory medical exams and established AIDS camps in which the affected were confined against their will (*El color* 402; *The Color* 356).[123] Certainly, Arenas could have become infected on any of the islands. The truth of his statement is obviously less important than the circumstances under which he made it, less important than his need to accuse Castro. What is relevant here—what is interesting in literary terms—is that although part of the obsession with origin is an attempt to mark out specific territories (Africa, Haiti, the United States) and to trace fixed routes along a geographic axis (east–west or vice versa), and another part of the conspiratorial obsession corresponds directly to the ideological postulates of the Cold War (the theory of the manufactured capitalist virus versus the natural theory), Arenas postulates a third way. Going beyond geography or the Cold War, Arenas identifies the origin debate as the product of a

[122] Editors decided to add this letter to the autobiography to fulfill Arenas's wish that it be widely read. Yet the length and format of the text seem to indicate a desire that it be published in the press and not necessarily as the last chapter of his autobiography. Its placement there produces a different idea of composition than the author had intended: the subject of AIDS frames the autobiography.

[123] The Los Cocos AIDS sanatorium, opened in 1986, at first received only 24 patients, but in the next decade that number grew exponentially and 17 other similar institutions were built.

global homophobia, calling it a reactionary international cooperative effort to destroy the dissident community. Arenas's world is no longer divided between cardinal points or their hotly debated ideologies: AIDS has triggered in him another sort of spatial awareness, between power and the historical powerlessness of homosexuality.

INFECTIOUS TOURISTS

The world was pointing its fingers in opposite directions and at different figures in a map destabilized by constant migratory movement. For the American discourse, which radiated out from the center to the rest of the world and whose scientific language decisively dominated the official account of the epidemic, those accused of transporting the infection—metaphorical bridges between a supposed origin and another supposed destination—were incarnated in what sociology calls ideal types but that perhaps, in the context of this social calamity, should be considered indicted types instead. These two types complement each other, but they are also differentiated by their "degree of mobility, the freedom to choose where to be" (Bauman 86). The infectious immigrant, the aforementioned scapegoat of the official discourse, is, I would argue, the least dangerous of all the HIV-positive travelers: he leaves his homeland without a return ticket because he cannot and even *must not* go back. The nature of his movement and the difficulties he faces make him less mobile; the migratory journey often ends with the first place he reaches, and the return trip ever retreats into the distance. His complementary opposite is the highly mobile infected tourist, who by definition possesses a return ticket. There are a number of iterations of this character: There is the traditional tourist, guru (says Zygmunt Bauman, not without a certain degree of irony) of the new era, and the vagabond who constitutes his inverse, a disdained other self for the tourist but also his submissive admirer. The vagabond is the involuntary tourist: he would like to be a conventional traveler but will never be one; he travels because he has no other bearable option.[124] In addition to these forms of tourism, there is also the flight attendant, that professional traveler, flexible like none other because of his incessant,

---

[124] The vagabond is distinguished from the immigrant in that the latter is someone who, by definition, travels in order to work and therefore ends up staying for extended periods, if not permanently. The former, on the other hand, travels at will, not because he is forced to but because he feels that the world at large is hostile to him. See Bauman (112–23).

indiscriminate movements in multiple directions. The flight attendant's journey *is* his work, and his mode of sexual fulfillment: for
him, work and pleasure are inherent elements of the transnational
flight. Among all the travelers, then, only he embodies the absolute
foreigner and therefore was the most feared and despised figure in
the early stages of the epidemic. All of these travelers were objects of
suspicion, but they were assessed by their potential mobility—that
is, their potential infection. At first, the presumably illegal Haitian
body took on criminal connotations that provoked a complete lack of
empathy for other immigrants, whether economic migrants or exiles.
Because of Arenas's Caribbean point of view, his being part of the
New York Latino community, he too occupied that uncomfortable
and even violent space of suspicion. But Arenas, an inveterate traveler
after his exile and an active member of a transhuman nation, did
not share that homophobic prejudice against the other traveler of the
epidemic—the tourist—widely blamed by the countries of the Soviet
bloc, by the African nations, by researchers, and later by a whole generation of European and American moralists who accused him of having put AIDS into circulation in his sexual pilgrimages. Blaming the
tourist was unquestionably another way to reproduce the prevailing
homophobic logic. Let's take a well-intentioned example that reveals
how internalized and internationalized homophobia had become. In
an article in *Life* magazine, a tormented American researcher travels
to Haiti to find out whether the virus "could . . . have come from the
American and Canadian homosexual tourists, and, yes, even some
US diplomats who have traveled to the island to have sex with impoverished Haitian men all too willing to sell themselves to feed their
families."[125] The intent is to clear the Haitian immigrant of blame,
presenting Haiti as a sexual victim devastated by waves of gay tourism
in Port au Prince, highlighting an American excess that bears the stigmatized mark of homosexuality. There is an implicit accusation here,
as well as a complete rejection of the possibility of pleasure in that
exchange of money and desire. This diagnosis is shaped by an aseptic
and even dogmatic view of medicine: its description corresponds precisely to what a *straight mind* (in the formulation of Monique Wittig)
might produce. The homosexual journey is seen as unambiguously
and exclusively oppressive and exploitative.

The human mind can end up hazardously trapped in the puritanical chasms of *straight* thinking. Without a doubt, the official theory

---

[125] Quoted in Treichler ("AIDS and HIV Infection" 380).

of the infectious tourist fed off a real context of inequality that only worsened as the epidemic and the century progressed. This inequality between the tourists who traveled for cheap sex in poorer and more exotic areas of the world—Asia, Africa, Latin America—and the perhaps futile resistance of their supposed victims did not go unnoticed either by the more transgressive authors of the Latin American HIV-positive corpus—Néstor Perlongher, Pedro Lemebel, and Arenas himself—or by critics. A number of postcolonial thinkers from a variety of traditions have drawn a parallel between the old orientalist journeys, motivated by all sorts of desires, that justified colonial interventions in the East, and these other journeys of sexual intervention. Erotic desire, claims Joseph Boone, was and continues to be one of the motivations for travel to distant lands: "The possibility of sexual contact with and between men underwrites and at times even explains the historical appeal" (Boone 90). In those "sanctuaries of noninterference" (the term is from nomadic writer William Burroughs), a set of possibilities comes together: fascination and abuse, enjoyment and exploitation. We should avoid falling into the reductive view of the journalist who watched the Haitian epidemic unfold at an enormous cultural and sexual remove from the crisis: those complex power dynamics produced a transaction mediated by money and sex, in which exploited and exploiter mutually benefited, blended together, and perhaps tragically infected each other with the virus. "In a restless world, tourism is the only acceptable, human form of restlessness," says a Polish philosopher (Bauman 94). That restlessness has always characterized the homosexual who becomes, when convenient, a universal tourist. The sex tourist, as stated earlier, embodies an endemic contradiction: that of being both an ideal of contemporary culture and an object of suspicion during the epidemic. It is this subject, with his multiple faces and many interpretations, that is examined, from the south, in the early work of Las Yeguas del Apocalipsis (The Mares of the Apocalypse)—an artistic collaboration between two Chilean writers and performance artists, Pedro Lemebel and Francisco Casas, between 1987 and 1995[126]—and in Lemebel's later narrative work. In the initial image of the traveler sketched out by these writers, who are so jealously protective of their places of origin, the international tourist is fused with the historical

---

[126] They assembled a total of 15 unforgettable works of avant-garde kitsch performance that put the body on the street: the artists' body—naked, transvestite, impoverished—representing the *locas* who died of AIDS and those tortured and disappeared under the dictatorship.

figure of the conquistador: he is the insidious emissary of an empire that attempts to invade Latin America, or Chile, through a viral, cultural, and ideological infection.

The first textual instance of that interpretation appears in an article on AIDS published in the now-defunct magazine *Nuevos aires* (1990–93; New airs).[127] The two transvestite writers contributed short but powerful columns that present the epidemic as the effect of a coldly calculated effort to destroy the local community. Under an eloquent title—"Un transiberiano llamado sida" (A trans-Siberian named AIDS)[128]—the poet Francisco Casas begins his text by alluding metaphorically to the disease as a train that joins European Russia with the Far East (another orientalist journey), a train called AIDS that bears within it, from one point to another, a lethal and illegal product. "El sida está estrechamente relacionado con la idea del viaje," writes Casas before mapping out the route by which it spread. "La enfermedad se transmite a través de las fronteras: de África a USA, de allí a Europa o viceversa" [AIDS is closely associated with the idea of travel. The disease is transmitted across borders: from Africa to the United States, from there to Europe or vice versa]. Casas uses "vice versa," a key phrase that indicates the reversibility of this movement, a suggestion still apparent in the statement that follows: AIDS "es la mitificación del viajante, el que trafica, *va o viene*, o sea, *el portador* que cruza la frontera-cuerpo, penetra los limites anales, intravenosos, con un desconocido polizón en su estructura" [is the mythification of the traveler, of him who traffics, comes or goes—that is, the *carrier* who crosses the border/body, penetrating anal or intravenous boundaries, with an unknown stowaway in his interstices]. And he once more repeats the idea of a journey between unnamed cardinal points, as if they were random: "El virus viaja anónimo entre dos puntos cardinales, y a su paso se reproduce, *coloniza* el cuerpo (lo invade hasta fijar su territorio)" [The virus travels anonymously between two cardinal points, and as it goes it reproduces, *colonizing* the body (invading it until it establishes its territory)].

---

[127] Unfortunately, this magazine is nowhere to be found now. It was not possible, even in consultation with the authors, to determine the exact date on which this article was published.

[128] The title alludes hyperbolically to the famous play by gay playwright Tennessee Williams, *A Streetcar Named Desire* (1947), translated into Spanish as *Un tranvía llamado deseo*. This play, in which class differences are a major theme, was made into a movie starring Marlon Brando and Vivian Leigh by Elia Kazan. Here, the local streetcar becomes a trans-Siberian train and AIDS replaces desire.

Examining the virus's insidious path allows Casas to move on to the political trajectory of the infection. The political element is contained in the verb *colonizar* [to colonize]: "El sida en Chile," writes the poet, "es una nueva forma de colonización, basada en el miedo y la represión sexual" [AIDS in Chile is a new form of colonization, based on fear and sexual repression]. An echo of this idea, reinforced and somewhat reformulated, appears in Pedro Lemebel's later work: "La plaga nos llegó como otra forma de colonización por el contagio. Reemplazó nuestras plumas por jeringas, y el sol por la gota congelada de la luna en el sidario" [The epidemic came to us like another form of colonization by infection. It replaced our feathers with syringes, and the sun with the frozen droplet of the moon in the AIDS camp] (*Loco afán* [1996] 7). The shift between the notion of colonization of time experienced by the Yeguas, made possible by the Chilean dictatorship and the Church, and the historical processes of imperialist domination referred to by both writers is a subtle one. What makes Casas and Lemebel's approach unique is that, unlike Reinaldo Arenas, they immerse themselves in the local version of oppression experienced by marginalized groups, tracing echoes of historical oppression in the present. For the Yeguas, the first colonization by contagion took place with the defeat of the indigenous world during the Spanish conquest, aided, as we know, by the unforeseen alliance of infectious diseases that the Americas—later reimagined or refounded as virgin because of the absence of certain antibodies—could not combat. "Los españoles," says Casas, "fueron portadores en sus cuerpos de la más sofisticada arma de exterminio [contra] el fiero pueblo Araucano" [The Spanish bore in their bodies the most sophisticated weapon of extermination (against) the fierce Araucanian people]. It was this same epidemic mechanism, they claim, that once more allowed the US empire to conquer them. It was a carbon copy of the imperial technique, but now the disputed territory was Chile: previously, the Spanish conquest had imposed Catholicism on the Mapuches (called "Araucanians" by the Spanish), and now the conquest carried out by the northern empire was imposing its neoliberal economic ideology on the local, *loca* variant of homosexuality, which in its own way repeated, or saw itself as repeating, the heroic resistance of the indigenous population.

Necessary here is a contextual digression regarding the abovementioned methods of ideological colonization (Spanish Catholicism, US neoliberalism) that Casas and Lemebel refer to in their writing. The epidemic, they tell us, forged a perverse alliance between two foreign logics that, unlike tourists, do not just pass through. They are opposites of a culture that the pair proposes as native. Casas identifies the origin of the national or sexual community (the boundaries between the two are unclear) in a racialized indigenous past; looking back, he imagines the Mapuche culture to have been both sexually diverse and yet immobile, isolated, free of any sin imposed by the Church and of the capitalist obsession with wealth. In the midst of the epidemic, Las Yeguas observed how the ideas of a religion that associates disease with sex and sex with sin were being revived. The association of these terms persuaded the national community to submit to the ecclesiastical doctrine that declared itself the defender of the nation's moral health. The most repressive wing of the Church, in alliance with the dictatorship's most conservative rhetoric, promoted abstinence as the only acceptable and safe way to control the spread of the virus. These figures refused to discuss other preventive methods, such as the use of condoms, and seized on AIDS, Casas claims, as the "antídoto más efectivo para establecer e institucionalizar nuestro comportamiento sexual" [most effective antidote to establish and institutionalize our sexual behavior].

The severe Catholicism that urged the disciplining of desire, that tried to "desexualizar la homosexualidad con justificación sanitaria" [desexualize homosexuality for health reasons, as Perlongher put it], was approved by a military dictatorship that also took advantage of the epidemic to reproduce discourses that scorned any exercise of freedom of thought and action except that of economic liberalism. This second form of ideological colonization was widely expressed in the adoption of neoliberal policies designed in the United States. Under a CIA-backed dictatorship, Chile became a testing laboratory for an economic practice that was then exported to the rest of the world.[129] Following foreign models, advised by Chilean economists trained at the University of Chicago, and shielded by the violence that weakened the opposition, the dictatorship privatized state industries, reduced state contributions to the public welfare system, and opened the nation's borders to economic intervention. In other words, it liberalized the economy without liberating the citizenry trapped in its fist. The ideology of the new capitalism, that machine for producing

---

[129] Chile, as a model of neoliberalism, has the best macroeconomic statistics in Latin America, but it is also one of the countries with the highest rates of income inequality among the 34 member nations of the Organization for Economic Cooperation and Development (OECD). The economic growth has benefited a select portion of the Chilean population while the promised trickle-down effect has barely reached those sectors that have historically been most vulnerable.

desires that survives off urges and compulsions to consume that must never be satisfied, would demand, for coherency's sake, a relaxation of restrictions on the sex trade. We can be even more specific: in 1982, amid popular discontent due to the world economic crisis affecting Chile, gay clubs opened in Santiago. Rather than reflecting official tolerance for homosexuality, the appearance of these clubs revealed the consolidation of free-market ideology in governmental logic (Robles, "History" 37). The sex trade demanded space in which to operate, but it, of course, ended up defying the mandates of the Church and its conservative faithful. The free market presupposes a necessary distancing from and even a contravention of the Church's moral values to trigger demand for and consumption of all goods, including sexual ones. These value systems gradually enter into conflict: while religious dogma opposes any loosening of restrictions on sexuality, economic policy first hesitates and then discreetly allows the maintenance of certain underground areas of sexual consumption that lubricate the system's gears.

Casas turns the idea of total consumption into a perverse image that uses the epidemic as a sign with two meanings and calls into question the two forms of colonization. In that image, the terror of the dictatorship becomes the terror of the disease, functioning as a new mechanism of consumption through the offering of safe sex (rejected by the Church): "El condón, maravilla de la tecnología moderna, artículo imprescindible para un coito efectivo y sin duelo [se vende] en una gama de diferentes texturas y colores que van del pasional rojo al gay rosa" [The condom, that marvel of modern technology, essential item for effective and regret-free coitus(, is sold) in a variety of different textures and colors ranging from passionate red to gay pink]. Casas adds,

> Es así como el mercado y la libre empresa se lanzan a la publicidad del terror promocionando la plaga más temida del siglo. Mientras unos se enriquecen a costa de un montón de maricas muertos, los gobiernos conservadores de las *buenas costumbres* advierten del peligro de la promiscuidad, refortaleciendo la familia, pilar fundamental de la institución cristiana, llamando a la población a la abstención sexual, o sea, al apareamiento controlado por la estructura del poder. En este caso, las minorías son anuladas por una perversa campaña destinada a hacerlas desaparecer, modificando su hábito sexual alternativo a uno delictual, reordenado en la prostitución y en la drogadicción.
>
> [It is thus that the market and free enterprise work to advertise terror, promoting the most feared epidemic of the century. While some grow rich at the price of a bunch of dead fags, conservative

governments warn about the dangers of promiscuity, reinforcing the family, a pillar of the Christian institution, and recommending sexual abstinence—that is, mating controlled by the structures of power. In this case, the minorities are wiped out by a perverse campaign to make them disappear, their alternative sexual habits reclassified as criminal under the name of prostitution and drug addiction.]

This is no exaggeration. The two imported systems are often in conflict, but there are also many similarities between them, as they both make use of *a bunch of dead fags* to strengthen their own position in the national community and do away with those subjects that pose an obstacle.

Let's return to the infectious tourist, which is where we were before this necessary digression. The foreign cultural models called out by the duo are still, in the *Nuevos aires* article, vaguely associated with the figure of the foreign tourist. That traveler carries the disease alongside empire—and not symbolically but completely verifiably. It was Casas's partner in the Yeguas who restored the allegorical element of the tourist figure, transforming the physical territory into a political one. In *Loco afán* (1996; Mad desire),[130] starting where Casas ended in 1990, the acid but exceedingly lucid Pedro Lemebel takes the figure in a more powerful and substantial direction for literature. The conquistador bearing a cross and smallpox reappears in the book's "*sidario* chronicles," transformed into a gay tourist who lands in Chile bearing dollars and HIV (and a sort of symbolic neoliberal *visa*, a contagious ideology that would destroy the already faltering unity of Chilean socialism). The infectious tourist is called Míster Gay (one of the many nicknames that Lemebel gives him) and is invariably white, muscular, virile, narcissistic, handsome, and globalized; within him, wrapped in his apparently "aséptica envoltura" [sterile exterior], lurks the invisible *stowaway*.

The virus, thus personified, becomes a metonym for a First-World citizen who literally and figuratively penetrates the Chilean nation. The infection is presented in the classic formula, as if Lemebel were accepting a rhetorical consensus about the disease. In this account, AIDS comes from some foreign place, from all those places that are not this one, and enters the territory from abroad: "La plaga *nos llegó*" [The epidemic came to us], writes Lemebel in the epigraph quoted above and then, in the article itself, employing a similar formula,

---

[130] These famous accounts were read by Lemebel on his program on the feminist radio station Tierra [Earth] and later published in a book also titled *Loco afán*.

reiterates that the virus is a sort of traveler or tourist *that arrived in Chile.* Like all epidemics, AIDS arrives, enters or penetrates, invades, attacks, or, as Arenas puts it, *falls upon* a place that had imagined itself immune. All these verbs of entrance that appear again and again in HIV-positive narratives are the textual traces of an attempt to demarcate a precise boundary and to establish a defensive position in the face of the enemy's incursion into the local space.[131]

But Lemebel deviates from the classic version when he allegorizes it, emphasizing that the virus/tourist's journey has been aided by foreign economic policies shaped by a foreign logic. And it is not just that the nation's immune system has failed but rather that the body politic—the dictatorship as an abusive representative of the national community—has welcomed the enemy with open arms. The military regime, Lemebel says, deliberately left the nation unprotected, lowered its defensive barriers, celebrated the entrance of all sorts of investors that benefited from the country's natural riches (Lemebel speaks metaphorically of the *dulce sangre* [sweet blood] of the nation) and from its earnings after economic liberalization and the privatization of state industries. This policy initiated during the military regime was expanded by successive democratic governments, which revised many laws but left the economic ones alone. The main idea here is that the nation has become a vulnerable body, threatened by an interventionist and highly infectious system/tourist (the infection of capitalist consumption) that contains the virus of neoliberalism. To complete the circle, in the final twist of the allegory, that tourist decides to remain in the country, like the economic model and like AIDS before it. It

---

[131] The rhetoric of importation appears again and again in the Latin American context. Among the examples are the Colombian nurse who described the disease as a "sida importado" [imported AIDS] and the Argentine critic Leonardo Moledo (1988), who echoed her almost exactly, calling it "un mal extranjero, un mal *traído* del extranjero, una de las tantas perversiones ejercidas contra nuestro país" [a foreign disease, a disease *brought* from abroad, one of the many perversions perpetrated on our country] (107, emphasis added). As Moledo saw it, the disease had been transported and *imported* to his country by the British at a precise political moment—that of Argentina's Falkland/Malvinas defeat: "El sida *llegó* a la Argentina en junio del 82.... No pudo haber elegido momento mejor para *instalarse* en la Argentina" [AIDS *arrived* in Argentina in June 1982. It couldn't have chosen a better moment to *move into* Argentina] (106, emphasis added). In this telling, the virus can attack the unprotected body of the nation through a double assault: one that comes from outside the nation (the British army) and a national one that comes from outside the dissident community (the repressive Argentine army under the dictatorship). Moledo argued that these two schools of masculinity, as Gombrowicz put it, gave the disease access to the young body politic.

is as if the epidemic—and here I quote again—"fuera un viajante, un turista, que llegó a Chile de paso y el vino dulce de nuestra sangre lo hizo quedarse" [were a traveler, a tourist, who came to Chile in passing, and the sweet wine of our blood made him stay] (*Loco afán* [1996] 23). The infectious tourist, like a metonymic figure of the economic system, of a real new culture of capitalism—the tourist and his virus *become acclimated*, as Lemebel's favorite poet, Néstor Perlongher, puts it. And upon staying, that infectious tourist becomes the symbol of a system's most sinister exploitation. But another doubling in the possible reading of this figure appears throughout the text. He represents a way of thinking, embodying it to such a degree that he seems to betray, as Lemebel sees it, the community itself and its most radical elements. When that handsome, wealthy gay man arrives in Chile, he abandons his credentials as an international traveler and stays, conquering even more concretely the bodies of the local sexual dissident community: one that does not feel masculine; that is not white; that calls itself, with a jubilant clamor, *la cola* or *la loca*. That global traveler sets aside his migratory spirit and becomes *acclimated* in Santiago, destabilizing the classical conception of the tourist as a disinterested and uncontaminated spectator who is always about to leave, positioning him instead as someone seeking to remain and transform the local community in his image. It must be made acceptable, Americanized. Apparent in his arrival is a blatant effort to facilitate the disappearance of a deeply subversive figure: the transvestite, the *flamboyant homosexual*, the man who takes on feminine signs as a way to rebel against Latin American culture. Lemebel's vision of the extermination of the *loca* thus coincides with Arenas's, from a contrary ideological stance but via the same opposition to dictatorships, when he claims that the infection is merely a tool of the dominant global ideology that seeks to do away with the marginalized dissident. Unlike Arenas, however, who thinks of the homosexual world as being vast and unified, a diverse world that can never be fractured, Lemebel presents the possibility of extermination as one that the system will carry out through the homosexual tourist: it is in the local context, within the community itself, Lemebel tries to tell us, that the global contrast between privilege and privation is mirrored.

Consumption That Consumes

The poetic project of *Loco afán* is to underscore the toll on the local community taken by the capitalist system adopted in Chile. The text works unapologetically from the local space, from the *loca*'s preferred place. Everything is *localized* to criticize a situation that had turned ominous. Its accounts provide a detailed look at *lo que el sida se llevó* (what AIDS took away) from the community:[132] the book presents itself as a rebellious elegy to all the victims of that tourist who infected the *locas* with the virus of his masculinity and the local space with his new consumer culture. Thus, the text explores the destruction of the local *loca* who occupies the prostitution districts that Lemebel knows so well: those corners of Santiago that "articulan el cruce entre el espacio metropolitano y la barriada marginal" [articulate the intersection of the metropolis and the margins] (Jaime Donoso 78) and not, as in Arenas, the intersection of the capital of socialism and the ultimate global city (New York). From this intersection, Lemebel celebrates the remarkable racial, sexual, and even linguistic diversity of the poor *loca*, rejecting standard Spanish and opting instead for a personal style of speech that includes vernacular and slang, cobbling together dissimilar semantic fields in a baroque argot that is additional evidence of a localist linguistic option. He maps out the place, the language, the point of view of the resistance against the invasive mainstreaming of everything, which is blotting out the transvestite and the transvestite's subversive potential. The persistent fixation on the local context in Lemebel's early work serves as a mechanism of resistance from the heart of the community at the crossroads of a profound change, one that is described in "La noche de los visones (o la última fiesta de la Unidad Popular)" (Night of the mink coats [or the last party of the Unidad Popular]) from *Loco afán*.

   In this account of opening there is a before and after the dictatorship, a before and during the epidemic that eventually takes the lives of all of the *locas* except the anonymous narrator. The tale begins on the night of the festive new year's celebrations of 1973, when the community is still united and popular and AIDS is only a specter on the horizon. These are also the months just before the fall of Salvador Allende and his revolutionary government project, one that had benefited the *locas*, though not in sexual terms. In a well-known manifesto written during the democracy, an embittered Lemebel reproached the Left, saying that "el marxismo [lo] rechazó tantas veces" [Marxism rejected (him) so many times], whereas in New York homosexuals

---

[132] "Lo que el sida se llevó," a reference to the translated title of *Gone with the Wind* in Spanish (*Lo que el viento se llevó*), is the name of one of the performances of Las Yeguas del Apocalipsis, first performed in 1989 on a street known for prostitution and a year later in front of the Instituto Chileno-Francés de Cultura in downtown Santiago.

were embraced (*Loco afán* [1996] *89*).[133] But in his literary version, Lemebel romanticizes the socialist past he supported, emphasizing how at that time, in the story's allegorical gala, "los matices sociales se confundían en brindis, abrazos y calenturas" [social differences were ignored in the flurry of toasts, embraces, and sexual desires] (13) among *locas* from every socioeconomic class. The military coup cleaved that symbolic embrace only a few months after:

Desde ahí, los años se despeñaron como derrumbe de troncos que sepultaron la fiesta nacional. Vino el golpe y la nevazón de balas provocó la estampida de las locas, que nunca más volvieron a danzar por los patios floridos. . . . Buscaron otros lugares, se reunieron en los paseos recién inaugurados de la dictadura. Siguieron las fiestas más privadas, más silenciosas, con menos gente educada por la cripta, del toque de queda. Algunas discotecas siguieron funcionando. . . . Quizás, la homosexualidad acomodada nunca fue un problema subversivo que alterara su pulcra moral. Quizás, había demasiadas locas de derecha que apoyaban el régimen. Tal vez su hedor a cadáver era amortiguado por el perfume francés de los maricas del barrio alto. Aun así, el tufo mortuorio de la dictadura fue un adelanto del sida, que hizo su estreno a comienzos de los ochenta. (15–16)[134]

[From there, the years tumbled out like a pile of logs collapsing and burying the national celebration. There was the coup, and the *locas* fled from the hail of bullets, never again to dance in the flowery courtyards. . . . They sought other places, they met up in the newly opened avenues of the dictatorship. Then came the after-curfew parties, private and silent, where fewer people had been educated by the grave. Some nightclubs remained open. . . . Perhaps accommodating homosexuality was never a subversive problem that would alter the nation's moral purity. Perhaps there were too many right-wing *locas* who supported the regime. Maybe its corpse-like stench was masked by the French perfumes of the fags in the wealthy neighborhoods.

---

[133] As described in the chapter on Chile in Tim Frasca's book, and in *Sangre como la mía* (Blood like mine) by Jorge Marchant Lazcano, in 1996 the center-left government coalition, headed by a Christian Democrat president, ordered a raid on two gay bars. Forty men were arrested, physically and verbally humiliated, and then forced to take an AIDS test (Marchant Lazcano 176). An important account of the situation in Chile can also be found in two major recent studies: *Bandera hueca* (2008; Hollow flag) by Víctor Hugo Robles and *Raro* (2011; Queer) by Óscar Contardo.
[134] The account gives us the details: the first Chilean case of AIDS was announced in 1984. The epidemiological crisis was declared a few years later, during the transition between the military period and a dubious democracy overseen from behind the scenes (and not so far behind them, either) by the dictator.

Even so, the dictatorship's deadly stink anticipated AIDS, which made
its debut at the beginning of the 1980s.]

The dictatorship implemented a complex set of political, social, and
economic transformations that wiped out the utopia of social unity
and violently divided the national community. On top of—or, rather,
taking advantage of—the totalitarian violence, a consumerist, suc-
cess-oriented, elitist code was imposed (sexual difference was less
important than class difference) that infected the local community,
enforcing a gradual masculinization that eliminated the French perfume of the wealthy *maricas* and the feminine behavior of the poor
locas from the lower class. This process also ended up dividing them:
the upper-class *locas* began to ally themselves with the dictatorship,
while those from the lower class were abandoned to their desperate fate. The anonymous author, who in later collections takes on
the identity of "Lemebel," observes the deterioration of the position
of the *loca*—Third-World, malnourished, effeminate, in open contradiction with a model of masculinity that is reinforced, codifying
difference and incorporating it into an acceptable model. The coup
de grace comes (says the author) even before AIDS, when the *loca*
gives up or succumbs to the temptations offered by the system: a
virile temptation that turns out to be viral. The subversive elements
(subversion understood as resistance to capitalism) of transvestitism
gradually disappear, and the *locas* give in to the frenetic apparatus of
capitalist consumption that is never satisfied, that only produces more
desire. As if satisfaction were an unhappy accident and consumption's
only objective were to accumulate sensations. As if that were its only
conviction, and any faith in resistance or community solidarity had
vanished.

This critique within the community has hardly been noticed by
critics, but at least one reader has highlighted how Lemebel sees
the history of transvestite culture as "a problematic trajectory that,
from radical beginnings, became a marketing strategy that has failed
to challenge unjust social structures" (Palaversich 104). Lemebel
notes—as a paradox and a warning—how imprudent complicity with
the system has put the community at risk. Because what sustains the
loca's desire can also destroy her. The author speaks of the danger
of falling under the "embrujo capitalista" [capitalist spell], whose
idealized figure is the body of the masculine gay man who in these
accounts always appears dressed as a tourist, with dollars in his wal-
let. In an interview, Lemebel wonders "to what extent homos have
been co-opted by the system. I believe that to liberate oneself from

the macho ideal that fills one's head is to affirm [a truer] identity" (Palaversich 104). That macho ideal pursued by the transvestite is expressed in the scene of one of the later chronicles in which the "maraquillas errantes" [roving twinks], despite the risks they face, hang out "en los alrededores del Sheraton a la pesca de [esos] gringos con hambre de poto latino" [around the Sheraton, cruising for gringos hungry for Latin ass] (Lemebel, *Adiós* 181). Need makes the greenbacks irresistible, so they opt for foreign money provided by an American tourist. Chumilou, one of many dead *locas* in "La noche de los visones," faces this dilemma. In the story of her poverty, the audacity of that consumption is justified by the reasoning that

> eran tantos billetes, tanta plata, tantos dólares que pagaba ese gringo....Tantas bocas abiertas de los hermanos chicos que la perseguían noche a noche. Tantas muelas cariadas de la madre que no tenía plata para el dentista....Eran tantas deudas, tantas matrículas de colegio, tanto por pagar....Entonces la Chumi cerró los ojos y estirando la mano agarró el fajo de billetes. No podía ser tanta su mala suerte que por una vez, una sola vez en muchos años que lo hacía en carne viva, se le iba a pegar la sombra. (*Loco afán* [1996] 18–19)
>
> [there were so many dollars, so much money that gringo was paying....And so many young siblings and their hungry mouths every night. So many rotting teeth in her mother's mouth, with no money for a dentist....There were so many debts, so many school fees, so much to pay....So Chumi closed her eyes and reached out to grasp the wad of bills. Surely her luck couldn't be so bad that this one time, just this once in all these years of doing it without protection, the shadow was going to catch her.]

In these narratives, a life is worth very little, and the need for money, which becomes a need for foreignness that in turn becomes a desire for men, forces the *locas* even to risk their lives. As if they were playing a game of Russian roulette in pursuit of neocapitalist privilege, only to realize, too late, that the cylinder was full of bullets. Lemebel draws a link between commodification and the epidemic, establishing a sequential logic in which the opening to the new, foreign economic ideology constitutes a progression of the epidemic. Consumerism operates within the discourse of disease.

Viral Vagabondage

Perhaps there has not been enough emphasis on this fact: the accused figure of the foreign tourist, temporarily hosted by an international hotel chain in Santiago, or in a dark corner of the capital city, *infects* the *loca* both with the desire to consume and with the dream of movement, another value of the capitalist era. The possibility of travel offered by the technologies of the new economy is eagerly incorporated into the fantasies of the Latin American *loca*. But her desire to leave is not based on Arenas's *pájaro* utopia—leaving in order to survive—nor is it only, or necessarily, an eagerness to flee dictatorial oppression since, as Lemebel notes, "el régimen militar nunca reprimió tanto al coliseo[135] como en Argentina o Brasil" [(Chile's) military regime never repressed the gay community as much as in Argentina or Brazil] (*Loco afán* [1996] 15).[136] The travels of the Chilean *loca* offer an opportunity for the free consumption of sex and suggest social advancement, although travel during this period, Bauman reminds us, is in itself a powerful method of stratification, as it does not erase social difference but instead underscores the differences between types of travelers. This situation is narrated not without a certain degree of sarcasm. In "La noche de los visones," the *locas regias*, the ones who can afford the trip to New York, go off to *buy themselves* AIDS in the heart of the empire. Pilola Alessandri acquires the disease in Manhattan: she is "la primera que la trajo en exclusiva, la más auténtica, la recién estrenada moda gay para morir" [the first one to carry it, exclusive importer of that most genuine, recently launched gay way to die] (16). The poor *locas* only have enough to travel to the northern south—that is, to the beaches of Brazil, a country that in 1985 was emerging from a long dictatorship and was perceived—as confirmed in other texts from the HIV-positive corpus—as a sexual paradise where "un sector de la clase media pasaba sus vacaciones, si el dólar lo permitía, ejerciendo de paso hábitos y fantasías reprimidos al amparo de un escenario más permisivo y libre" [a portion of the middle class spent its vacations,

---

[135] Here we encounter one of Lemebel's classic wordplays: from *loca* to *cola* [tail, ass], and from *cola* to *coliseo* [coliseum].

[136] It is well known that the Argentine dictatorship was very harsh on homosexuality. The protagonist of *Adiós a la calle* recounts that things only began to ease up at the end of the dictatorship, "pero era evidente que a los más jovencitos o a los más llamativos los seguían cazando de los pelos como si los militares todavía anduvieran patrullando las calles, y esos policías de civil seguían haciendo de las suyas" [but it was clear that the youngest or most flamboyant continued to be hunted down as if the soldiers were still patrolling the streets, and the state police kept doing their thing] (Zeiger, *Adiós* 29). For a historical account of homosexual repression in Argentina, see Foster (2001) and Brown (2002).

exchange rate permitting, temporarily indulging in repressed habits and fantasies in a freer, more permissive place] (Moledo 108).[137]

Moledo ends by turning the mirror around to show us that not only do the *locas* approach the infected tourist in the local territory but they also, straining their meager budgets, move across borders seeking sex that becomes synonymous with foreign AIDS. The *locas* want to come off as tourists, the idolized figure, but they only manage to achieve a feeble imitation (dangerously caricaturesque, says Bauman): that of the happy vagabond. In her travels abroad, the *loca* never manages to embody her dazzling masculine, disciplined *other self*; she can only imitate it, still breaking the norms and undermining the social order. After all, although tourists and vagabonds are both avid consumers, the latter are only *defective* consumers whose "potential for consumption is as limited as their resources" (Bauman 96). Furthermore, they "add nothing to the prosperity of the economy turned into a tourist industry" (96). In the abstract the vagabond *loca*'s defective consumerism is the cause and effect of her unstable social position, pure spending without receiving in turn, a squandering that ends in destitution; nevertheless, in a more concrete context—that of the virus's travels—that consumerism is defective in that it also directs consumers to their death. It confirms not the limitless continuation of consumption but the certainty of its end, of the extermination of the vagabond consumer. The Latin American *loca* comes across the virus in the constant movement of displacement, and she returns from her travels having lived experiences but earned nothing more, with no other *asset* but the infection itself and a ticket to the only destination left—the cemetery.

So: death comes and destroys, democratically. The disease, for Lemebel, is a "repartidor público ausente de prejuicios sociales" [public distributor without social prejudice] (*Loco afán* [1996] *23*). But it does not affect all in the same way. The narrator ironically notes that while Pilola dies a glamorous New York–style death, La Palma, who spends everything she has on her trip to Brazil, comes home dying and stripped of all glamour. As is fitting for vagabonds, the AIDS they experience is "generoso...con cuanto perdido hambriento le pedía sexo. Casi podría decirse que lo obtuvo en bandeja, compartido

---

[137] The Argentine claims that, because in the 1980s "el sida ya hacía estragos" [AIDS was already wreaking havoc] in Brazil, there spread through the country "el temor de que los viajeros trajeran el virus, tanto en sus valijas como en sus linfocitos T4 para contaminarnos" [the fear that travelers would bring in the virus, whether in their suitcases or in their T4 lymphocytes, to infect us] (Moledo 108).

y repartido hasta la saciedad" [generous…with any drifter hungry
for sex. You could almost say it was delivered on a platter, doled out
till they'd had their fill] (17). These *locas* who leave their place of
origin end up vulnerable, unprotected. It is not that they fall off the
map; rather, they are marked by multiple routes of global contagion
in an expanded area of contact—the world. Although their deaths
are differentiated by class, they all participate in the production and
transport of the virus. They all collaborate, Lemebel says—not just
the infected tourist who carries out the virus's work before dying, but
also the *loca regia* and the *loca vagabunda*. The contrasts between
them become blurred; the false liberated utopia of foreign consumption is imposed, and while it might once have been seen in the community as the end of a historical oppression, in the body of the dying
loca we find the places most critical of the new capitalism. Lemebel
offers only one possible escape, one that is allegorical and not at all
certain: remaining and resisting the system. Because the only character in this book who does not travel[138] is also the only one who
survives to write the story. That narrator, that stationary witness, is
the model figure established in the fixed point of the marginalized
periphery, resisting the deadly fever of unprotected consumption,
contemplating the sepia-tone photograph of the disappeared to pay
them heartfelt homage.

SICK SINCE BEFORE

The cartographic distinctions and their subjects, the infected travelers, become less and less effective in evaluating AIDS: the categories
become blurred and blend together. The men of the epidemic are
mobile subjects across immobile territories: there is a tension there,
but also an opportunity to extend those spaces and overlap them. If,
as seen in Arenas, as hinted at in Lemebel, every traveler bears his
national identity, and if identity is linked to a territory, when that
identity is internalized, geography, too, experiences displacement. For
this reason, there are domestic and foreign geographies or individuals, immigrants and emigrants who bear their origin and use it to
read their own experience, vagabonds who try futilely to be tourists,
and stationary locals who see themselves as being beset by successive

---

[138] In later books, the author would also embark on journeys to foreign lands, but
in the book discussed here, the narrator still travels only around the city.

waves of travelers from foreign cultures. All of them, as a group, come to define a definitive impossibility: that of identifying an origin, of outlining the shape and tracing the perimeters of immunity. And so the only locality that remains is that of the current place, from which they communicate an interpretation of the crisis. It is this that we find in later stories: absolute dispersion, the need to focus the eye to examine the movement of the overlapping spaces.

I would like to dally for a moment on a narrative that depicts the spread of the disease while also sending a more ambiguous ideological signal than that of AIDS's activist authors (Arenas, Perlongher, Lemebel). It is a minor short story, one that avoids metaphors, that flees allegory, one written in the clear language of a more recent generation. In "Hombres en habitaciones pequeñas" (1997; Men in small rooms), by the Chilean writer Sergio Gómez, we can read the way the spatial categories of infection are shattered. Gómez writes during the era of survival, but his story is set when the disease is still fatal, not chronic. It attempts to establish the routes by which the virus has been brought to Santiago, to the body of the ailing man who is "muriéndose en un feo hospital público" [dying in an ugly public hospital] (136). Parrita is dying, and two of his friends are waiting in a dismal public square in front of the hospital for him to appear. It's not hard to guess what they talk about: how the disease is transmitted, what situations could result in infection. The possibilities are as numerous as the speculation is futile. In a scene vaguely reminiscent of *Waiting for Godot* (but without Beckett's existentialist core), the two homosexuals wait for their friend to appear at the window. They wait—hopeful but uncertain—to discover whether Parrita has died. Parrita does not appear, but it isn't visiting day, and Lillo and Leiva, the two friends, wonder whether they have arrived at the agreed-upon time, whether a shape in the window is that of the patient. But this is only an excuse for their real interest: filling the anxious wait with old stories, stories repeated a million times but not always recalled completely, that confirm the existence of a shared past. The conversation advances the possibility of reconstructing the path of transmission, if only to the extent permitted by their gossip—and gossip, as a mode of narration, is also endlessly and arbitrarily extendible. It soon becomes clear that the effort put into reconstructing that route comes out of a need to identify the moment of contagion—that is, to calculate whether one of them could have contracted the virus.

Leiva's and Lillo's accounts are hardly satisfying, details from a predictable script. Parrita is in love with a television actor, Renato

Madariaga, who was also his first companion in childhood sexual games. During the Chilean dictatorship, the actor went into exile in Paris (one of the cities of the Latin American sexual diaspora and an epicenter of the epidemic). Like a number of famous real-life homosexuals, Renato "dijo que se había ido por culpa de Pinochet, pero esa no era la verdad. Todo el mundo sabía que se había ido por maricón; aquí lo ahogaba el ambiente" [said that he had left because of Pinochet, but that wasn't true. Everybody knew he'd left because he was a fag: the atmosphere here was suffocating him] (127). Leiva is not as wealthy as Renato, but he is just as gay and has also endured that oppressive atmosphere. Nevertheless, he draws a distinction between political and sexual oppression that would be impossible in Arenas's accounts, where the two spheres converge. Dissidents are treated quite differently under the two dictatorships, even if a parallel restlessness inspires their exodus. It doesn't matter what excuse they have. Though homosexuality still cannot be openly displayed, opposition to the dictatorship is acceptable, even admired, in the context of the arts. Another idea at work in Renato's past is that beyond the nation's borders, oppression does not exist—or at least it does not suffocate the way it does within them. Yet we must read Lillo's reaffirmation of what had become a cliché in the community—"Afuera, en el extranjero, lo consigues todo" [Out there, in other countries, you can have everything] (127)—with a grain of salt. That foreign space in which *different* men could have everything is transformed: the *everything* that they so prized has become risky. That *everything* is merely ironic, or contradictory: all of the freedom of the past has led to Parrita's current confinement in the hospital.

The romance with Parrita, as the protagonists tell it, begins upon Renato's return from exile, where he has been given *everything*—a diploma in theater from the Sorbonne, sexual freedom, and, on his return, a major television contract, celebrity and success, and even a girlfriend. And those who stayed, in staying, had achieved *nothing*. Renato has returned from his journey "más abierto y conocedor" [more open and knowledgeable], while the local homosexuals "no estaban preparados para algo así" [were not prepared for anything like that]—which will prove "fatal," "fatalísimo" [deadly, incredibly deadly] (128). Next, in a plot point right out of the soap operas Renato stars in, comes the unexpected arrival of Renato's official boyfriend, a European who is, significantly, orientalized. He is "un árabe mitad español y mitad moro, de un color de piel increíble, aceitunado" [an Arab who is half-Spanish and half-Moorish, with skin an incredible olive color] (128).[139] The newly arrived boyfriend, who bears all the classic signs of foreignness—he is *strange*, an exoticized outsider—is portrayed in the gossipy dialogue as the most infectious of all of the travelers, or at least the most likely point of origin for the infection that has reached Parrita: "¿Tú crees que la enfermedad se la pasó Renato? [pregunta Leiva]. Tal vez la trajo desde Europa aquel turco aceitunado y al final de la cadena se la pegó a Parrita" [You think Renato gave him the disease? (Leiva asks). Maybe that olive-skinned Turk brought it from Europe and at the end of the line it got Parrita] (129). The suspicion appears in the form of a question and positions Parrita at the end of the chain of international propagation that brought the virus into the local territory. Parrita could be the victim of not one but several journeys: Renato's journey into supposed exile and his journey home again, and the touristic travels of the foreign, racialized lover who, though he comes from Europe, is not seen as European. But the linear logic is destabilized by Lillo's response: "No creo. Parrita estaba enfermo desde antes" [I don't think so. Parrita's been sick since before] (129). Here, the familiar script is altered, undermining the expectation that the figure of the traveler, which appears in a number of variations in this text, is responsible for the disease. Parrita has been infected *since before* coming into contact with the travelers. Parrita is therefore not at the end of the chain but at a sort of beginning that is also a continuation. The question about origin eliminates the possibility of infection: Parrita, his friends tell us, has been a carrier for "por lo menos . . . dos veranos" [at least . . . two summers] (129).

This fictional text by a more contemporary author approaches the crisis by leaving behind the border discourses of infection found in Arenas, Casas, and Lemebel, authors who reimagine the nation as an originally pure space, the victim of successive, and always foreign, acts of epidemic aggression. The protagonists of "Hombres en habitaciones pequeñas" confirm the idea that has taken root in the social imaginary—a North–South route and vice versa, East–West and vice versa—and then undo that route and localize it in the nation. Situating the syndrome in the local territory meant abandoning the question of origin: at the end of the 1990s, it no longer made sense to think about the virus's origin. It was now understood what AIDS

---

[139] This character is reminiscent of transatlantic Gonzalo in Witold Gombrowicz's novel and of Aceitunita, the young man in Augusto D'Halmar's novel *Pasión y muerte del cura Deusto*, both discussed in earlier chapters.

was, that it was not just a homosexual disease, that travelers and locals alike were potentially infected and infectious. It no longer mattered where the virus came from, because it was here and everywhere and there was still no cure: perhaps that ultimate cure is the Godot of this story and of the epidemic.

CHAPTER 3

Back to the Nations of Death

The boundaries of the space for sexual dissidence shrank during the peak years of the epidemic: the fiction of liberation that promoted reintegration into the world, a fascination with cosmopolitanism, and a utopian transnational community suddenly found itself at a dead end. The disease eliminated movement—or redirected it. Travel changed, becoming more oriented toward seeking places of refuge. It ended in hospitals, hospices, AIDS camps: all involuntary places of residence, heterotopias of death that at their most morbid are places where people go to die. These places are the antithesis of travel, notes Georges Van Den Abbeele, because all travel presupposes some distance from what we call the place of origin. These places are both areas of motionlessness and also a reversal or a return: the return to the confinement of the nation or of the quarantined spaces that serve as normative allegorical representations for it (though the word *quarantine* does not really capture the fluctuating temporality that characterizes AIDS internment). Death glittered in the distance as the longed-for destination of so many young people that the syndrome had made suddenly old. And those aged youths awaiting their end formed a new HIV-positive community, located in the antipodes of the imagined community of those energetic rebellious sons of the nation—the Gombrowiczian *filistria*—and of Arenas's *patria pájara*, whose members, as already noted, were always ready to take flight outside their territory, even as they bore the double locality that made them unique. Examinations of the *pájaros'* efforts to flee the syndrome began to appear in literature. Some understood that there was nowhere to go. That was Reinaldo Arenas's terrible realization: "Ahora la única fuga que me queda es la muerte" [At this point, the only escape for me was death] (*Antes* 9; *Before* ix), he writes in both his autobiography and his fiction. Others, though, concocted scenes of repatriation in which the author's reality—his nostalgia for home as he languishes, his rage, his fear that his return will be only a foretaste of death—is clearly operating somewhere in his unconscious as he writes. Even in those texts, literature finds a way to problematize those home-like spaces of refuge that are soon also understood as allegories of the homeland. *Allegory* is a word that should be used in moderation, but it is essential in this context, because although no new interpretation is necessary to confirm the allegorical shift from the family home to the nation-home,[140] some effort is required to understand that the hospice and the hospital that appear in HIV-positive texts are also allegories for the nation. The hospital and its substitutes are a point of origin, a transitional *home* that a person abandons to start life, the place that must be left behind to enjoy freedom (in this respect, the hospital is just like home), and the institution that must be returned to when one's own illness or that of others threatens. In *El desbarrancadero* (2001; The precipice), writer Fernando Vallejo describes his return from Mexico to Medellín and his childhood home—"al manicomio, al moridero" [to the madhouse, to the dying place] (90), to a "Colombia en chiquitito" [miniature Colombia] (151)—as his brother, who has also returned, but from Cali, is dying. "Si supieras," the narrator tells the winds, "en lo que se ha convertido mi vida y este país y esta casa" [If you only knew what my life and this country and this house have become] (98). His brother's death brings him back to the home cum hospital, to the nation of death that is familiar but not his own. Yet for the healthy body that has the power to speak and also for the termi-nally ill body found in so many other texts, that return to the hospital has restrictive echoes of home: drifting interrupted, sex denied, the future definitively withdrawn. There may be nothing so domestic as the imagined space of the nation. Even if the hospital were another allegory of the nation-home, it would be established not as a formative account but as a dysfunctional space: one of defeat and decease. To put it another way: in narratives of the syndrome, the hospital is a place to die and a morgue; it is the cemetery where the communal tragedy, the negative allegory of the nation, is rewritten.

Hospital Homeland

The greatest proliferation of allegorical areas of confinement is found in the theater, where the imagination ranges through a number of

---

[140] This is a classic interpretation. Consider, for example, Doris Sommer's reading in *Foundational Fictions* (1991).

different territories. Onstage, the scenography is shaped by a translation of a work that is only an interpretation: the director and actors construct spaces that the text only hints at. This is apparent in the silent reading in Copi's *Una visita inoportuna* (1987; An inopportune visit), a posthumous work, written in French and first staged in Paris in 1988,[141] that may be the first theater piece in the Latin America–in-exile HIV-positive corpus. Without a doubt, the work of this Argentine playwright, writer, and caricaturist is one in which the space of representation has unusual importance. It is not one space but several that overlap. This space is alternately the room in the public hospital where the sick man awaits his end and the protagonist's homeland (an allegorization of the home); it is also a hotel and even a morgue. All stopping points before the cemetery. And in its final transformation, breaking the realist pact, the space is revealed for what it actually is: a stage on which famous death scenes from classical theater and world literature are performed. The spatial metamorphosis is subtle and must be analyzed in detail. The work pushes to be read as a performance of the drama of life and death. The hospital, the homeland, the theater are all vital places. In them, the respectively real and symbolic births of people and characters take place— but these places are also the anteroom to the end of existence, both real existence and the existence that is foreshadowed with the fall of the curtain when life or the work comes to an end. That curtain or the book opens, and this is what we see: at the beginning of *Una visita inoportuna*, written as part of the absurdist theatrical tradition, all the characters come together around the bed of a young-old man, an ailing actor named Cirilo. The text creates fictitious figures, the protagonists of quarantines and farewell scenes: a professorial and overdramatic doctor, a perverse nurse, a loyal friend, and one of Cirilo's nephews who identifies himself as a journalist—that is, as the *last spectator* of the epidemic.[142] The initial scene takes place in

---

[141] The premiere took place in the Théâtre de la Colline in 1988 under the direction of Jorge Lavelli. It came to the Argentine stage in 1992 and was published as a book in 1993.

[142] It is significant to note Copi's ambiguous stance on the Journalist, a key figure in the epidemic because of media sensationalism and the negative propaganda about AIDS during that period. Copi harbored a deep mistrust of the notion of *truth* in representation but, like many authors of the HIV-positive corpus, he felt a need to capture the *real* impact of the disease in his writing. Perhaps for this reason, Copi includes him as "nuestro último espectador" [our last spectator] (Copi 59) and gives him the role of chronicler to carry out through fiction what the nonfictional author refused to do.

the hospital, but it is reminiscent of a family gathered at the bedside of the protagonist, who feels like he's in his own home. And I say *his home* thinking also of Copi, who was an adolescent in Buenos Aires and an adult in Paris—there he would write and stage most of his work; there he would be diagnosed and die at the end of 1987. Cirilo is a condensed version of the image that Copi constructed throughout his 20 years of playwriting, and it is perhaps for that reason that at the end of his life Cirilo appears in a public hospital in Buenos Aires and not in Paris. Copi left his natal homeland behind when he was 23 and never returned, but it is there that the author sends his alter ego, repatriating him (or himself) in the imagination, as if Copi, at the end of his life, thought of his homeland and its hospitals as the only possible place of return.

But there is more—there is always something to add when reading Copi. We witness not only death in that Argentine hospital but also, ironically, life. We see the characters celebrating the second anniversary of the virus in Cirilo, yet another possible biographical allusion to the amount of time that passed in the author's real life between his diagnosis in Paris in 1984 and the activity, also in Paris, of writing the work over the course of 1986. The infected guest of honor receives, as a father would, birthday gifts for this strange creature of his, exclaiming ironically to the people who entail his symbolic family, "¡Qué encantadora idea haber pensado en el cumpleaños de mi sida!" [How lovely to have thought of my AIDS birthday!]. This multiple inversion is interesting: the ailing person as a parent accompanied by the child/virus that will eventually kill him. After all, the doctor sarcastically predicts that Cirilo "vivirá lo que viva su sida" [will live as long as his AIDS does] (Copi 29)—that is, the life of the still invincible virus in Copi's Paris will end the life of its carrier.[143] Cirilo seems feminized, and death, too, is represented by a feminine character: also in attendance is Regina Morti, the *queen of death*, an Italian opera diva whose histrionic femininity, notes Eduardo Muslip, evokes the figurative presence of the transvestite.[144] Her *inopportune visit* announced in the play's title indicates that she has arrived to carry off Cirilo early,

---

[143] A similar idea appears in one of Pedro Lemebel's chronicles, in which the *loca* is "embarazada" [pregnant] with AIDS, and giving birth to it will be the final act of her death. See "El último beso de Loba Lamar" (*Loco afán* [1996] 41–50; The last kiss of Loba Lamar).

[144] Death here is not a woman but a transvestite, a recurring motif in the HIV-positive fiction of Lemebel, Perlongher, and Sarduy. Death not only snatches away the transvestite's life but also is a synecdoche of her.

but he resists leaving the hospital, his only, if transitory, home. The hospital's identity as a merely temporary residence, as a transit zone between life and death, is reinforced in the comparison that Regina Morti, as compulsive a traveler as the virus, makes between that place and a luxury hotel:[145] "Los tratan bien [a los enfermos] en la Salud Pública. De haberlo sabido me hubiera ahorrado fortunas en el [hotel] Plaza cada vez que vengo a Buenos Aires. Tomaré una suite en este mismo pabellón" [They treat (the sick) well at the public hospital. If I'd known that, I would have saved a fortune on staying at the Plaza (Hotel) every time I come to Buenos Aires. I'll get a suite right here in this wing] (25). Cirilo idealizes the hospital, wanting to see it as a sort of home, but death reminds him that it is only a stopover, a place to stay while she is waiting to carry out her task. Regina, death and diva, wrapped in her black robes, then settles in beside the young or perhaps old actor to await a real and theatrical dramatic moment for her last act, but the play keeps putting off that moment into the future. In reality, the doctor says, he should already be dead, and "las causas de ese exceso de salud" [the causes of that excess of health] must be investigated. It is the doctor who tells him to "enorgullecerse de sus reiterados triunfos sobre la muerte. Es usted un héroe en este templo de la ciencia" [be proud of your repeated triumphs over death. You are a hero in this temple of science] (28). One might also wonder about the source of that *excess of health*, those *repeated triumphs* that so surprise the doctor. Does the dying Copi see returning to the homeland as increasing his resistance to the virus? Does he idealize the nation as the only place in which survival is possible? Will it be a final act of triumph? It is difficult to refute this notion: why else would one return to a land of restrictions and the denial of liberty? The fictional Copi has chosen his homeland as a place of refuge because outside it, in the extratextual space, the epidemic is intensifying, and at the time the calamity did not yet appear to have reached Argentina on a large scale.[146] But we can also conjecture, following the text, that return is only a postponement, as it is then suggested that, in real life and in fiction alike, no HIV-positive person escapes death. Except that death itself becomes a representation, mere simulacrum.

[145] The words "hostal," "hotel," and "hospital" all come, etymologically speaking, from the Latin word indicating a space of welcome and hospitality.

[146] Although it is possible that Copi knew that the first case of AIDS in Argentina was discovered in 1983, there is no evidence that at the time it was as widespread there as it was in France at the end of the 1980s.

The author has the doctor ask a crucial but rhetorical question: "¿Cree usted que la muerte verdadera que le acecha tiene algo que envidiarle a la muerte que se envuelve en negras vestiduras en un escenario?" [Do you think the real death that's stalking you has any reason to envy a stage death wrapped in black robes?] (28). The text constructs an identity that is part reality and part representation, and the two soon become nearly indistinguishable. Both deaths are going to take place: one within the hospital of the theater, and the other in a hospital that turns into a space of representation. Cirilo will be simultaneously a terminally ill patient and the actor *representing* the death of a sick man. In this recursive maneuver—this theater within the theater—it becomes difficult to see a way out, and the way out is also something to fear: "¿Cuándo voy a morir *dentro de la realidad?*" [When am I going to die *in reality?*], asks Cirilo (28). "¡Nunca morirá querido maestro! ¡Su nombre nos sobrevivirá a todos!" [You'll never die, beloved maestro! Your name will outlive us all!], the doctor answers cheerfully, employing the myth of the artist's posterity (28). But Cirilo as a character believes in reality, and Copi seems thereby to call into question his own resistance to mimetic representation.[147] He tries to distinguish between the various additional identities: the dying character, the actor playing a sick man, Copi the writer, Copi the person: "No hablo de mi nombre. Hablo de mí" [I'm not talking about my name. I'm talking about me] (29). It becomes gradually more difficult to determine when he is talking about reality and when he is not, as the boundary between those two spaces blurs. His first dramatic death—in which Copi pays homage to Federico García Lorca's death at five in the afternoon[148]—is pure theater within theater, and thus a triumph of life offstage; his second, which is Shakespearean in tone—it quotes Hamlet's death—must be the real death. Again, though, this death quotes another, and it takes place within the theater. Death, then, moves away from reality.

---

[147] There is a certain contradiction in this latter Copi, whom Delgado calls the author of "*poéticas irrepresentativas*" [unrepresentative poetics]. Montaldo, on the other hand, sees reality in Copi as a literary incentive to invent. Because here the dramatic personal experience haunts not only the unconscious of his writing but also, as is apparent, his most acute consciousness.

[148] Copi makes intertextual use of the homosexual Spanish writer's famous poem "Llanto por la muerte de Ignacio Sánchez Mejías" ("Lament for Ignacio Sánchez Mejías"). Not only does Cirilo indicate that he will recite Lorca's lines that night, but at the end of the text, when the time is "las cinco en punto de la tarde" [exactly five in the afternoon], he says, "Es la hora" [It's time] (65).

Theater and mimesis are at odds; instead, theater becomes a zone of uncertainty or of possibility, an imaginary zone where people flee a deadly fate. Death in the theater is a representation, while real death traps the corpse in a closed, fixed space: the cemetery.

We should note the contrast that Copi presents between the fluctuating space of pure representation, the longed-for but transitory space of the homeland (as represented by the hospital), and the dreaded, eternal space of the cemetery. The sick man is trapped between those two times and two spaces: the theater, where Cirilo amuses himself with death, and the cemetery, where he wants to house his friend/lover, who has buried many acquaintances and has made burial his profession. This friend is building him, as an "obsequio póstumo" [posthumous offering] (19) a huge mausoleum in La Recoleta[149] so that Cirilo can receive visits—visits that are once more inopportune and to which Cirilo is already objecting. "¡No quiero que me entierren en ninguna parte!...¡No crea que me va a arrinconar cuando esté muerto! ¡Viejo necrófilo!...No tengo la intención de comunicar a nadie mi próximo domicilio" [I don't want them to bury me anywhere!...Don't think you're going to pin me down once I'm dead! Old necrophile! I have no intention of telling anyone where my next place of residence will be] (20). Toward the end, Cirilo (or Copi) is reluctant to die in reality, to be domesticated in the only place that feels foreign to him. In the hospital version, he refuses to leave the theater that has been his home, to depart from his homeland. And in that gesture of resistance we can perhaps spot a revelation: the premature certainty that the space not only marks a geographic position but also becomes the axis of the political argument, the sudden awareness that the epidemic cannot be thought of as something that takes place outside the nation but instead ineluctably includes it. That return to fiction is a way of indicating that the situation must be understood as local. Local in Paris, yes, but even more so in Copi's Buenos Aires, in Sarduy's Havana, and in every nation in Latin America. Copi makes AIDS symbolically travel back, nationalizes his symptoms, relocalizes the catastrophe so that it becomes clear that the epidemic goes beyond the abstract lens of the global and must be examined in the concrete space of the crisis. With Copi settled in his homeland once more, it is clear that despite

---

[149] La Recoleta is famous not only for its elegant cemetery but also for having been the center of homosexual courtship during Copi's youth. Gombrowicz refers to this place in *Trans-Atlántico*.

being in exile, the dying dissident has never stopped being and feeling Argentine. The HIV-positive body of the citizen is thus repatri-
ated; while exile meant illness, it is the homeland that must now take
care of it, offering it *hospitality*.

FOUNDATIONS OF THE CUBAN AIDS CAMP

Severo Sarduy is another Latin American writer who lived, like Copi,
in Paris during those terrible years. He, too, near death, *mentally*
returned to his place of origin to settle accounts. The renowned novelist, who emigrated before Castro's revolution and never returned to
Cuba, received his diagnosis in a Parisian hospital in 1987—the year in
which the Argentine playwright died. Sarduy's constant hospital stays
overwhelmed his spatial imagination, and he began to think about
the disease from another angle. Although in 1984 he associated the
syndrome with the representational convention of the voyage—the
ship of lepers that crosses the novelistic landscape of *Colibrí*—only
a few years later he would associate it with stability and reduce it
to confinement. It is difficult to pinpoint the precise moment when
Sarduy's point of view changes: strictly speaking, the experience of
hospital internment that first stalks him precedes the discovery of his
own illness. Gripped by the terror beating at the heart of Paris's cosmopolitan homosexual community, Sarduy sees others' hospital stays
as foreshadowing his own future. In one narrative from *El Cristo de la
rue Jacob* (1987), written around the time of his diagnosis, the author
cum protagonist describes leaving his summer retreat—the voluntary
reclusiveness of literary work—in search of an adventure. He waits
beside a highway until a truck, carrying a load of sheets "de dios
sabe qué leprosería[150] o qué hospital" [from God knows what lepro-
sarium or hospital] pulls up beside him.[151] At a sign from the driver,
"Sarduy" climbs into the back of the vehicle, and among the laundry
from what might be an AIDS camp, the two men only masturbate,
"sin duda por miedo al sida" [no doubt for fear of AIDS] (*El Cristo*
55; *Christ* 69). The presence of the hospital space makes it impossible

---

[150] At the time, the word *leprosería* (leper colony) was used interchangeably with
sidario to refer to Castro's AIDS camps. The poems in Reinaldo Arenas's *Leprosorio*
(1990) refer to the ravages of the AIDS epidemic.

[151] The truck as a vehicle of contagion is a trope for African and Asian AIDS. The
transmission along these vehicles' routes, note some authors, is a metaphor for the
process of globalization along national borders. See Patton and Sánchez-Epler (17)
and Binnie (107).

to forget the epidemic—the odor or the whiteness of the sheets is a deterrent—and powerfully evokes the community's isolation. The awareness of danger is apparent in the impulse to write that book: in those same years, Sarduy writes *El Cristo de la rue Jacob*, a detailed examination or exploration of his skin (*archaeology* is the term he uses) in which he reads every blemish and scar as a trace of the past. It is as if he were translating the marks that life has inscribed on the surfaces of his body. That examination in turn provokes a series of texts; Sarduy tells each scar's story, writing their biographies. Yet his ultimate objective—and this is my conjecture—is to use that inquiry to confirm the absence of—or perhaps to find—the purplish marks of sarcoma. Toward the end of the chronicles written before his diagnosis, the author associates a wart to be removed with the imminent death of a friend in a Paris hospital. Only after his own diagnosis and admission to the hospital does Sarduy begin to describe his experiences as a sick person, using a diary format that tracks his dreaded confinement—the diary, we must point out, is the preferred form for writing about illness, and Sarduy, too, employs it even as the writing itself resists the convention. Two texts depict the experience of hospitalization. One is the short "Diario de la peste" (1991), written during one of his stays in Paris's Laennec Hospital, a few blocks from the Rue Jacob after which the chronicles are named, where the author was trying to recover from a complicated case of pleurisy. The other is an aphoristic text called "El estampido de la vacuidad" (1993; The roar of the void). These brief entries are the background or foundation upon which he eventually constructed the image of the colonial mansion in *Pájaros de la playa* (1993), the place in the novel where the terminally ill *pájaros* spend their last days.

If I may digress for a moment, before discussing the spatial parallels between the old Laennec Hospital in Sarduy's personal memoirs and the colonial mansion in the narrative, I will refer to the accidental history of the novel, which began as an interruption to Sarduy's work right at the end of his life. In his "Diario de la peste," he notes that before he fell ill his intention had been to write *Caimán* (Alligator), which would join *Cobra* (1972), the aforementioned *Colibrí* (1984), and *Cocuyo* (1990; Firefly) to complete his "zoological tetralogy." As he explained it, the series would take the form of a food chain in which, by the end, "el Caimán insular se hubiera comido a la ondulante Cobra, y esta al Colibrí, volador fijo, y este al fosforescente Cocuyo. Caimán queda[ría] solo al final, pero con los otros animales incorporados y enlazados en su interior. Emblemas mudos de la devoración sucesiva," adds Sarduy, "jeroglífico que es una pregunta: ¿Quién se come a Caimán?" [the insular Alligator would have eaten the writhing Cobra, and this latter in turn would have eaten the Hummingbird, stationary flier, which would in turn have eaten the glowing Firefly. Alligator (would be) alone at the end, but with the other animals incorporated and joined together inside him. Mute symbols of successive devourment, a hieroglyphic that poses a question: Who eats Alligator?] ("Diario" 33). The author thus leaves open a question that is not just zoological but also political. Without a doubt, Sarduy proposes here one of his complicated games of free association in which he deliberately leaves certain essential information out of the tale. One of the details omitted is that the island of Cuba is shaped like an alligator,[152] so the question of who is going to eat it can be read in political terms; one possible answer is that it will be devoured by Marxism or, alternatively, by capitalism. If we stick for now only to the literary aspects, the riddle will be easier to guess: *Caimán* was never written—the epidemic swallowed it whole. But something else also interfered: the need to write another novel. Sarduy abandoned *Caimán* to write more autobiographical sorts of texts and *Pájaros de la playa*, not only the most autobiographical of his novels[153] but also, in the words of Sarduy himself, the most readable. Yet it is a novel, I would like to add, contradicting the author, that in a way belongs to the zoological tetralogy. In its pages, Caimán appears as a character, though not the protagonist, alongside, as we will see, a number of other animalized characters.

End of the digression, if that's what that was. *Pájaros de la playa* is a text that, without rejecting the author's boundless imaginary, strays from the earlier path to narrate the space of the epidemic— the mansion-turned-morgue—and its protagonists. The mansion comes to be inhabited by a new HIV-positive community of men. In the past they were athletes who ran along the beach, "atareados en esa ofrenda cotidiana a la salud" [absorbed in their daily offering to health] (*Pájaros* 11; *Beach* 9), as if the body were the insignia of

---

[152] As Julio Cortázar wrote in some sentimental lines praising revolutionary Cuba, the country is a "caimancito herido y más vivo que nunca" [injured baby alligator, fiercer than ever]. See the complete poem in Cortázar (1971).

[153] "*Pájaros de la playa* [es] el adiós novelado del cubano Severo Sarduy [quien narra] con la desolación y el decoro de quien con eso se despide y *se escribe*, arrojado del sí y al borde del abismo de lo incoloro" [*Pájaros de la playa* (is) a farewell in novel form by the Cuban writer Severo Sarduy, (who narrates) with the desolation and dignity of a man who is saying goodbye and *writing himself*, cast out of himself and on the edge of the colorless void] (Ullán 1780).

a powerful, productive nation for which failure was unimaginable, but these beach *pájaros* will soon be—in fact already are—golden figures from the prehistory of AIDS, now infected and aged before their time. The novel's major characters also come together in that mansion inhabited by AIDS patients: The Cosmologist functions as the *last spectator* (Copi *dixit*) in writing his own *diary of the epidemic*, not as a simple journalist but as the "historiador de la enfermedad y no solo su víctima" [not only its victim but the historian of the disease] (Sarduy, *Pájaros* 76; *Beach* 55). Like Sarduy,[154] with real scientific rigor and horrifying anguish, Copi sets out all that is known and unknown about the AIDS that afflicts him. Caimán, the reptilian medicine man who tries to cure the infected with his herbal potions and plasters, and the sick man, Caballo, both of them lovers of Siempreviva—another alter ego of the author but possibly also an alter ego of death[155]—who in her previous life, a life that played out 40 years earlier, was a wealthy Cuban woman named Sonia. Now, dressed as a young girl even though she is a bedraggled old lady, she moves into the mansion as if it were an "hotel de lujo" [luxury hotel] (*Pájaros* 31; *Beach* 23) that offers temporary lodging to all of Sarduy's main characters and those whom "la energía abandonó" [energy has abandoned] (*Pájaros* 19; *Beach* 15). Located "más allá de la autopista" [beyond the highway] (*Pájaros* 19; *Beach* 15), on the margins of industrial progress, the colonial mansion is a desolate, dilapidated place that most closely resembles Laennec Hospital, where Sarduy stayed in 1991, a building whose construction, according to his account, "data del siglo XVII, los muros húmedos o carcomidos" [dates back to the seventeenth century, the walls damp or crumbling] and full of cockroaches that nobody makes the least attempt to get rid of ("Diario" 33–34).[156]

Space evokes the intimate topography of experience, houses memories, even serves as a refuge for some forgettings that are, as Gaston Bachelard puts it, always lodged in a territory that is familiar to us.

---

[154] This character not only writes a diary of the disease like Sarduy but is also obsessed with the cosmos, one of the author's passions: astronomy and astrology figure in a great number of his works.

[155] Siempreviva is one of death's nicknames. In Fernando Vallejo's HIV-positive novel *El desbarrancadero*, a feminine figure of death is called "la siempreviva, la compasiva, la artera, mi señora Muerte, cabrona" [immortal, compassionate, cunning, my lady Death, bitch] (70). Here I choose to think of Siempreviva as a character who represents a Sarduy who rejects death.

[156] Laennec Hospital was condemned in 2000.

The mansion also recalls places that the author has visited, both in his earlier fiction and in his AIDS memoir. The mansion in *Pájaros de la playa*, with its "muros aun sólidos y arabescos, [sus] arcos peraltados y azulejos en el dintel de las puertas, [sus] cinco pasillos de mosaico blanco y paredes encaladas que conducen al jardín [y a su] torrecilla" [Moorish walls that still stand solid, (its) sloping arches and tiled doorway lintels, (its) corridors with whitewashed walls and white mosaic floors, (and its) little turret] (*Pájaros* 19; *Beach* 15), corresponds to La Regenta, the orientalized mansion/brothel described a decade earlier in *Colibrí* as a place for sex-change surgeries and libidinous encounters between men. La Regenta was a place of political upheaval, marked by the carnivalesque sign of desire that inevitably recalls the eccentric palace of uninhibited sex in Witold Gombrowicz's *Trans-Atlantyk*, discussed earlier. But the mansion/brothel that in 1984 presupposed the *possibility* of a contagious disease outside its walls reappears in 1993, transformed into the epicenter of an illness that is all too *real*. The mansion in *Pájaros de la playa* is presented as the reverse of the palace of sexual freedom: it leads it to ruin. It is no surprise, then, that discussions of this novel have taken it as a given that the colonial mansion resembles not so much a brothel as a hospital, that in fact it might be a literary translocation of the Santiago de Las Vegas Sanatorium, popularly known as Villa Los Cocos, a prerevolutionary country manor where the controversial first Cuban AIDS camp was established in 1986. Because that was what Los Cocos was: an internment camp—free but compulsory—for carriers of the virus, located in a neighborhood on the outskirts of Havana. It would later be replicated in other parts of Cuba "en atención a la demanda" [in reponse to demand] (Zayón and Fajardo 13). It is quite likely that Sarduy knew about those places, whose objective was, according to texts produced in Cuba, to halt the spread of AIDS "mediante el expeditivo método del internamiento forzoso" [through the efficient method of forced internment], which provoked "un sinnúmero de conflictos de opinión, tanto en el exterior como en la propia Cuba" [endless debates, both abroad and in Cuba itself] (Zayón and Fajardo 12). Whereas the Cuban AIDS camp confines a youthful, sexually active, and often asymptomatic population, Sarduy's mansion only contains people who are dying of the disease, for whom the place is not one of forced isolation but the *pájaros'* only possible perch before beginning their final flight. In its fictional incarnation, various spaces overlap within the mansion: the jungle brothel of *Colibrí* brought into the present day, always on the island, and the experience of the urban Laennec Hospital, which Sarduy significantly calls Long

Beach in his diary, noting that after spending nearly a month there recovering from pleurisy, "muchos me encontraron un aspecto tan saludable que parecía que volvía de la playa" [many thought that I looked so healthy, it seemed like I was coming back from the beach] ("Diario" 34). All of these scenes—the Paris hospital with its dilapidated colonial atmosphere; the fictional brothel turned AIDS hospice; the Castroist, castrating sanatorium for infected Cubans—blend together into a single desire: a desire for Cuba, to which the author will never return. Sarduy's decision to place the house of his death on the island of his birth allows us to sense an urge that is also expressed in Copi's posthumous work. As death approaches, these writers, who lived their whole adult lives in Paris, developed their work there, were diagnosed and treated in that city's hospitals, repatriate their respective alter egos. And they do so in literature, I conjecture, not so much as a measure of their longing to return but as a sign of the failure of the global project, as an indication that the crisis is local in nature and can only be understood as such.

The Political Meaning of Return

Sarduy not only localizes his alter ego but also creates an entire HIV-positive community on the island. An alternative community that points at the misdoings of the national community and, by extension, at the failed political utopias that dominate the present and past of its history. In that critical operation, space and time intersect: the cartographical operation presents Cuba as a concrete place of internment and death that resists all global abstraction; this approach to time places in allegorical tension two political moments that are also emblems of opposing ideologies: the deadly present of the Cuban Revolution and the time that preceded it 40 years earlier. This previous period is embodied by a single alter ego of the author: old Siempreviva comes to the place of death as the current version of elegant prerevolutionary Sonia, who exhibits the characteristics of the Cuban upper middle class. Two eras in a single body: it is as if in Sarduy's imagination the country were still living in simultaneous epochs that do not negate each other because they both represent failed utopias. The Cuban author thus highlights a context for the global crisis: the collapse of the twin political utopias of the modern era, teleologies of progress that many dissidents believed in until the arrival of the epidemic and the disenchantment that accompanied it. One: the communist system, whose egalitarian promises soon classified the island's homosexuals as bourgeois traitors—Arenas was its most vocal victim, along with Sarduy, who never returned. And the other: the capitalist system, which in its historical development used freedom as an ideological weapon against its most vulnerable subjects, under the banner of a global community project that could not fulfill its promise of liberation for dissidents. Pedro Lemebel was also quite vocal in critiquing this system; in a calculated settling of scores, he figuratively carried AIDS back to New York in 1984, carrying a placard in a gay pride parade that read, "Chile returns AIDS." Sarduy employed those fierce denunciations of the two systems in the symbolic sphere of the novel. He argues that the epidemic should be reconceived as a local phenomenon, rejecting the utopian and, in more than one sense, false political notions imposed on the community. He suggests critically reexamining the two great foreign utopian policies offered as metaphors for the disease.

The alluded-to dystopia is clearly at work in Sarduy's choice of the island. The island, besides being a familiar landscape, is the predilect territory for utopias in the Western intellectual tradition. It is that chimerical zone in which any social transformation seems possible. It is the place where freedoms can be established that do not exist anywhere else, and in this sense it is foundational: the island is always an alternative space for communities that are opposed to the communities already established. Or at least that was the idea behind the first utopian island in world literature, described by Sir Thomas More in 1516. His tale, the account of a voyage that is both fictitious and polemical, describes the systems and customs of an island nation whose inhabitants practice religious tolerance, choose to live in groups in caves, and reject private property. It is a truly community-minded society that depicts, impugns, and inverts the real established spaces of society as it is conventionally constituted (Foucault, "Of Other Spaces" 24). More's island contradicts European political ideas in a radical way, so much so that it ended up costing the author his life on the gallows. But his political treatise structured as fiction served as a platform for subsequent utopian thinking; it doubtless sustained the revolutionary ideas of the twentieth century and is cited in Severo Sarduy's final, posthumous novel. Nearly four decades after the Cuban Revolution, *Pájaros de la playa* retraces the path of the utopian thinking of socialism that had combated that of capitalism, exploring its progress in the fictional past (the part of the plot situated 40 years before the rise of Fidel Castro) and showing it in the narrative present to be a wholly dystopian dream: the island of utopia transformed into a place of death.

The past tense of the novel features Sonia, a modern character who represents the arriviste ambitions of the bourgeoisie (she is, etymologically speaking, the *wise one* although phonetically she is a dreamer—a *soñadora*). The Sonia of the past organizes an extravagant party with the aim of seducing the Architect, an idealist (another dreamer) who, like the inhabitants of More's utopia, tries to create a new society in an underground cave. He tries, in other words, to *sculpt* the island in accordance with a community-oriented model that symbolically prefigures Fidel Castro's communist project. Sonia sets out to distract him from that revolutionary ideal, which she does not share, attempting to redirect the Architect's social passions into sexual ones. The plot employs and parodies the foundational fictions of the nineteenth century: the union of these two characters, who serve as allegories for two opposing political projects for contemporary Cuba, fails utterly. As the couple ascends the hill in Sonia's shiny, brand-new, smoke-belching Bugatti, their escorts, the albino twins, comment, between blasts of the horn, that the exhaust from the engine is the "perfume…de la modernidad" [perfume…of modernity] (*Pájaros* 142; *Beach* 103). It is among those toxic perfumes of modernity that Sonia and the Architect come together sexually, in an act that is also an allegorical alliance between the two political models, but soon afterward the modern blue Bugatti falls off a cliff. The very modernity of the fledgling social project is destroyed by Sonia's bad driving, which is both literal and also a metaphor for economic management. The broken body of the Architect lies amid the wreckage, while capitalist Sonia miraculously survives. Thus, the impossible union of this ideologically dissimilar couple is validated, and the fleetingness and fragility of a libidinal or passionate political agreement is highlighted. The joining together of these two political ideologies, represented allegorically by a capitalism that equates progress with consumption and an idealist communism anchored in a community-minded paradigm, fails utterly. The possibility of a middle ground disappears. In this episode, the novel reinforces the idea of the double fiasco of the "twin political ideologies of modernity" (Siebers 5).[157] Capitalist Sonia, wise one or dreamer, is the one who lives on with

---

[157] Another minor element is nevertheless interesting: the ideological crisis is also represented by the albino twins who accompany the couple in the Bugatti—twins described as "igualitas" [identical] (*Pájaros* 84; *Beach* 61) who appear in all of the author's narrative work, and who in this novel want above all else to stand out. Sarduy prefigures Siebers's (1994) formulation by allegorizing capitalism and socialism both as a pair of lovers who cannot be together (Sonia and the Architect) but also as twin siblings (the albinos are transvestites) who attempt to be seen differently. Sarduy thus indicates that these utopian projects of social progress are parallel in their aims yet ideologically exclusionary.

the energy of illusions. She survives, if barely, the loss of her double complement, but she arrives in the future—the present of the plot—transformed into an old transvestite, decrepit, ravaged by AIDS but still lustful, and rebaptized as Siempreviva. Whereas 40 years earlier we witnessed the anticipated collapse of socialist ideology, now the gravely ill Siempreviva is a symbol of the crisis of the utopia of capitalism. She who was once glamorous Sonia arrives at the mansion/morgue loaded with piles of junk and old dresses. She hides away with the AIDS sufferers who were once agile *pájaros*, watching them disappear while she wards off death using natural remedies provided by Caimán the medicine man, a figure whose alternative medicine calls science into question in the critical moment of the crisis. Siempreviva also puts herself into the hands of Caballo, who administers a sexual treatment to stimulate her desire to be young once more, to stay alive forever and honor her name. Her body is the territory in which certain contradictions of the moment are manifested: consumption—of bodies, creams, pills, magazines—becomes synonymous with life. Consumption is also what keeps the system running; it is its ideological foundation. Yet consumption is also a risk: the disease arises from that very consumption, underscoring how the political system has fundamentally abandoned the community aspect, its utopianism. The mansion, located beyond the highway, symbolically on the far side of the utopias of modernity,[158] is what remains of the building that housed the failed community government, the ruined residence, marginalized and inhabited by the very people responsible for the period of seeming global health under capitalism in its glory days. Senile Sonia/Siempreviva grows ever more sickly, patched up, wholly postmodern but, above all, *post* everything—postnational like so many homosexuals and postutopian like all dying people. She meets a truly Sarduyian end, refusing to succumb to the ravages of the disease on her own body and on the body politic. Living up to her name, she reformulates the scene of death, aided by memory: the Architect's tale of a strange species of moon bees whose hives—another model of community living—are perfect, of an "arquitectura que el hombre aun no conoce" [architecture of which man is still ignorant] (*Pájaros* 146; *Beach* 106). The sophisticated flying insects are ruled by an elderly queen bee that perhaps ruled over other workers before them;

---

[158] "A/*utopi*/sta" [highway] contains the word "utopía" within it. I read here another possible linguistic game as a coded way of insisting that the mansion is far from any progressive utopia.

a young drone feeds her "una miel verde que la robustece y trans-forma" [a green honey that strengthens and transforms her], and then the queen bee leaves, "no se sabe si a morir sola o a regir a otro panal" [we don't know if to die alone or to reign over another hive] (*Pájaros 146*; *Beach* 106). At the end of the work, Siempreviva understands that those words are a premonition: treated with Caimán's poultices, she becomes that queen (another name for transvestites) that flies off perhaps to establish a new hive, a new society. That possibility remains open. Sarduy does not relinquish the future, even though the present epidemic obscures it from view.[159]

Inhospitable Hospices

On the outskirts of an anonymous Latin American city,[160] we find another house-turned–twilight home, one that opens to the city's sick when, once the disease is declared local, all the other areas of the city where homosexuals circulated are closed off. This homophobic purg-ing of the public spaces—from the streets to the hospitals—leaves the HIV-positive community without a place in its own city. The height-ened fear caused by the epidemic, and the resulting social justifica-tions for the obligatory punishment and eradication of its supposed carriers, mark a symptomatic *adiós a la calle* (farewell to the street).[161] It is not just a supervised shutdown of nocturnal activities but a real stampede: the streets of the capital city have already been somewhat dangerous for prostitution and clandestine homosexual pleasure, but the fear of infection makes them a zone of guaranteed extermination, of paranoid revenge. The visible and invisible effects of the syndrome also lead to the shutting down of the nightclubs and saunas, and even the emptying out of the hospitals. It is in these circumstances that *Salón de belleza* (1994; *Beauty Salon*), a novel by the Mexican-Peruvian

---

[159] Sylvia Molloy has pointed out another possible intertextual reading, in which Sonia/Siempreviva is a nod toward the character of the same name in Anton Chekhov's *Uncle Vanya* (1899). At the end of the play, Chekhov's Sonia offers a defense of hope: "What can we do? We must live our lives. Yes, we shall live....We shall live through the long procession of days before us, and through the long evenings; we shall patiently bear the trials that fate imposes on us; we shall work for others without rest....I have faith, Uncle, fervent, passionate faith....We shall rest....We shall see all evil and all our pain sink away in the great compassion that shall enfold the world" (70).

[160] Despite its apparent anonymity, cultural details such as the reference to the Banda de Matacabros (Goat-Killer Gang, a group that attacks transvestites) mark it as Peruvian.

[161] This is the title of an Argentine AIDS novel by Claudio Zeiger (2006).

writer Mario Bellatin, is set: the community's forced removal from the urban landscape; the need, in that desperate moment, for the establishment of a private space that can take the community in. Just like Sarduy's mansion-turned–AIDS sanatorium, Bellatin places his salon-turned–death camp "en un punto tan alejado de las rutas de transporte público que para viajar en autobús hay que efectuar una fatigosa caminata" [far from any form of public transportation (so that) to get here people had to walk a great distance] (*Salón* 34; *Beauty* 13). Only on the periphery of the modern Latin American city can the territory be modified: from the utopia of feminine beauty to the dystopia of homosexual death. The salon, which once took in women who sought to be fixed up or even transformed, is slowly made available to injured transvestites who need more and more *fixing* or assistance after a beating. This shelter is only a preview of the final transformation of the salon, which overnight closes its doors to its customers and to the beaten men and reopens them to the HIV-positive community. The transition is described thus: "En los hospitales los trataban [a los travestis] con desprecio y muchas veces no querían recibirlos por temor a que estuvieran enfermos. Desde entonces y por las tristes historias que me contaban, nació en mí la compasión de recoger a alguno que otro compañero herido que no tenía a donde recurrir. Tal vez de esa manera se fue formando este triste Moridero que tengo la desgracia de regentar" [The victims of the attacks were treated with contempt when they were brought into the hospitals. Often they weren't even allowed in for fear of infection. Which is why I began to help wounded comrades who had nowhere to go and perhaps that is the beginning of this sad Terminal I have the misfortune of running] (*Salón* 15; *Beauty* 5). The owner of the place, a transvestite who also acts as the narrator, wants to create "un lugar verdaderamente diferente" [a truly unique place] that is not lacking in originality (*Salón* 46; *Beauty* 57). It is perhaps in this notion that we note some initial dissonance: How can he make this place different? Unique compared to what other places? He does not say. We can only conjecture that it will be different from hospitals or other sanatoriums opened by religious institutions.[162] The

---

[162] In Latin America most hospices for AIDS patients were opened by nuns or clergy. However progressive they were, Néstor Perlongher notes that these religious figures saw "algo positivo en la peste, la posibilidad de provocar una reacción en relación al comportamiento sexual de las comunidades homosexuales: obligar a las personas a revisar su propia sexualidad y su modus vivendi" [something positive in the epidemic, the possibility of provoking a reaction with regard to the sexual behavior of the homosexual communities: forcing people to reconsider their own sexuality and their modus vivendi] (*El fantasma* 62).

reading suggests that the metamorphosis of the salon is not merely aesthetic. The function of the space also changes: it goes from nurturing feminine beauty to nurturing transvestites' wounded bodies to nurturing (if you can call it that) death.[163] In this current period, which constitutes the fictional present, the salon has become a refuge for the terminally ill after the closure of a number of spaces previously open to the dissident community: the downtown streets where the narrator used to go out as a transvestite, the sauna owned by a Japanese family that he used to visit (its erotic vapors vanish in the terror of contagion, and its chipped white tiles make it a symbolically sterile zone).[164] The Terminal thus becomes the only local space whose doors remain open to those who have nowhere to go, offering the community not a place for sex but temporary lodging for "una muerte rápida en las condiciones más adecuadas" [a quick death under the most comfortable conditions] (*Salón* 50; *Beauty* 38). The Terminal, says the narrator, is no longer just for his friends: it loses the affectionate intimacy of friendship in the final moment of suffering and is reshaped as a community space accessible to all men whose bodies are possessed by the disease, even if they are strangers and do not admit to being—or even are not—homosexual. (The narrator does not draw these sorts of distinctions, perhaps because he assumes that AIDS and homosexuality are synonymous.) In sharing AIDS, they

[163] Mario Bellatin has indicated that the idea for the novel came out of an article he read in a newspaper: "Allí decía que había un peluquero que recogía enfermos de sida en un barrio marginal limeño. Esta anecdota me pareció que podía ofrecer un espacio rico para crear. A partir de ese momento ingresó mi propia invención" [It said that there was a hairdresser who was taking in AIDS sufferers in a poor neighborhood on the outskirts of Lima. It seemed to me that the anecdote could provide a rich space for creation. My own imagination took it from there] (de Lima). The anthropologist Blanca Figueroa, who headed up the largest study of homosexual hairdressers carried out in Lima, stated in a personal communication in 2009 that of the 144 hairdressers interviewed, not a single one was aware of the story.

[164] Saunas, which appear again and again in dissident accounts, as a heterotopian space first for uninhibited sexual engagement and later for the unconstrained spread of the epidemic, become "el punto de discusión más ardiente de la delicada cuestión del sida" [the most heated point of debate regarding the delicate question of AIDS]. Néstor Perlongher notes that, paradoxically, the saunas were first built for hygienic purposes, and some of them still function according to a therapeutic model: "En los más modernos saunas gay, en una verdadera perversión de la función higiénica, el del sexo desplaza cualquier otro calor: se trata de locales orgiásticos con salas especialmente oscurecidas para la confusión de los cuerpos sudorosos" [In the most modern gay saunas, in a complete perversion of their hygienic function, the heat of sex displaces any other heat: they are orgiastic places, their rooms deliberately darkened so that sweaty bodies can tangle together] (*El fantasma* 65).

all become part of a community of equals whose only other alternative would be to go back out into the streets and die of the disease or in the widespread violence. The decision to take them into that place that, according to its owner, is not "un hospital ni una clínica sino sencillamente un Moridero" [a hospital or a clinic; it's simply the Terminal] (*Salón* 21; *Beauty* 11) and "un lugar para morir acompañado" [a communal place to die] (*Salón* 24; *Beauty* 13), is therefore necessary and appropriate. But although its compassionate objective at first seems convincing—as quoted above, the narrator notes that it was perhaps helping the wounded that inspired "the beginning of this sad Terminal [he has] the misfortune of running" (*Beauty* 5)—and although the task of heading it seems like a humanitarian mission that must be accepted, it gradually becomes clear that the crisis is causing a sinister transformation in the narrator's worldview. The state has stepped aside and allowed the novel's protagonist to make all of the decisions, not only taking charge but also becoming lord and master of the rejected bodies. There is, after all, no jurisdiction over these bodies that matters in the case of abuses, as the Italian philosopher Giorgio Agamben warns in his book *Homo sacer* (1998). As the state identifies a political actor as undesirable and withdraws his status as a citizen, he is left outside the boundaries of its protection, at the mercy of every act of unpunished violence. In marginalizing him or stripping him of his rights and turning him into merely a body ("bare life" is the phrase the philosopher uses, to differentiate it from civil life), the state assumes that *something*—neglect, hunger, cold—or *somebody* will carry out the elimination that the state prefers not to take care of itself: extermination is socially very costly and requires that explanations be given. Abandoned by the national community of which they were never truly a part, these dying men are left to an ignoble death or to the possibility that anyone might claim the right to end their lives.

The hairdresser notes that it is to protect them from that terrible fate that he decides to take them in, but upon becoming the "regente" [regent] of the place (as he calls himself),[165] he himself comes to serve the logic of repression. In the winding chronology of *Salón de belleza*, it becomes difficult to "señalar un momento específico en el que el altruismo se convierte en violencia" [point to a specific moment in which altruism turns into violence] (Pratt, "Tres incendios" 101). "El

---

[165] *Translator's note*: While "regente" is used to mean "manager" in many Latin American countries, it carries with it clear echoes of a monarchical structure. In using the verb "regentar" to describe his role in the salon, the narrator identifies himself as not just a manager but a ruler, the ultimate arbiter of all that takes place there.

mal no tenía cura," argues the hairdreser. "Todos aquellos esfuerzos no eran sino vanos intentos por estar en paz con nuestra conciencia. No sé dónde nos han enseñado que socorrer al desvalido equivale a apartarlo de las garras de la muerte a cualquier precio" [There was no cure. All our efforts were merely vain attempts to ease our conscience. I don't know where we got the idea that helping sick people means keeping them away from the jaws of death at all costs] (*Salón* 50; *Beauty* 38). In the plot, which plays out between the narrator's ambivalent disquisitions, the reader comes to doubt even the original altruistic intention. It becomes apparent, in a close examination of his account, that the hairdresser is imposing a policy of increasing confinement on the sick, transforming the Terminal into an extension of the final solution. Why else would he impose such harsh rules and maintain such strict panopticon-like vigilance? He creates an absolute barrier: The families and friends of the sick are denied entrance— they can only contribute money, clothing, and little else. Doctors and healers are also forbidden, as are both medicines and medicinal herbs. No visits from religious leaders are allowed, and the use of crucifixes, icons, and prayers of any sort is prohibited. In addition to these prohibitions against any measure to relieve suffering, residents of the Terminal are also denied the possibly palliative effect of the company of others: lovers and family, sick men whose illness is not yet terminal, and all sick women are prohibited. Nobody checks to find out why the cold wind is creeping in through the cracks, why the ration of soup gets smaller and smaller even as donations increase. Though the narrator's explanations are not trustworthy, his actions seem so justified that it is no surprise when the police force, which acts as a sovereign entity in representing the state's interests, appears to collaborate with him as he fends off the neighbors attempting to force their way into the space in order to destroy it. The hairdresser and the police form a temporary alliance against civil society, which has begun to challenge the way the space operates outside the boundaries of society. The neighbors see the Terminal as a possible source of infection; the police, however, seem to understand the space's real function and sanction its operation on the margins of the law, putting it once more in the hands of its only administrator. "No sé de dónde me viene la terquedad de llevar yo solo la conducción del Salón" [I don't know why I insist on being the only one to take care of business here] (*Salón* 31; *Beauty* 21), the narrator says. The statement is a rhetorical one, of course, because at no point has he been willing to give up total control of the space, to relinquish the power he wields, perhaps for the first time, over the bodies of others.

That power is discursively shaped and legitimized by a neat argument reminiscent of euthanasia: the "larga agonía que se vestía de esperanza" [long-term suffering…disguised in a kind of hope] (*Salón* 30; *Beauty* 20) must be cut short. Yet the narration itself provides the counterargument: not all of the sick wish to endure the harsh conditions in the Terminal. In one of the most disturbing and powerful moments in the novel, the protagonist prevents a terminally ill young man from escaping: "Fue tal la paliza que le propiné, que muy pronto se le quitaron las ganas de escapar. Se mantuvo en la cama echado, esperando pacíficamente que su cuerpo desapareciera después de pasar por las torturas de rigor" [I beat him so badly he quickly lost all desire to escape. He lay calmly in his bed waiting for his body to disappear after the inevitable pain and torture] (*Salón* 36; *Beauty* 23). I return here to Agamben to note the causes of that imposed violence, in which not only has compassion disappeared, but also the sick individual has been stripped of all agency and even subjected to "las torturas de rigor." We see that when mere life or bare life is defined as an absolute preoccupation, it is expelled from the sphere of action in the political realm. And the space of expulsion in which those naked bodies end up is, in our culture, the concentration camp: there we find the state of exception that governs contemporary social life; there the excluded are sent; there terror reaches its peak, showing that any "apparently innocuous space [can suddenly become a] space in which the normal order is de facto suspended and in which whether or not atrocities are committed depends not on the law but on the civility and ethical sense of the police" (Agamben 175).

In Bellatin's death salon, we see precisely this transformation: from a clinical setting where innocuous forms of material succor and psychological relief take precedence, to a figurative concentration camp where the level of cruelty depends solely on the decision of the ailing hairdresser (his illness here is not merely physical), who is backed by state support. Thus, the space set aside for "good death" proves sinister, evidence that only in discourse is the dystopian nature of the project of modernity configured as the possibility of progress. This failure of political idealism laid bare by Agamben is, paradoxically, vividly echoed in the epigraph at the beginning of the novel: "Cualquier clase de inhumanidad se convierte, con el tiempo, en humana" [Anything inhuman becomes human over time]. This idea is the key that emphasizes, from the very beginning of the book, the unsettling continuity between the dream of utopia and the reality of dystopia. In fact, David Morris has argued, every utopia can generate its own nightmare, and Tobin Siebers agrees: "Attempts to distinguish between utopian and dystopian thinking are ultimately bound to fail. Utopian desire is the desire to desire differently, which includes the desire to abandon such desire" (3). That continuity is reinforced in the reversible relationship that the plot establishes between the human (the humanist ideal), the nonhuman (its correlate in other species), and the inhuman (that which negates the possibility of the human): this is a fundamental problem in the biopolitical tradition to which Agamben belongs.

In addition to the infected individuals, the other *protagonists* of *Salón de belleza* that are subject to the manager's designs are the fish acquired during the salon's glory days. In keeping with the salon's transformation into a place of death known as the Terminal, the fish tanks used as decoration suffer the same fate: they become a miniature concentration camp whose aquatic inhabitants are sadistically forced to play out the brutal limits of the survival instinct, which leads them, allegorically speaking, from the realm of the nonhuman to the decidedly inhuman. The fish tanks and their fish, the narrator's experimental subjects, provide a mirror image of what is taking place in the salon: the fish are plagued by fungus and diseases, becoming untouchable like lepers, consumptives, and AIDS sufferers throughout history. They become predators of the weakest among them—the ailing hairdresser is one of those predators. Like the human patients in the Terminal, the fish experience opportunistic illnesses associated with neglect, illnesses that kill them off while the hairdresser impassively watches. He coldly observes the behavior of the fish and of the sick, the way that both "se aferran de una manera extraña a la vida" [still somehow cling to life] (*Salón* 32; *Beauty* 19) and in the final circumstances that drive them to the destruction of their own community. "Sin remordimiento alguno," the narrator confesses, "dejé gradualmente de alimentarlos con la esperanza de que se fueran comiendo unos a otros" [Without any feelings of remorse I gradually stopped feeding them and hoped they would eat each other] (*Salón* 15; *Beauty* 5). The narrator's emotional indifference and later his sadistic actions emphasize his dehumanization in the face of suffering, and he eventually loses count of how many men and fish are still alive and how many have died under his dominion. The paradox is clear: it is difficult to differentiate between dehumanization and a policy of dignified death. Here, though, the phenomenon is taken to an extreme.

The fish become ghostly subjects, and their tanks come to mirror the morbid project that is being carried out in a less obvious but equally cruel manner with the ill. The deterioration of the ethic of compassion seems more extreme than a mere Darwinist *laissez faire*—the reading proposed by critic Estela Vieira (2002). Here, the logic of the survival of the fittest is obsolete, as nobody in the Terminal is going to survive. There is a sinister symmetry and complementarity between the infected fish tanks, the terminal AIDS camp, and the nation that contains and excludes them. In those replicas of the nation in miniature, the implacable machinery of the production of death holds sway as society's only path, perhaps its only possibility. The fundamental principle of citizen consent to ensure good governance at the hands of the state is undermined here: Agamben argues that the representation of the political should not be thought of in terms of citizen rights agreed upon in a social contract, given that the only possible agreement is one of exceptionality in which the actors included in it are, in agreeing, automatically excluded from the political sphere. In other words—Agamben's—human life is politicized only through the abandonment of a citizenry to a power defined by its ability to produce death. The novel confirms that the elimination of marginalized spaces and communities is required in current political systems. The hairdresser gives in to this requirement. His power is growing: he is not just a manager but a sovereign. His words are deeply ironic: "nunca el negocio fue más floreciente como cuando el salón se convirtió en Moridero" [business was never so good as when the beauty salon was converted into the Terminal] (*Salón* 69; *Beauty* 58). The protagonist suggests that only by changing focus—from producing beauty to producing death—does the workspace find its place and its purpose within the nation. The concentration of power and cold efficiency in a single person, as well as the Terminal's booming business at the peak of its activities (here we find echoes of the logic of Nazi genocide), are nevertheless doomed to failure because they are not sustainable over time: the hairdresser himself is infected and sees no possible successors among the other residents. The transitory power that made him feel "inmortal" [immortal] has made him unable to "preparar el terreno para el futuro" [prepare for the future] (*Salón* 73; *Beauty* 62), which is essential for ensuring the continued effectiveness of any established system. Blinded by his authority over those human and nonhuman bodies, he has not perceived the possibility of his own disappearance: his power has been his blind spot as he gazes into the mirror, until "al descubrir las heridas en mi mejilla las cosas acabaron de golpe" [when I discovered the sores on my cheek, it all ended right then and there] (*Salón* 54; *Beauty* 42). With that sudden blow—a coup d'état perpetrated by his own body—he is forced to imagine shutting down the Terminal: flooding it like a fish tank, burning it down with all the ailing residents inside it, or, his ultimate decision, restoring the salon to its original form. This restoration of *past splendor* is, without a doubt, the most enigmatic moment in the novel: among all the possible ways of repudiating the place of death, why restore it to what it was in its beginnings, and why eliminate any trace of his own presence? The narrator builds a pyre and burns the garments that conferred on him his transvestite identity like someone abandoning a project altogether, as if that rejection of the self were the only possible way to end the crisis, as if he were rejecting the possibility of the future. The intimate topography of the work space that was also home, of the hospice for the injured that never tried to be a hospital, and even of the concentration and extermination camp where the nation is finally revealed, becomes, in its final metamorphosis, a mausoleum full of mirrors where only the voice of the narrator as he prepares to die now echoes.

FLIGHT TO THE INTERIOR

The authors of the Latin American HIV-positive corpus construct clinical universes that allegorize the homeland as a failed medical institution (Copi), as an example of exclusion on the margins of civil society (Sarduy), and as the defender of a regime of death that operates in parallel to mainstream society and on orders from above (Bellatin). These configurations inspire renewed fantasies of escape that play out both in the real world and especially in literature. Let us turn now, already at the local level, to escapes that take place within the space created by the new mechanism of confinement in the nation. As the nation cannot offer definitive solutions or relieve symptoms, and as it replicates in the AIDS camps old methods of medicalized exclusion and is transformed into a portent of death, the ill must flee that place of isolation, even if they cannot escape abroad. Copi's protagonist is admitted to a Buenos Aires hospital, from which he then attempts to escape so as not to end up in the cemetery. One of the terminally ill residents of Sarduy's mansion, which could well represent the Cuban AIDS camp Los Cocos, hopes to shed his own flesh. He writes in his final novel, "Mi espíritu ya no habita mi cuerpo; ya me he ido. Lo que ahora come, habla y excreta en medio de los otros es pura simulación" [My spirit, no longer inhabiting my body, has left me. What now eats, sleeps, speaks, and defecates amidst the others is only a simulation] (*Pájaros* 21; *Beach* 16), while Sarduy's alter ego Siempreviva tries to escape by leaping into flight like the queen bee she is and heading toward an uncertain future. But Sarduy writes from afar and literaturizes reality, while the forced confinement of Bellatin's AIDS camp makes escape a dangerous option that leads directly to the beating suffered by the young man in the Terminal.

During a trip to Havana, Pedro Lemebel narrates a less figurative escape of a sick man in compulsory confinement. Freely combining autobiography and fiction, "Lemebel" begins his account "El fugado de la Habana" (The Havana fugitive)—from the book *Adiós mariquita linda* (2005)—outside the AIDS camp that serves as a frame for the elegiac narratives of *Loco afán*, entering the only country that has instituted the forced internment of infected individuals. During the sixth Havana Biennial of Art in 1997, "Lemebel" meets a young painter who has escaped from one of the AIDS camps (called, using Soviet terminology, clinical gulags[166]), which were a source of great controversy abroad and even in Cuba itself. It is also known, however, that "entre la población del país, muy ignorante al principio sobre el VIH y sus posibles formas transmisivas...esta medida gozó de un ligero y egoísta consenso favorable" [among the country's population, which was at first quite ignorant about HIV and its possible methods of transmission...this approach enjoyed a slight, selfish consensus approval] (Zayón and Fajardo 12). The segment of the population that was most supportive of the regime thought it their duty as citizens to embrace the internment policy, even if a patient was asymptomatic, even though the virus's latent period could last more than ten years.[167] Control,

---

[166] The medical shift in the usage of this Russian word, which refers to forced labor camps for political prisoners, is significant. The popular expression is cited by Zayón Jomolca and Fajardo Atanes in the prologue to their Cuban AIDS anthology *Toda esa gente solitaria* (1997).

[167] Only in 1994 did the Cuban government loosen its controls and allow citizens who had been proven *responsible* to return to work. This change in AIDS camp policy coincided with the appearance of an initial combination of two drugs (there would later be three) that improved the prognosis of the syndrome and reduced the possibility of contagion.

then, is maintained not just by the state but by the entire nation, which ensures that the state's orders are carried out for the good of the nation's citizens. Anyone who flees must hide not just from the police but from an entire population serving a police role: a human panopticon that not only condemns escape but is also willing to denounce it. Freedom exercised in defiance of the law becomes a form of social death that is perhaps more violent than the confinement decree itself.

Yet "Lemebel" is a foreigner who is unable to recognize, much less turn in, a fugitive like Adolfo, the young HIV-positive protagonist of his chronicle. The account of how Adolfo contracted the disease in adolescence follows a convention mentioned earlier: he is infected through an unprotected sexual encounter with a foreign tourist. But this story differs from the usual one in that the tourist carrying the disease is female and also in that the harsh treatment of the epidemic in Cuba is completely exceptional, unique in the world. At the time, it was a surprise even to the Cubans themselves: "Entonces yo no sabía qué era ese lugar [el sidario], por eso me presenté voluntariamente" [Back then I didn't know what that place (the AIDS camp) was, which is why I went there voluntarily] (Lemebel, *Adiós* 57). Also against his will, he remains a permanent prisoner in the "hospital del sida" [AIDS hospital]. One jail, the AIDS camp, within another: the island where Adolfo attempts to pass undetected. After escaping, after spending "tres días caminando oculto de los caminos y la policía" [three days walking, hiding from the roads and the police], Adolfo arrives in the capital city, where he is forced to remain "encerrado varios años hasta que cambiaron las cosas" [several years in hiding until things changed] (88). The city closes in around him: his flight becomes the object of ideological criticism. His own comrades and friends attack him, telling him, "Chico, tienes que entregarte, tienes que someterte al reglamento de salud pública, debes regresar al hospital y dejar que la revolución se haga cargo de tu vida. No debes dejar que el individualismo te lleve por caminos reaccionarios" [you have to turn yourself in, you have to obey public health regulations, you have to go back to the hospital and let the revolution take charge of your life. You can't let individualism carry you off down reactionary paths] (89). In this narrative, Cuban society does not judge the illness by its origin— neither as a capitalist infection nor as a homosexual disease—but it does criticize Adolfo harshly, faulting his decision not to submit to the state and to embrace instead a reactionary individualistic ideology. In the logic of Castroist paternalism, it is the state that should provide the rules and have control, as it does not trust the decisions of individuals who act outside of the social norm that dictates equality, at least in theory, for everyone.

Adolfo embodies the traitor, the same position that Arenas occupied at the start of the Revolution. And although the system became liberalized in 1997, he cannot freely return to society because he is due some time in the clinical gulag. As he says in the text, "Ahora no vuelvo ni amarrado porque todavía tengo esa cuenta pendiente. Aunque ahora ... el sistema del sidario es más libre [y] uno puede salir firmando un compromiso de no contagiar a nadie, de no singar con nadie, de no conocer a nadie" [Now I wouldn't go back there even if forced, since I've got that pending sentence. Although ... the AIDS camp system is freer now (and) you can get out by signing a promise not to infect anyone, not to screw anyone, not to meet anyone] (*Adiós* 88). The tale of this infected Cuban man highlights the various layers of his confinement: the closed-off territory of the island and its ideology of revolutionary salubrity that prevents him from exercising his individuality; the AIDS "hospital" where he has a debt to pay that, out of disobedience, he will never dispatch; his own body that must be repressed sexually and even emotionally. Even after his escape, the young man remains mentally a prisoner of his disease, and it is to the private space of Adolfo's consciousness, trapped by illness, that "Lemebel" is referring when he asks about the perhaps truly revolutionary and liberating possibility of love: "¿Y si te enamoras?, le pregunté yo, cortándole su mirada de plumas violentas. Entonces puso cara de sorprendido. Eso ya no es para mí. ¿Quién podría amar a un sidoso sin pena, con un amor que no esté pintado de compasión?" ["And what if you fall in love?" I asked him, cutting off his feathery glare. He took on a look of surprise. "That's not for me anymore. Who could love someone with AIDS without pity, with a love not tinged with compassion?"] (88). Here, "Lemebel" is the person who makes that necessary transgression possible, who temporarily facilitates an escape that is not just physical or sexual but also emotional: "Yo también soy una araña leprosa" [I'm a leprous spider, too], he tells him (88), equating them to persuade him to enter a romantic relationship, to make lonely Adolfo part of a sort of community mediated by sex. And so this improbable couple—the Latin American foreigner and the ailing Cuban—begins to make its way through Havana's busiest streets. The Chilean writer offers the possibility of freedom, but the next morning Adolfo has disappeared, consumed by fear: the iron cage can become a psychological home, one theorist has argued, and escaping it will require more than just the promise of solidarity or love.

CHAPTER 4

Female Disappearance Syndrome

The pages of Latin American AIDS offer a problematic look at the representation of the infected, portraying unsettling methods of gender-based exclusion of female carriers of the virus. HIV-positive women hardly appear in the writing of the epidemic, and the few transvestites are subject to ridicule and increasing violence as carriers of a particular *femininity* in the biological body of a man (Gilman, "AIDS and Syphilis"). This exclusion was not only the result of a direct intervention by traditional society against those affected or suspected of being affected by the disease, against all those it saw as undermining the self-sufficiency of capitalism. Dramatically, the texts also reveal the internalization of those prejudices by the sexual minorities themselves, prejudices that they used against each other. The main sufferers of the epidemic were caught up in a tide of mutual suspicion that predated the crisis. And it was AIDS that sparked the conflict between the two most afflicted communities: women (especially feminists, who added the virus to their agenda combating all forms of male violence) and sexual dissidents (especially transvestites), who saw AIDS as embodying a historical discrimination.

What should have been a productive alliance against the epidemic— the joining of the minorities' political forces, the summing of knowledges—became ruptured and also shared loss. And the figure that emerged from the ruins of that alliance, that symbolically survived, embodied the values of masculinity understood less as a biological marker than as a cultural construct, a symbolic load placed upon and even embedded in a body. Masculinity as a set of values that becomes entrenched in society through the naturalizing use of categories that oppose the construct, cultural and otherwise, of femininity. There are, of course, some female victories in the struggle between the genders in periods of crisis, but they are partial and sometimes Pyrrhic victories that reinforce the socially conceived weakness of femininity in contrast to the body of the heterosexual man or of the homosexual who follows a more virile, socially acceptable model. But in study-ing Latin American AIDS, we might also suggest that society took advantage of the crisis to prop up an old political notion, displaying its unshakeable faith in a masculinity that it viewed as vigorous and healthy and using that actor to embody an ideal of the future, a single possible mode of survival. Although a number of authors rebutted that idea, some HIV-positive texts embraced it.

In drawing connections between apparently unrelated episodes, we can examine the single nexus linking the denial of female and transvestite bodies with the resulting reinforcement of a masculinized homosexual subject in whom the social expectations of heterosexual-ity are codified. As I argued previously, infected women are nearly absent from the initial accounts of AIDS, even though female carriers formed a growing segment of the infected population. Even as their numbers increased, they continued to be described as an anomaly in the prevailing narrative of the virus, in which the female body, when ill, is afflicted with an illness that is not hers. Her figure remained buried, so to speak, under the overwhelming HIV-positiveness of the dissident community. The astonishing social, media, and then literary dominance of dissident militancy came out of an urgent need to take a political stance. The epidemic brought an end to whatever silence remained in Latin America's dissident communities: the mas-sive coming out triggered by the syndrome brought HIV-positive subjects into the national consciousness, socially *positivizing* them through their numerous and undeniable public presence. But that introduction into society, which for several years seemed absolute, was not free of subsequent problems. Secondary effects included the reinforcement of the historic link between homosexuality and ill-ness, the ratification of a false and unfortunate—even deleterious to society—notion that the syndrome selected, exclusively and with sinister precision, homosexual bodies. But the communities did not have many options: nobody was going to offer them rights if they did not go out into the streets to demand them. The homosexual appropriation of the landscape, which in its (committed, compel-ling) way reproduced the rhetoric of social discrimination, also had tertiary effects that critics have so far hardly addressed: the medi-cal and literary invisibility of women, a *negativity effect* in the crisis (Foertsch 57). While men engaged in the struggle, denouncing poli-cies of homophobic hostility and calling out the state for the lack of prevention measures and medical care, women largely watched from the sidelines, shielded in an illusory discursive immunity that the embittered female protagonist of a late novel describes thus: "Somos la generación [de mujeres] que no entendió ni admitió la realidad del sida, que guardó silencio y prestó oídos sordos a la advertencia" [We are a generation (of women) that did not understand or recognize the reality of AIDS, that remained silent and turned a deaf ear on the warning] (Cacho 77).

Women at first expose a *negative* statute in HIV-positiveness: the female body is robbed of its possible viral load, delaying the entrance of women's voices and experiences into the narrative of the epidemic. They appear in their own texts and those of others as secondary and peripheral characters to HIV-positive men, or as sunk in fear, even in a paranoid trance. Yet infection was avoided on the page: the consequences of unprotected intercourse were warded off, the dreaded disease remained mere speculation. The sick woman's body was for a long time superfluous to the epic epidemic, and when she did appear, she was formulated as a "mujer que se pierde" [woman who is lost] (Zeiger, *Adiós* 90), "una mujer con un pasado y un presente, o tal vez varios pasados y ningún futuro" [a woman with a past and a present, or perhaps several pasts and no future] (158). The latter appears, if rarely over the tragic course of the syndrome, in two complementary forms described earlier: the infectious, victimizing prostitute, whose ongoing, mobile sex work was a precise counterpart to the male prostitute or promiscuous dissident, and her opposite, the innocent victim of someone else's (a male partner's) straying who submissively resigns herself to her fate.

THE SOLITUDES OF WOMEN

I return to the problem that occupies me here to examine representations of the tension between HIV-positive homosexuals and negativized women (women who were not accepted as possible carriers, infected females punished for their sexual freedom or perhaps responding only with solitary stoicism). The rivalry between the groups (discrimination, dismissal, closeted misogyny) that prevented them from joining forces against the epidemic was no doubt mutual, but its effect perversely contributed to the exclusion, nearly to the point of complete disappearance, of any sign of femininity—both the body of the female and that of the transvestite, which bears or projects, as noted, its own femininity. Among the rare instances of HIV-positive writing by women, I will look at two novels by popular authors that both shape and confirm a shared viewpoint, repeating certain widely accepted stereotypes instead of upending conventions.[168] These texts incorporate deeply entrenched ideas, adopting a feminine gaze to examine and perhaps validate the tension between genders generated by the epidemic. In *La nada cotidiana* (1995; The daily nothing), writer Zoé Valdés portrays an exiled Cuban, La Gusana, in Madrid. The protagonist (like the author) has left the island during the austere Special Period and settled down in Europe. It is there that the novel begins: her marriage of convenience to an elderly Spaniard is not sexually satisfying, attempts to repair their relationship have failed, and the symbolic bridges and points of cultural contact between the two worlds gradually collapse. The protagonist complains of this in a letter to a friend in Havana before diagnosing the sexual situation itself:

> Dirás que por qué entonces no me busco un amante. Aquí [en Madrid] ciertamente hay niños preciosos, de esos de cutis rosado, ojos limpios y negros, pelo azabache, boquitas rojas como la sangre.... Unos verdaderos Blancanieves, listos para envenenarlos con manzanas. Pero mi vida, ¿qué crees? La mayoría son homosexuales, no quieren cuento con una. Porque si al menos le metieran mano a los dos bandos, tú sabes que yo...no tengo prejuicios. Pero ellos son recalcitrantes con los pipis. Las totas, vaya, no hay quien se las haga poner por delante, lo de ellos son los rabos. Y de eso estamos todas en falta. Fíjate que yo ando siempre con un paquetico de cinco condones en la cartera, pero se me van a pudrir. Los compré nada más aterricé en Barajas, en el mismo aeropuerto. Pues boté la plata. (100–101)
>
> [You're probably wondering why I don't find a lover. Here (in Madrid), there are definitely beautiful boys, with rosy cheeks, clear dark eyes, jet-black hair, little mouths as red as blood.... Real Snow Whites, ready to be poisoned with apples. But guess what, darling! Most of them are gay, want nothing to do with you. If they at least played for both teams, you know I...I'm no bigot. But they really are quite stubborn with their willies. They're not the least bit interested in cunts; they're all about cocks. And none of us girls have that. I actually carry a little box of five condoms in my purse, but they're going to fall apart on me. I bought them as soon as I landed in Barajas, right in the airport. A total waste of money.]

The accuracy of this statement is less important than the frustrated expectations and isolation it expresses: the homosexual community

---

[168] The variety of texts written by male writers allows us to pick and choose among the most provocative ones, those written in favor of or in rebellion against the social situation. HIV-positive texts written by women are few and far between, but though they are more conservative in nature, or precisely because of that, they deserve critical attention.

of the developed world, as Reinaldo Arenas noted in New York, has done away with bisexuality and not only alienated the gay community in the 1980s United States but also women—at least some liberal ones like La Gusana—in 1990s Madrid.[169] What is new to the protagonist exiled in Spain is that the *gais* (as they are called in the Iberian Peninsula) have become *stubborn* in their difference, in their choice of a same-sex partner, and refuse to consider women. Even in the expanded space of a newly global world, women who are not conventionally married and have had to compromise to achieve some degree of sexual freedom are sexually marginalized. In concluding her confession, La Gusana ironically notes,

> No creas, ahora seguro te desmayarás que hasta he pensado en meterme a lesbiana. Una ve aquí tanta película con tetas enormes y paradas, nalgas duras, mujeres toqueteándose que se te moja el blúmer y sin querer te viniste mirando a dos tipas chupándose los pezones y los clítoris.... Pero el sexo con las mujeres, cuentan algunas revistas, es más peligroso con respecto al sida, porque a los tipos les encasquetas el preservativo y ya, pero todavía para las perillas no se han inventado las cámaras antiefluvios, o como quieran llamarle. (101)
>
> [You're not going to believe it—you'll faint dead away when I tell you I've even considered going lesbian. You see so many movies here with huge, perky boobs, firm buttocks, women fondling themselves, that your panties get wet and suddenly you've come watching two girls sucking each other's tits and clits.... But sex with women, some magazines say, is more dangerous when it comes to AIDS, because you can just slip a condom on a guy and be done with it, but there aren't any raincoats for women's little nubbins yet.]

This unique moment, this discussion of sex between women and the risk of AIDS in the lesbian community (by then a huge taboo), posits sex between women as a profoundly unprotected realm: it is the most daring act of all. Bisexual and lesbian sex are both forbidden, and to make things worse, La Gusana can't imagine returning to the arms of that "viejo tirapeos" [old fart] she'd never even have hooked up with "si no hubiera sido porque no aguantaba más la libreta de racionamiento" [except that (she) couldn't stand the rationing anymore] (100). I have focused on this minor episode because it not only sketches out once more the marginalization of women in the sexual

---

[169] Arenas, too, is nostalgic for the widespread practice of bisexuality, or *bugarronería*, on the island. He complains acidly of that loss, just as Valdés's La Gusana does.

realm but also expresses resentment of the men who marginalize them and expose her to the heightened *danger* of lesbianism. The marginalization of the female protagonist of one contemporary Mexican novel is perhaps even more dramatic. In Lydia Cacho's *Muérdele el corazón* (2006)—very local, more recent, irretrievably HIV-positive—the protagonist also feels betrayed by the male gender and maintains a strict distance from men: first from her husband, who admits to being bisexual when she accuses him of having given her the disease, and then from the transvestites she meets in a therapy session. Over the course of her evolution, we see the contradictions she experiences, a married woman who has followed all society's mandates of faithfulness and obedience. Upon discovering that she is HIV-positive, Soledad lives up to her name, angrily withdrawing and attempting to punish the husband in whom she had placed her trust. There is a clear intention to teach a lesson about the irresponsibility of the married man and patriarch who embodies the social ideal of sustenance- and protection-providing masculinity. In the convention that shapes this novel, infidelity, associated with sexual excess, is expressed both in the husband's adultery and especially in his bisexuality, which together entail a double betrayal that leaves the protagonist unprotected and ultimately infects and kills her. It is a symbolic staging of a perverse form of domestic violence, consistent with the feminist demands made by the author in other texts. The writing employs a rhetoric of punishment for the violence implied by that betrayal and operates from the intractable place of female suffering: her death at 33 years of age, covered in sores, evokes the crucifixion, making women the innocent martyrs of sacrilegious men. In the process of dying, silent as the Mater Dolorosa, she gets her revenge on the sinning man, refusing to forgive him and stripping him of the positive attributes of his masculinity. The wife replaces him as a family protector with a number of different women who are close to her: her dead mother, who remains present in memory; her mother-in-law, who represents the infected; the female friend who after the husband's death even takes his place in the family. This feminine community is radically, even viscerally, opposed to the bisexual, HIV-positive husband and the community of ailing homosexuals that she briefly visits in search of sanctuary. In that scene, an unexpected homophobic violence erupts. Soledad's first discovery when she attends the anti-AIDS group meeting is that she does not belong. She first asks, rhetorically and repeatedly, "¿Qué hago aquí?" [What am I doing here?], and then follows it with a bitter observation that is actually directed at her husband: "Solo dos mujeres, pensé. ¿Por qué tantos hombres si los hombres nunca van a nada que tenga que ver con sus emociones?" [Only two women, I thought. Why so many men, when men never go to anything that has to do with their emotions?] (Cacho 79). But the attendees are not *normal* men (this is a key word employed in the novel) but *other* men, transvestites whom she observes with uneasiness and suspicion. The psychiatrist leading the session is a "cuervo" [old crow] who takes advantage of the infected young people. The transvestites are "extraños remedos de mujer" [bizarre imitations of women]. She finds therapy "patética" [pathetic] and deems it useless, full of recriminations and resentments that she, despite the "injusticias" [injustices] that she has had to endure, does not believe are shared. Her tone is not compassionate and supportive but instead conveys the paradoxical superiority of being, herself, a woman who is discriminated against. The transvestites, on the other hand, "son los discriminados de los discriminados; no solamente viven en un país que niega la sexualidad y aborrece de las personas con VIH, sino en una patria que le cierra atemorizada la puerta del closet.... Mi país condena sin piedad a las personas diferentes" [are doubly discriminated against: not only do they live in a country that denies their sexuality and abhors people with HIV, but they live in a nation that shuts the closet door on them in terror.... My country mercilessly condemns people who are different] (81–82). After uttering that revealing "my country," the protagonist proceeds to confirm that she belongs to the national community that perpetrates that double discrimination against difference. Her rejection is absolute: "No quiero volver a estar ahí, entre ese dolor ajeno," she says. "No quiero conocer el [miedo] de aquellos, aquellas habitantes de la isla del ostracismo sexual" [I don't want to go back there, in the middle of those people's pain. I don't want to know the (fear) they feel, stranded on the island of sexual ostracism] (82). Coming full circle, Soledad goes back to the vision she had previously formed of dissidence, even if in the abstract. Although she hadn't thought homosexuality "mala...en sí misma" [bad in and of itself], now, "esta tarde, en este cuarto, rodeada de hombres actuando abiertamente como extraños remedos de mujer y solo algunos con apariencia varonil" [this afternoon, in this room, surrounded by men openly acting like bizarre imitations of women and only some of them masculine in appearance], her attitude changes (84). This is a turning point. Now she openly condemns homosexuality:

Si el día de mañana me pidieran los muchachos del grupo contra el sida que marchara con ellos en defensa de sus derechos, no lo haría. Una parte de mí dice sí, tienen derechos humanos, derecho a actuar en lo

privado como mejor les plazca; la otra me indica que al hacerlo público, al aceptar marchar con hombres travestidos, justifico ante mis hijos que ser homosexual es bueno y eso no es verdad. (85)
[If the guys from the anti-AIDS group came to me tomorrow and asked me to march with them in defense of their rights, I wouldn't do it. Part of me says that yes, they have human rights, the right to behave however they please in private; but the rest of me says that by making it public, by agreeing to march with transvestite men, I would be telling my children that being gay is good, and that's not true.]

Her personal crisis produces no empathy for others. The protagonist feels threatened, her heternormative values called into question, which she expresses in this observation about transvestites: "Es como si nosotras no existiésemos, [como si] el sentimiento amoroso fuera privativo de [esos] hombres" [It is as if we did not exist, (as if) feelings of love were reserved for (those) men] (Cacho 84). Soledad rejects the figurative "mimicry" of femininity, femininity that she chooses to perform until death because only thus, she believes, can she continue to belong to normal society and maintain her privilege within the set of practices that define heterosexuality as envisioned by heterosexual men.

Muérdele el corazón, then, problematically reproduces and reinforces a conservative social mandate promoting a return to a world that punishes any deviation from masculine sexuality. *It is not true that homosexuality is good*, argues the protagonist in a veiled accusation about the origin of her infection and also about the danger her children are in. If homosexuality is not good, adds the novel, it must be contained; at the very least, that community's participation in the social sphere must be restricted. Their *human rights*, it argues, must be limited to private matters and never be permitted public display. The story establishes itself within a normalizing system that allows the protagonist to become a spokesperson for the most conservative discourse. Discriminated against by society, she discriminates against minorities even more despised than her own. And here we encounter an insurmountable critical problem: the systematic rejection of women prescribed in writers' historical canon is repeated, in a way that is symmetrical but inverted. Yet here it is the protagonist who carries out this rejection, relegating not only transvestites but also women to a position in which they are divested of their rights as citizens. The female protagonist of this Mexican text imposes on the transvestite, and by extension on all sexual dissidents, the same silence and the same rejection that femininity has undergone, and celebrates her own "derecho a la privacía y a la confidencialidad" [right to privacy and confidentiality] (43), emblems of proper womanhood. She puts other groups that suffer discrimination in *their* place and sets herself up in competition with those whom she judges to be imitating her. In this complex equation of female jealousy toward those other men (so eloquently captured in the novels of Lydia Cacho and Zoé Valdés), we see the impossibility of a political alliance that might defend against the shared discrimination experienced during the epidemic. This at-first harmless competition between women, transvestites, and homosexuals was later resolved, in other, more radical texts, through a gradual and complete elimination of the feminine sign: of women and of transvestites.

A *SHARED* RISK

We must examine this conflict from another angle. In Copi's posthumous work, we can observe the historical presence of mutual resentment and exclusion of femininity on the part of the homosexual community. Copi ironically relives what Tim Frasca (2003) calls *closeted misogyny*: the ailing protagonist of *Una visita inoportuna* (1987) disdains death, a feminized though sexually ambiguous figure who threatens to carry him off to the "reino de los muertos" [realm of the dead].[170] The sick man categorically refuses to go with her, saying—almost shouting—that he is not going to go off with a woman "después de toda una vida huyendo de ellas" [after spending my whole life avoiding them] (48). Copi's statement is ambivalent and full of sarcasm, identifying death, regardless of biology, with femininity. But it also reflects the situation of marginalized elements of the population: there is an evident underlying discord, a score to be settled. Feminists, above all, were sharp readers of this hostility, which was in some sense a product of the rebellion against the historical subjugation of women and of the struggle for power in the social sphere that only intensified when modes of joint action against the state had to be negotiated and each group felt compelled to defend its needs and to insist on its own importance.

---

[170] Many characters in HIV-positive novels who seem to be women later turn out to be transvestites, marking in yet another way the exclusion of the female body. In Copi's posthumous work, characters flee from death when they see it as a woman but accept it when it is clear that death is a transvestite. In Severo Sarduy's *Pájaros de la playa*, the character of Sonia seems to be a woman 40 years earlier, but in the present she is Siempreviva, a transvestite who might represent death.

Accusations were hurled back and forth, and not even the Chilean writer Pedro Lemebel came out unscathed. Lemebel was among the initial organizers of an urban campaign to salvage femininity under threat: femininity performed by the transvestite's own body, and the associated bodies of women. Lemebel and Francisco Casas, his partner in the previously mentioned artistic collective Las Yeguas del Apocalipsis, set up their defense of the HIV-positive *loca* in alliance with Chilean feminists, who, for their part, focused on their own gender's predicament. But like any collaboration between heterogeneous communities, the collaboration between the homosexuals (especially the *locas*) and the female activists was extremely fragile, built as it was on an unstable foundation of circumstantial solidarity that arose out of specific strategic needs. The alliance, which formed under the dictatorship and continued into the democratic period, could only benefit both communities: Chilean sexual militancy inherited tactics for political struggle that were passed down by the feminists, while the women in turn were able to take advantage of their colleagues' knowledge about education regarding the prevention and containment of sexually transmitted diseases.

Nevertheless, the rapid spread of the virus sparked tensions between the tentatively aligned rival parties. There were mutual recriminations, allegations of unfair competition. Speaking together in an interview given in 1989, Lemebel and Casas comment on these difficulties, noting that some feminist activists have accused them of "copa[r] los espacios femeninos ganados por ellas" [occupying the feminine spaces that women had won] (Salas 29). Las Yeguas, who adopted and adapted some of the tactics of the radical feminists who took to the streets in the 1980s to protest the disappeared and a number of other social and political problems, say they have not occupied anything and reiterate their commitment, their fundamental decision to "estar con las mujeres" [be with women] (29). Nevertheless they immediately add a less categorical and certainly more ambiguous statement: "Estamos con las mujeres," they say, "pero sin paternalismos; todo golpe en el hombro nos parece raro. No queremos vestir más a la novia, nosotras somos las novias negras" [We are with women, but without paternalism; any pat on the shoulder seems odd to us. We don't want to dress the bride anymore; we are the black brides] (29). The statement repeats, quite definitively, that the *locas* are committed to fighting *with* and not *for* women, but the formulation is equivocal, as it makes explicit that they will no longer be collaborating—dressing the bride—and expresses a desire to go further and become *black brides* themselves, to compete (if I extrapolate on the metaphor) for the same groom. It offers a veiled warning of a struggle to impose different forms of feminine presence in a single territory, and it is that effort, Lemebel and Casas argue, that the feminists resent. As American activist Janice Raymond (cited in Millot) has reminded us, "transsexuality is the latest male ploy designed to ensure man's continuing ascendancy in the battle of the sexes, men now compete with women on their own ground and pose the immediate threat of turning them into a dying species" (13). We sense in these metaphorical statements a competition to wear the wedding dress that is not merely figurative.

In the complex period of the transition to democracy and the emergence of AIDS, of greatest concern was how to deal with the epidemic; how to shatter taboos in a homophobic country that forbade prevention campaigns and railed against the use of condoms so as *not to encourage young people to have sex*, how to normalize homosexuality while also pushing a more egalitarian message about the disease. The prevailing rhetoric was one of "riesgo compartido" [shared risk] that underscored the existence of a danger for the "población general" [general population]—the only way to make the governments react. This approach would turn out to be, at least according to some critics, a double-edged sword: the rhetoric of shared risk contributed to the *dehomosexualization* of AIDS (Frasca, "Men and Women" 16), erasing the homosexual agenda from the public discussion and erasing homosexuals themselves from the map of political concerns. For those who fought both for their right to sexual diversity and against AIDS, it became crucial not to cede ground; meanwhile, for the feminists, who worried about the invisibility of HIV-positive women in the social imaginary, it became necessary to take a more active stance. They began to compete for visibility in the crisis, perhaps motivated by the idea that capturing the state's attention could save their lives.

This contradiction between solidarity in the face of catastrophe and rivalry over representation can, I suspect, help shed light on the most provocative statement in the interview with Las Yeguas del Apocalipsis. Asked specifically about the AIDS epidemic, they say, with ominous merriment, "Esto del Sida es otro mambo, no es una enfermedad homo, le da a todos los que tienen ano" [This AIDS thing is something else—it's not a homo disease, it gets anyone who's got an anus] (Salas 28). Yet this statement also rejects femininity. Making veiled allusion to the so-called general population, the Chilean performance artists posit the anus as a *democratic* zone of possible contagion for any body. The apparent premise is that in addition to the genitals that differentiate the anatomy of each biological sex, all citizens have in common the possession of an anal sphincter and thus run the same risk. But in privileging the anus as an infection zone, they assume that there is only one route by which the virus enters the body. By proposing this direct, rectal route as an exclusive one, they eliminate the possibility of other zones of inoculation, rhetorically erasing the singular genitality and sexual machinery of the female body and the reproductive uniqueness that certain organs grant women. That body is castrated, equalized, and ultimately discursively subjugated to the bio-logics of the transvestite. The physical particularities of the female body are paradoxically suppressed, negated, and even negativized in a gesture that is intended to be inclusive.

I am interested in this idea because this gesture that simultaneously includes and excludes women not only is provocative but also has a certain predictive value: the Yeguas statements are from 1989, and the schism took place soon afterward. This discordant tone was characteristic of the times, not just in Chile but in the whole Western world. And it intensified as the number of infected women grew and the feminization of AIDS at last began to be discussed, if only after an unconscionable delay and with moralistic undertones. In that crucial moment, there was an urgent need to recognize women as carriers, giving them public and state recognition: to protect them. They were owed that recognition—but so were men, and that competition, the mutual resentment between the two genders, gave rise to discord. In that process of recognition, after all, women were made—in some cases made themselves—the only *innocent* victims of the epidemic (as if there were *guilty* victims or even somebody to blame; as if the disease had actually been caused by people who had succumbed to sexual liberation and its temptations). In many places, the emergence of women in the media as the "most vulnerable" infected individuals coincided with the beginning of prevention campaigns and attempts to domesticate women, promoting sex within married couples over previous or parallel relationships, and promoting women's maternal role and the state's caretaking role with the most innocent of all: children. And it was precisely this idea that ended up creeping into the more referential literary representations.

THE THEATER OF HYPERFEMININITY

Not only was Pedro Lemebel one of the few activist artists who paid attention to the situation of women, but he was also among those who early on identified the masculinization process taking place in the social imaginary at the end of the twentieth century. His chronicles tell the story of transvestites, whose posture as female hovers somewhere between the purely imitative and the openly parodic.[171] They single out the *loca* as the era's most heroic, unforgettable figure,[172] defending her human rights as yet another political victim of the dictatorship that permitted the entrance of AIDS. Their political objective is to highlight those events that ensure a grim future for the transvestite, who inhabits a binary intersection of genders. First comes the military coup that, by imposing its classist and racist ideology, divides the poor *locas* from those of the upper class. Then there are the economic effects of Chile's return to neoliberalism under the dictatorship, which contrasts the Latin American *loca*, provincial and flamboyant, with a Míster Gay who descends from the "Olimpo primermundista" [First-World Mount Olympus] (*Loco afán* [1996] 22); in Lemebel's neobaroque version (and here I am including elements from a number of different texts), he is a tall, blond homosexual who penetrates borders opened by globalization, a handsome, muscular, commanding gay man who is portrayed as the polar opposite both of the *loca*'s Dionysian debauchery and especially of her femininity. That gay man is, in Lemebel's metaphor, an ultramacho foreigner who brings with him an imported HIV to annihilate the most vulnerable members of Chilean sexual dissidence. This is the epidemic's final blow: an operation to destroy the disordered, unproductive Latin American *loca*, the local *loca* associated with community-mindedness and emotionality. In this viral, virile infection, the syndrome literalized some of the processes of transverse masculinization in the Chilean social imaginary, assiduously and efficiently aided by authoritarian, disciplinary policies of a neoliberal bent. All the virulence of the First World was unleashed on transvestites, who took on, in a context remarkably absent of women (having been *supplanted* by the *loca*), the performance of a construct that, as the author foresaw it, was threatened with extinction.

---

[171] There is some critical disagreement as to how to read the figure of the transvestite. Some see in her a sort of imitator of hegemonic norms and of stereotypes that reidealize the rules of heterosexual society (Leo Bersani), whereas others see him as a cultural actor who carries out a subversive appropriation of the feminine role in patriarchal society, parodically performing the female body (Judith Butler).

[172] Lemebel reinscribes and radicalizes the legacy of José Donoso in *El lugar sin límites*, says Gabriel Giorgi in an unpublished article, reproducing the *loca*lizing process carried out by Néstor Perlongher in Argentina in the wake of Manuel Puig; and by Reinaldo Arenas, who tore back Virgilio Piñera and José Lezama Lima's masks of apparent masculinity to reveal their homosexual aesthetic.

This process of masculinization foreseen by Lemebel is not unique to HIV-positive writing but is instead the effect of a possibly universal aspect of culture in the capitalist world. Mary Louise Pratt argues that the exclusion of women is seen with alarming frequency in the novelistic imaginary of the 1990s.[173] She identifies in a particular group of Latin American works the mass disappearance of bodies that represent femininity. This exclusion corresponds, Pratt suggests, to certain masculine anxieties (anxieties that are, in fact, not exclusively heterosexual) regarding women's growing presence in the professional, political, and intellectual spheres. In other words, it is an anxiety about the feminine refusal to accept the premise of subordination imposed by the antiquated clauses of the social contract; about the increasing demands for their rights as citizens; about their withdrawal from, and sometimes even their rejection of, the matrimonial and maternal role. The argument is that narrative at the end of the twentieth century grapples with the gradual dismantling of the nineteenth-century contract governing the relationships among citizens and political equality among men—specifically, among male bodies whose connections were limited to emulation or identification, to competition and even rivalry in which the erotics of desire were suppressed.[174] This contract, Pratt explains, could only be carried out on the basis of another complementary, implicit, and supposedly prior pact, sexual in nature, in which women had ceded their civic and economic rights to their husbands.[175] Without this ceding of rights, the social contract could not function, could not ensure the legitimacy of a masculine government for the nation or the control of male citizens over women. Yet the mechanism of the contract presupposed heterosexual power relationships that were unfounded in reality.

[173] The novels discussed by this critic are Alberto Fuguet's *Mala onda* (1991; *Bad Vibes*), Mario Bellatin's *Salón de belleza* (1994), Diamela Eltit's *Los vigilantes* (1994; The vigilantes), Fernando Vallejo's *La virgen de los sicarios* (1994; *Our Lady of the Assassins*), Mayra Montero's *Tú la oscuridad* (1995; *In the Palm of Darkness*), and Ricardo Piglia's *Plata quemada* (1997; *Burnt Money*).

[174] I am referring here to the concept of *homosociability*, popularized by Eve Sedgwick and queer studies but originally found in Leslie Fiedler's book *Love and Death in the American Novel* (1966). This concept defines masculine relationships in which homosexuality is masked and sublimated in other modes of masculine interaction.

[175] Here Pratt follows the thesis of feminist political scientist Carole Pateman in *The Sexual Contract* (1987).

Stripped of that social armor, the writers have responded by producing fictional spaces—that is, social imaginaries—that set out on
the page the disintegration of the pact between the sexes. They do
not reconfigure new social and sexual contracts with women; they do
not even attempt to renegotiate them. It is unclear what role women
might play on this new stage: indeed, the narrative opts to eliminate
them both symbolically and even literally. It either denies them entry
to the written stage or drives the plot to such an extreme of violence
that women themselves choose to marginalize themselves or wait for
death. Significantly, against the backdrop of the syndrome, the same
textual operation, a deeply entrenched way of thinking, is apparent in
novels written by women. We see it in the situation of Zoé Valdés's La
Gusana, who in her pursuit of freedom must become party to a marriage compact, and in doing so becomes trapped in a dysfunctional
relationship in which her desire to escape is punished with rejection
by men who *stubbornly* refuse sex with women, and through their
sexual abstention generate a fear of infection by women. In the case of
Soledad, Lydia Cacho's conservative protagonist, the disease that her
husband gives her forces her to return home and shut herself in there,
adopting, in her weakened position, a submissive model of femininity that moves from rage to resignation and whose only *dignified* exit
is death (her husband, on the other hand, survives her and is left in
charge of the family).

Pratt does mention some radical cases in which the fraternal bond
between men becomes sexualized, and thus "lo femenino es recu-
perado por los cuerpos masculinos" [femininity is restored by male
bodies] ("Tres incendios" 94). The acceptance of sex between men
may partially explain why so many texts from the 1990s that fea-
ture homosexual men—many of them HIV-positive—fail to note any
need to ally with women: the feminine role was filled by the transvestite, and the figure of the woman therefore became superfluous. In
Pedro Lemebel's chronicles, affinities with femininity are only part of
the exultant performance of a simulacrum, a rhetorical strategy—an
alliance—that proves contradictory, if not meaningless: in Lemebel's
writing, the extratextual commitment to being with women fails.
When it comes to symbolic configurations, Lemebel confirms the
absence of the female body from his writing. What's more, this does
not take place in a vacuum: it has precedents in homosexual literature, in which the feminine body is marginalized because it does
not serve as an erotic element in the text and is sexually substituted

by the feminized body of the *loca*.[176] In the recessionary libidinal economy of the viral narrative, that policy of exclusion of the female body becomes firmly established. Inserting the *loca* as a substitute for woman in the "teatro de la hiperfeminidad y de la artificialidad del género" [theater of hyperfemininity and gender artificiality] (Giorgi, "Historias") illuminates the very material absence of the feminine that precedes the *loca*'s predicted disappearance. Faced with the epidemic horror that was wiping out Latin American transvestites, there did not seem to be room or time either to foster solidarity with the collective and individual female body, or to expand the ways that the infected were characterized.

The Masculinization of the Social Imaginary

The outbreak of the epidemic profoundly transformed the gender situation found in *Salón de belleza* (1994), the aforementioned Peruvian novel by Mexican writer Mario Bellatin. This text, in my view, radicalizes the split from and the rejection of femininity that is also evident in Lemebel's work, but here the mechanisms of exclusion are not inevitable but instead generated in a calculated, violent manner. The syndrome marks a watershed moment between a past in which the salon catered to women and helped make them beautiful, and a present in which those female bodies, and even the feminine masquerade previously performed by the protagonist, are completely rejected. The entire period that in the novel's complex chronology precedes the crisis represents the time of a life "que puede llamarse disipada" [that you could call...dissipated] (*Salón* 47; *Beauty* 34), a life that includes its share of unproductive disorders, of desires that defy the heterosexist norms with which the transvestite complies during nights of eager prostitution in the city center, clothed as a woman. The protagonist also performs his daytime work as a hairdresser in female garb, which does not make his customers uncomfortable: "Solo a las mujeres parecía no importarles la atención de unos estilistas vestidos casi siempre con ropas femeninas" [The women didn't seem to mind being attended by male stylists dressed in women's clothes] (*Salón* 24; *Beauty* 13). Although the salon claims to be unisex, its only customers are "mujeres viejas

---

[176] In the Hispanic world, the effeminate male (not just the transvestite) has until very recently been the only recognized and recognizable homosexual because he matches the stereotype that defines homosexuals not as men who simply desire other men but as men who in their desire assume or usurp the feminine role. It is that unstable and destabilizing place that seems to be condemned to the pathological extinction noted by Lemebel.

o acabadas por la vida [bajo cuyo] cutis gastado [es] visible una larga agonía que se [viste] de esperanzas" [old worn-out women (beneath whose) worn-out skin a long-term suffering (is) visible, disguised as a kind of hope] (*Salón* 30; *Beauty* 20). The hairstylist and his employees, also dressed as women, devote themselves to making the other women beautiful, which within the system of the novel means restoring those elements that make them feel magnificent: revitalizing them, reviving them, restoring the femininity destroyed by the aging process.

The spatial and temporal elements of the beauty salon are brought together under the banner of a feminine absolute by which women and homosexual men establish a mutually beneficial relationship. The appearance of the disease triggers a transformation of that society: the salon becomes a place reserved exclusively for providing a quick and efficient death to the terminally ill—and only the ill. Far from being a unisex space, the salon becomes *monosex*, reserved only for young men who, ravaged by AIDS, can die in the company of others in the same condition. This spatial metamorphosis is reflected—as if in the mirrors that line the walls of the beauty salon—by the change in the protagonist's outlook. With the salon's transformation into the Terminal, the protagonist nominally ceases to be a hairdresser and instead calls himself the regent, assigning himself the power to decide how the lost souls in his charge will spend the rest of their lives. Significantly, the narrator does not call himself a nurse, which would suggest an intention to provide support and care for the ill even if he could not cure them; pity is a trap into which we are deliberately drawn at the beginning of the novel. Instead, the narrator uses the authoritarian and ever-watchful language of sovereignty to describe his mission: caring for the dying is expressed not as altruism but as the certainty of annihilation. Settled in his new role, the former hairdresser rejects feelings of compassion. The few moments of tenderness toward those men (whom he calls *huéspedes* [guests] because their stays are only temporary) are soon replaced by dehumanized indifference and by the exercise of absolute power symbolically associated with a violence that is understood as masculine.[177] As

---

[177] At the beginning of an important article on violence, Pratt wonders rhetorically, "¿La violencia tiene sexo? Definitivamente sí. Tanto en la estadística como el imaginario social, los agresores normativos son masculinos, los agredidos masculinos y femeninos. Y entre los agredidos, la categoría de víctima se reserva, como indica su género gramatical, prioritariamente para las mujeres, es decir los cuerpos hembras" [Does violence have a gender? Most certainly it does. Both in statistics and in the social imaginary, the normative aggressors are male, and those who are attacked are male and female. And among those who are attacked, the category of "victim" is reserved, as its grammatical gender (in Spanish) suggests, mainly for women—that is, for female bodies] ("Tres incendios" 91).

the epidemic worsens, his control over the Terminal becomes more and more rigid and ruthless; he imposes many rules that seem more fitting to a prison than to a hospice, including the prohibition of entry to women. His former customers, who represent the dwindling hope of recovering lost beauty, the pious Sisters of Charity who offer succor and prayers, and women dying of AIDS are all forbidden entrance. "Venían a mi puerta en pésimas condiciones," the impassive narrator explains. "Pero yo desde el primer momento me mostré inflexible. El salón en algún tiempo había embellecido hasta la saciedad a las mujeres, no iba pues a echar por la borda tantos años de trabajo sacrificado. Nunca acepté a nadie que no fuera de sexo masculino" [They came to the salon in very bad condition.... I stood firm from the very beginning. The beauty salon had once been dedicated to beautifying women and I wasn't willing to sacrifice so many years of work. Which is why I never accepted anyone that wasn't a man] (*Salón* 34; *Beauty* 23–24). And although he himself then concedes that at first he had thought about "aquellas mujeres que tendrían que morir en la calle con sus hijos a cuestas" [all the women who would have to die in the streets with their children clinging to them] (*Salón* 34; *Beauty* 24), all too soon he stops thinking about them, stops listening to their pleas and their offers of money. Internally, the voice of that other segment of the infected population is silenced. The plot presents a hierarchization of violence: although the dying bodies of homosexual men are admitted *for* death, female bodies cannot even access that realm; women are doubly exiled from the contract that perversely serves as the foundation for that new space for the HIV-positive community. Women—those reproductive bodies that were only acceptable as a model of beauty or paradigm of an aesthetic quest intended to seduce and satisfy men, those bodies that appear as a vision of a transvestite ideal—have lost all utility. The failure of this aesthetic ideal triggered by the epidemic has made femininity superfluous, Pratt notes, to the point that the female body is erased even among the alternative community in the Terminal. In other words, the body of the HIV-positive woman has lost the only attribute that gave it value, and upon losing its potential for beauty, that body is shown to be useless. This problem, which can easily go unnoticed within the novel's complex plot, nevertheless illuminates a program of exclusion that becomes even more systematic toward the end of the book. The process of eliminating feminine elements ends with the signs of the infection itself: "Las cosas acabaron de golpe" [It all ended right then and there] (*Salón* 54; *Beauty* 42), the narrator announces. "De golpe," he says, making no effort to avoid the dictatorial echoes that the word *golpe* (a word used in Spanish to name, among other things, a coup) evokes in Latin America. Sudden, too, is his decision to strip, to burn his women's clothing: the dresses, the feathers, the sequins, the narrator tells us, inviting us to share his disdain for all the things that once granted him his symbolic identity as the queen regent—or simply the queen—of the Terminal. Thus, the erotic aspect of an entire aesthetic—the pursuit of feminine beauty in a male body, associated with his sexual conquest—comes to an end with the protagonist's imminent disappearance. This disappearance should be read as a sort of suicide carried out by the femininity borne on his body, a suicide that is merely an extension of the politics of exclusion discussed earlier. Pratt has proposed that female bodies become expendable in the imaginary of the end of the century, and that femininity is restored by transvestite bodies, as seen in a dual disappearance that unites all that is feminine: both women's bodies and the bodies that mimic them, the biological sex and the cultural construction of that sex. The thanatic reasoning and euthanistic rhetoric of the Terminal end up deactivating the transgression of feminized sensuality, of all the feminine mechanisms that the epidemic has made synonymous with death. In "AIDS and Syphilis," Sander Gilman argues that with the advent of AIDS, homosexual men come to represent not the traditional stereotype of the feminized man but a fusion of the ailing infected man, who must be cured, and woman as the source of the disease, who must be destroyed. That fusion symbolically provokes a drive to eliminate the transvestite body. The association of AIDS with sexual disorder sets in motion a symbolic disciplinary mechanism for which the absolute suppression of any sign of femininity is formulated as the only way to reestablish order, an order that is nevertheless utterly desolate and sterile.

The process of substituting and symbolically eliminating femininity that takes place in the Terminal is also reflected in *El desbarrancadero* (2001; The precipice), an HIV-positive novel that kicked off the twenty-first century, though its fictional present goes back to the same crucial period explored in *Salón de belleza*. Written by the Colombian Fernando Vallejo, who in addition to being the author is also identified with the irate narrator of this autobiographical fiction, the novel portrays the men of the family (except the narrator) *going off a cliff*: first the father dies suddenly of cancer, and later the brother, Darío, the narrator's companion in adolescent homoerotic adventures and adult orgies in New York City, dies of AIDS. In the narrative present, which takes reality both as a foundation and above all as a model, the character "Fernando" travels from Mexico, the country in which he has gone into exile, to his native Colombia. There he finds that his homeland is a slaughterhouse in which all men are at risk. Vallejo calls it both a "matadero" [slaughterhouse] and a "país de Tánatos" [country of Thanatos]; he addresses the nation, which in his work is a woman who victimizes men: "asesina, malapatria, país hija de puta engendro de España, ¿a quién estás matando ahora, loca?" [murderess, evil country, bastard spawn of Spain, who are you killing now, you madwoman?] (118). I should note again here that the feminized homeland is one that victimizes its citizens. But the homeland also serves as a representation of the nation and its citizenry, and thus it is the "pobre patria exangüe" [poor exhausted nation], victim of generalized violence, that is rocked by "derramamientos de sangre y de petróleo saqueado por los funcionarios, sobornada por el narcotráfico, dinamitada por la guerrilla, y como si lo anterior fuera poco, asolada por una plaga" [the spilling of blood and of oil plundered by bureaucrats, bribed by drug traffickers, dynamited by guerrillas, and, as if all that weren't enough, devastated by an epidemic] (78). It is these hardships that beset the citizens of Great Colombia, but the novel focuses with particular interest on what happens within "Colombia en chiquitito" [miniature Colombia] (151): the family home that serves as another place of death in which the narrator's father and brother are victimized by the woman of the household. The house is headed by a mother who has no proper name; she is simply nicknamed La Loca. The narrator also calls the nation a madwoman in the rhetorical question cited above—¿a quién estás matando ahora, loca?—and it soon becomes clear that the question is meant for both: the nation and the mother. La Loca is the cancer that has (to paraphrase the narrator) spent 60 years sucking out the father's soul, and she is also the epidemic that is killing Darío, even conspiring to kill him. She is, the narrator tells us, "más dañina que un sida" [more destructive than AIDS] (69). The mother embodies absolute, castrating female domination,[178] which the narrator describes with evident tension: at bottom, after all, he still fears an

---

[178] Contradicting classical psychoanalytic theory, which sees the castration of a boy as a paternal exercise to prevent incest with the mother, here castration, which is of the phallus as a symbol of power and not of the actual penis, is carried out by the mother to prevent incest with the brother. Significantly, the mother is also accused of separating the two brothers, although the novel does not explain why.

irreversible feminization that would strip him of his manhood and cancel out the masculine power he treasures and histrionically acts out throughout the book. Significantly, in writing this unforgettable childhood scene, Vallejo reaffirms those gender roles (genitals as metonymy) that culture deems natural and necessary: "Así procedió la Loca [a tener hijos], y yo, el primogénito, que no era mujer sino hombre, varón con pene, terminé de niñera de mis veinte hermanos.... Yo lavaba, planchaba, barría, trapeaba. Ordenaba como si tuviera vagina y no pene, y lo que yo lavaba, planchaba, barría, trapeaba y ordenaba la Loca lo ensuciaba, arrugaba, empolvaba, empuercaba, desordenaba" [So La Loca kept having kids, and I, the eldest, who was not a woman but a man, a male with a penis, ended up as a nanny to my twenty siblings.... I washed, ironed, swept, mopped, wiped. I tidied as if I had a vagina and not a penis, and everything I washed, ironed, swept, mopped, wiped, and tidied, La Loca would dirty, wrinkle, stain, begrime, disorder] (54–55). The accumulation of verbs and the insistence with which they are repeated rhetorically underscore the hatred felt by La Loca's eldest son, possible successor to the father as dominant over his siblings and over his own mother. She always turns out to be more powerful and ends up dominating him, transforming him, just as she had his father, into a servant. Among those crimes attributed to "la permisiva, la disoluta, la reina loca, la Loca anárquica, la parturienta" [the permissive, dissolute mad queen, anarchic, parturient La Loca] (68), the one that the narrator perhaps resents most is that his mother has interfered with the brothers' love and driven them apart. In recalling that other childhood memory, Vallejo's irate antimaternal diatribe takes on a loving tone toward Darío that contrasts with his hatred for his mother: "De niños, cuando éramos él y yo solos y aun no nacían los otros, nos unió el cariño. Después el genio disociador de la Loca nos separó. Después la vida nos volvió a juntar, con sus muchachos. Y juntos seguimos hasta el final en que nos acogió en su asilo de ancianos la que empieza por eme" [As kids, when it was just the two of us and the others weren't born yet, we were united by affection. Later, La Loca's talent for breaking things up split us apart. Later, life brought us back together, with (Darío's) boys. And we stayed together until the end, when the woman whose name starts with *m* took us in at her nursing home] (154). We should reflect on at least two elements in this biography of the brothers. The first: that their fraternal love contains an incestuous desire that their mother has tried to prevent, one that will never be consummated because the brothers ward off any possible mutual desire by sharing lovers.[179] The second: that Fernando and Darío had to abandon their mother so they could be together again and be *with Darío's boys*, and that they must continue to reject her in the present in order to remain together (thence, perhaps, the enormous discursive violence against the mother who dominates the home). And maybe here we should pause to wonder about that return home, to that *refuge* belonging to the mysterious M., whose initial stands as much for "muerte" [death] as it does for "mujer" [woman] and "madre" [mother]. Why does the plot bring the brothers back to the realm of their mortal enemy, of the mother/death who castrates, dominates, and annihilates the masculine bodies and desires in the household? I conjecture that it is in the maternal home, where "Fernando" was symbolically feminized as a child, that things must come full circle, that he must regain the masculinity that was wrested from him. A masculinity that demands total opposition to femininity: he must domesticate his mother's discourse and that of all women/mothers, and situate himself in contrast to his younger brother, who is said to resemble their mother in his fits of madness and bad humor. "Con los años [y con la enfermedad] se le había agriado el genio. Cada día más y más se le expresaba un temperamento de Rendón [apellido de la madre], como si ese fuera su primer apellido. Y tras el mal caracter el retraimiento. Se había vuelto hosco, sombrío. Se estaban sumando en él los dos sidas, el del virus y el de la vejez" [With the years (and with the illness), his temperament had soured. Every day he seemed more and more like a Rendón (the mother's last name), as if that name, and not our father's, came first in his surname. And behind

---

[179] As in homosociability, a latent but hidden form of masculine homosexuality, women *channel* the desire between men. Similarly, in their shared homosexuality, the young boys could be channeling their brotherly desire in order to avoid incest. Class ideology is also at work in the brothers' amorous complicity. Recalling his childhood, Fernando talks about his adventures with Darío in the old Studebaker: "La cama ambulante lo llamaban, y se le revolvía el saco de la hiel a esa ciudad pobretona donde solo los ricos tenían carro. Maricas, nos gritaban cuando nos veían pasar, cargada nuestra máquina prodigiosa de bote en bote de muchachos. ¿Maricas? Eso era como Cuba gritándoles imperialistas a los Estados Unidos" [It was known as the bed on wheels, and they were all green with envy in that impoverished city where only the rich had cars. Faggots, they'd yell when they saw us go by, our marvelous machine stuffed to the gills with boys. Faggots? That was like Cuba yelling "imperialists" at the United States] (134).

the unpleasant personality, a deep reserve. He had become sullen, somber. He was being laid waste by two AIDS, that of the virus and that of old age] (49). The brother who is closer to the mother becomes weakened by the disease, by contrast reaffirming the strength and robust health of his older brother, who remains the only survivor, the only man in the house.

It is important to note the gradual disintegration of the symmetry between the brothers. Although there have been many similarities between them in the past, those abruptly come to an end when they decide to get tested for HIV. In the Russian roulette of the epidemic, the narrator's brother, who "con sida o sin sida era un caso perdido" [was a lost cause whether he had AIDS or not] (Vallejo 11), has become infected. The positive test result underscores all the differences between the two. Darío seems to be the less reasonable one, less restrained, the one who has less willpower to resist sex. "Fernando" pleads with him, reminding him, "Uno tiene que escoger en la vida lo que quiere ser, si marihuanero o borracho o basuquero o marica o qué. Pero todo junto no se puede. No lo tolera el cuerpo ni la sufrida sociedad. Así que decidíte por uno y basta" [People have to choose what they want to be in life: a stoner, a drunk, a cokehead, a fag, or what have you. But you can't be everything. The body can't take it—and society can't, either. So pick one and be done with it] (20). It is the narrator himself who questions his advice: "¿Basta? ¿Decirle basta a un huracán?" [Be done with it? Can you tell a hurricane to "Be done with it"?] (46). Darío contracts the virus, while his older brother abandons what the novel has cast as a Dionysian impulse. The disease passes over the more disciplined brother, the one who not only fulfills but also defends the symbolic order. The plot presents "Fernando" as being obsessed with taking on the role of teaching the values associated with the masculine sphere. Although in previous novels Vallejo portrayed his fictionalized self as an elitist defender of linguistic correctness and of the precise exercise of exact sciences, in *El desbarrancadero* the author boasts of being a "sabio sin diploma" [sage without a diploma] (25) who is able to argue with the doctors about the curative power of their medicines. "Fernando" experiments on Darío's passive body, while the doctors, that "caterva de charlatanes doctorados" [gang of certified charlatans] (25), are unsettled by the opportunistic infections that proliferate in the dying man's body. As the dying brother grows weaker—his will to fight back is beaten into submission by the combined assault of virus and medication—the healthy brother is revitalized by a power born of exhibiting a knowledge consistent with the cultural convention of masculinity. If we accept that gender is shaped by cultural configurations that come to seem natural through use, we might then be able to agree that, despite his subversive style, his controversial vocation, and his dark and even self-effacing humor, the novel's narrator reinforces a hierarchical distinction between genders—archaic in its origins but still quite current—that is reproduced in the two brothers. The initial equality between the brothers, who form an allegorical couple, comes to an end when healthy, knowledgeable, and authoritarian "Fernando" grants himself the right to decide about Darío's life, even contemplating euthanasia: killing his brother himself and leaving the family home for good.

The impact of the disease on the filial relationship repeats the binary opposition of genders that pervades Fernando Vallejo's worldview, one that tends to revile anything associated with femininity. Echoing the most persistent discursive maneuver in his novels, here Vallejo once more attacks fertile women as "vaginas delincuentes empeñadas en parir y parir y parir y parir perturbando la paz" [delinquent vaginas that just give birth over and over and over again, stirring up the stillness] (131). Women arrived, he says, like another plague "tras las siete plagas de Egipto [y] no contentas con llenarnos el mundo de hijos y el mar de pañales cagados, se dieron a quitarnos estas putas los putos puestos que con tan ímprobos esfuerzos hace doscientos años, a machete y sangre, con sudor y lágrimas, le habíamos quitado al español" [after the seven plagues of Egypt.... Not content with filling the world with children and the sea with dirty diapers, those bitches started taking the bastard jobs that we, with two hundred years of enormous effort, with machetes and blood, sweat and tears, had taken from the Spanish] (79). Vallejo's discourse rails against the increased agency of women noted by Pratt, but in every possible area of production: their labor both on the job and in the birthing bed. The backdrop of the epidemic in the novel suggests another negative association with femininity: women as producers of a "plaga humana" [human plague] (87), femininity identified with illness. Resisting the pathologized femininity represented by all women—including his mother and her "insania perpetuadora" [endless insanity] (56)—and both the femininity of his brother and the dreaded, even hated, feminization process itself, "Fernando" embraces and asserts masculinity as the only way to survive, as the only value for the current era. In its rigid rejection of anything that undermines the supremacy of masculinity, the discursive construction of *El desbarrancadero* goes back in time and calls for an unfortunate culture-wide resistance to femininity.

CHAPTER 5

Happy Hour?, or The Cocktail Era

The widely trumpeted announcement that the deadly epidemic was turning into a chronic condition meant an immediate upheaval in HIV-positive writing: now that the death sentence had been suspended indefinitely, how would literature deal with the epidemic? But the pharmacological promise of 1996—the cocktail of drugs, the long-awaited happy hour—took a while to become universally available,[180] and it took an equally long time for the improvement in the situation of the infected to be reflected in the literature. Many post-cocktail texts continued to gaze back on a past that still resembled the present all too closely. Even in narratives that make meticulous note of the pharmacological advances—from toxic AZT to two-drug combination therapy to tritherapy—the underlying perspective is similar to that of texts that look backward: though they certainly narrate new situations, the fear of infection and of death remains active, drifting through the texts. Argentine texts that make note of the new treatment do not see it as a relief: there pervades instead an acute anxiety about living a life whose schedule is dictated by a medical regimen.

Existence, now shaped by the rhetoric of self-discipline—taking pills on a fixed, constant schedule—introduces a system of normalization that is implicit in the new therapy. Aware of their own physical fragility, which is exacerbated by each dose, the characters also seek ways to resist, wild outings that slip the collar of daily routine and offer moments of

---

[180] Access to the tritherapy varied widely across Latin America. In Argentina, which I will discuss in this chapter, the Supreme Court in 1997 ruled that the state had to provide the medications to its citizens for free. Nevertheless, Marta Dillón argued, the drugs were not always available at the distribution centers, and people had to go back again and again "a buscar algo para ir tirando" [looking for something to tide them over] (55). In addition to the risk of discontinuity in the state supply, of course, there was also the risk of increased resistance to the drugs, which would make them useless.

uninhibited sexual intensity that undermine the discourse of bodily control. Sex reappears after a long literary absence: it is the most remarkable awakening of this period in the literature, and it is at precisely this point that a transformation takes place. These texts explore the place of sexual relationships in the carrier's newly extended life—sex as a practice that wavers between responsible condom use and risky spontaneity. They also dwell on two concerns that are only possible when life can be projected forward into the future: anxiety about finding lasting love, and fear of solitude, the hated companion of the sick person. These uncertainties compel the narrators to document how to face survival, and especially with whom to face it. In fact, it is these worries that guide the efforts of the HIV-positive present: how and with whom should one move forward into the future? In texts by contemporary authors who write narratives rooted in the present, there is a clear need to share but also a fear of commitment, as if that fear were a reformulation of the fear of infection. This desire to share without commitment shapes a contrary movement within the narrative. The narrator seeks both to draw nearer to others and at the same time put spatial and emotional distance between them, using various intermediaries where there should be constant, fluid communication. The dramatization of an ever-present, ever-possible danger unfolds in a series of behaviors shaped by the technologies fetishized by globalization. And this is without a doubt another new element in writing about AIDS at the time: the appearance of mechanisms that, though they facilitate endless hookups, also function in the literature as an impediment to being together.

CALL WAITING

The old telephone won't stop ringing, and the tape keeps playing the same metallic phrase that serves as the title of Argentine writer Guillermo Saccomanno's story: "Deje su mensaje después de la señal" (1994; Leave a message after the beep). Next we hear voices doing just that: leaving messages for Cecilia, the protagonist. Again and again, the voices of her mother, her father, her sister-in-law, a workmate, a recently divorced friend who keeps calling back as the hours pass and no one answers. At the same time, with indefatigable determination, the rough words of Fabbri are recorded, demanding, perhaps more urgently than anyone, an answer. But Cecilia has decided to pretend that she is not at home. She seems to be protecting herself from the endless anxieties of other people, anxieties produced by a world that "parece estar llegando a su fin" [seems to be coming to an end] (77), a city out there "convulsionada por la tormenta" [rocked by the storm] while she takes shelter in her "búnker" [bunker] (90). Soon it becomes clear that her strategy is one not just of avoidance but of containment, intended to avoid having to face with others the things that *torment* her inside. It is the period immediately prior to the cocktail that will change the course of the epidemic, a period in which rumors of the appearance of an effective treatment are already circulating, and Cecilia still has not managed to process a series of unfortunate events: her partner has died of AIDS, and now Fabbri, her therapist, her confidante, her occasional bisexual lover, perhaps the love of her life, has just received the deadly diagnosis. Aware that she too might carry the virus, she withdraws into her apartment/bunker and into herself—her body is another fortress—to fight it alone. Her reluctance to talk about the illness—the confessional compulsion that was so common in accounts of AIDS in the 1990s—her silence, I repeat, is manifested in the one-sided interruption of communication. I write *interruption* and not *termination* because the lack of communication here is not absolute: Cecilia does not lift the handset (as if merely touching it might confirm her infection), but she does listen to the monologues that others leave for her on the machine.

The telephone and its contemporary accessories—the answering machine, call waiting—thus turn out to work against communication: rather than serving as a *medium*, they function as a *filter*. With them, communication is impeded and interrogated: Can the apparatus keep her in touch with others without having that contact imply risk? Can technology isolate her from contagion without dooming her to eternal solitude? These questions are not answered in Saccomanno's open narrative, which only plants the doubt in the reader's head. What is interesting here is that the telephone, a device that is a metonym of contemporary social communication, is called upon to centralize messages, featuring in the story as a new model of community mediation in a closed space that is not an AIDS camp but a woman's lonely home. This is a contrast with the closed spaces of the past that bore echoes of the prison or the concentration camp— and it is a substantial difference. Although with the initial appearance of Latin American AIDS came *absolute* isolation—as an effect of the discourses of abstinence promoted in a variety of circles[181] and a result

---

[181] According to Linda Singer, during the worst years of the crisis, opposing groups were in agreement about controlling sex: conservatives because they associated it with a moral ill; some feminists because they believed that the exploitativeness of pornography, as an effect of sexual liberation, put women at risk; and gay activists because they wanted to halt the spread of the disease (177).

of the quarantine policies in clinical spaces—Cecilia's contemporary confinement hardly protects her. Hers is a voluntary seclusion in the middle of the capital city, where the telephone significantly functions as a link with the outside world that she can access at will—or at least that is the initial impression. The story indicates a wish to communicate that is nonetheless never fulfilled. At Sunday's and story's end, Cecilia finally breaks her isolation, lifts the receiver, and calls him back, but what she hears on the other end is the metallic voice of an answering machine repeating the same words in her ear: *deje su mensaje después de la señal*. At the end of the text, the storyline insists on an evident disconnect between the characters that is articulated by the apparatus that was supposed to create a connection.[182] The centrality of telephonic mediation and its absence in this story thus confirm a contradictory message about the post-cocktail HIV-positive mindset, one that facilitates contact with others but also puts it on hold. This contradiction, which becomes more pronounced in later Argentine texts, also indicates certain changes in the way the social imaginary of the epidemic is articulated. What is suggested in Saccomanno's story and repeated later in the cocktail texts is a dilemma about community: if we recognize that *communication* and *community* share an etymological past—that of having *in common*, of being or living together, in the words of Roland Barthes—we cannot refute the idea that any interference in communication symbolically indicates a conflict at the community level. The experience of wanting closeness and rejecting it is translated into expressing the desire to be connected to and participate in an extended community, a community that is made possible by means of communication but that does not necessarily ever become self-aware or united. Put another way, the local and global homosexual community is more *in touch* than ever, yet the medium enabling that togetherness hampers the possibility of encounters that are not just concrete but stable over time, encounters that would allow the community to build networks not just of affinity but of companionship. The new media mediate the community but also serve as an excuse to postpone commitment.

The specific circumstances that drove the writing of this new HIV-positive imaginary resulted in a looser relationship with others' bodies and a closer relationship with one's own: with the prolongation of

---

[182] The telephone itself was born of a paradox: Alexander Graham Bell, to whom the nineteenth-century invention is attributed, would have created the apparatus to communicate with his wife and his mother, both of whom were deaf.

carriers' lives, and as their public presence became more acceptable in the larger Western cities,[183] there was a decline in the more political aspects of the community, which had united to face death together and especially to condemn society's complicity in their genocide and demand their rights as citizens. That struggle was derailed by the momentous development of the cocktail: the groups argued over what policies to pursue, were riven by substantial class differences (critical differences, given the high cost of the medication), and competed for the funds set aside for treatment. As the antivirals became more universally available, the objective of the struggle that had united them now drove them apart; everyone pursued his own agenda.[184]

The more combative and radical spirit of the dissident sexualities began to founder, and a more disengaged lifestyle arose, one perhaps more in keeping with the individualism promoted by the new culture of capitalism. In addition, the fiction written by these new carriers of the virus shifted its focus, taking an approach that was divorced from politics (understood as activism that makes demands): the protagonists struggle alone, often pained by their survival, which requires a high level of personal responsibility and routines that exacerbate the narcissistic relationship with their own ailing bodies. The suffocating monotony of the medications mobilizes the subjects of contemporary writing, who seek to escape the harsh pharmaceuticals less by being with others day to day than through the intensity of successive and often ephemeral sexual encounters aided by virtual communication media. This desire is no longer directed at flesh-and-blood bodies; it is sublimated in imagined bodies that achieve, though gradually less and less, physical form. Saccomanno prefigures this situation in a brief but important scene. Not only has Cecilia shut the message bearers (the community that seeks her presence) out of her bunker, but also, behind their backs, she has refused her family, friends, and lover her physical presence and affection, choosing instead the company of

---

[183] In more progressive cultures, there has been a tendency to cease condemnation and to moderate violence through the law. This process no doubt differs from place to place, but new laws have helped stop the violence. The "aluvión confesional" [flood of confessions] discussed by journalist and novelist Claudio Zeiger is an effect but also a cause of the reduction in violence. Of course, that change still requires public recognition of a sexuality that "sigue siendo algo que se debe confesar (o sea, que en algún rinconcito del corazón tiene un resto de pecado o de delito implícito)" [is still something that must be confessed (that is, in some remote corner of the heart it retains a trace of implicit sin or crime)] (2001).

[184] This is the case in all of the Latin American countries studied by Tim Frasca (2005).

bodies recorded on a videotape: with them, she relinquishes herself to the sexual pleasure that she has been putting off. Those bodies are nothing but surface, but the pornographic scenes they perform are so exciting and satisfying for Cecilia that nothing and nobody seem lacking outside the montage of their studied poses and recorded images of their genitals on the screen. After the final close-up, she is spent. "No hay como el sexo grupal" [There's nothing like group sex] (91), she thinks, not without a certain irony, when the session is over. (And in the logic of this story, it would not be inappropriate to add what is implicit but never expressed in words: *There's nothing like group sex, especially when nobody is at risk*.) The concrete presence of another human body has been displaced by onscreen characters who provide pleasure with guaranteed safety that sexual contact cannot offer. The post-cocktail HIV-positive imaginary favored this model of virtualized sexuality, which internalized the need for safe sex while sidestepping the widely recommended abstinence—because if there are other participants in the scene, then we cannot really talk about abstinence. This is sex mediated by technology, pointing toward a hypertrophied reality saturated with images to which the individual surrenders even though he or she knows in advance that it does not correspond to physical reality, as sociologist Jean Baudrillard calls it, trying to distinguish it from the naturalized hyperreal or virtual reality that, he argues, is *experienced* as being true). In this process, reality has lost its referential power, becoming instead a *simulation* that is not a simulation, duplication, or parody of reality but that precedes and actually constitutes the perception of reality. In the case of this scene, the others on the screen are an acceptable and even preferable simulacrum because they are present yet lack affective or physical weight—that is, the burden of risk. Their signals are comforting: their disembodied voices or words, their images that can be rewound and reviewed on the screen or discarded. Sex and by extension all relationships are subject to virtuality—that is the message recorded after the beep. And there is no effort to stigmatize contemporary technology; the literature of the cocktail era does not condemn these approaches to relationships but rather documents a moment of uncertainty, of contradiction, celebrating the possibility of a new way out that offers an escape from coercion but also indicates the community's suffering.

Safe Sex by the Telephone

"Tengo que escribir" [I have to write], begins the diary of HIV-positive poet Pablo Pérez. The initial scene (of writing) takes place during another hot, stormy February in Buenos Aires. As in Saccomanno's story, the autobiographical protagonist Pérez is sitting by the telephone. In *Un año sin amor. Diario del sida* (1998), written as the cocktail was first introduced (1996), the author not only waits for the phone to ring but even anxiously desires it: "Hace tiempo que nadie me llama, hace tiempo que no escribo y cuando me siento a escribir siempre interrumpe algun inoportuno. Pero esto es una simple trampa, me siento en un simulador de escritura para estimular a la campanilla del teléfono" [It's been a long time since anyone's called me, it's been a long time since I've written anything, and when I sit down to write, something always interrupts me. But this is a simple trap: I feel like I'm simulating writing to make the telephone ring] (19). Everything in this room—the old record player, the new answering machine, the computer where "Pablo Pérez" writes—all of it conspires against his solitude. Thanks to these three devices, somebody ends up appearing at the other end of the line to pull him out of his anguished isolation. Throughout this documentary-style text, narrated under the *peso del presente*[185] [weight of the present], the writing space (where Pérez *simulates*) becomes the backdrop for waiting: the delay is described to make it seem shorter; Pérez writes in silence, summoning the ring of the telephone. Writing, here, is not a passive action but the mechanism that will trigger the call. Before sitting down to fill the pages of his diary, "Pérez" has composed a number of personal ads in which he has described himself, as one might an appealing piece of merchandise, to attract a reader of the classifieds in *NX* magazine.[186] The calls he is waiting for will, if they come, be in response to one of those ads. "Ya está," says "Pérez" about one of them. "Ya lo entregué, y va a aparecer así: '30, 1.73, 60, tipo latino, buen cuerpo, tendencia *slave*,[187] a veces muy obediente. Busco *master* o amigo varonil,

---

[185] In her lucid survey of contemporary Argentine literature, Beatriz Sarlo argues that there is a paradigm shift between the historical or interpretive focus of the novels of the 1980s and the documentary or ethnographic bent of literature from the 1990s onward. It is not that the past has disappeared but instead that there appears "el peso del presente, no como enigma sino como escenario a representar" [the weight of the present, not as an enigma but as a context to be portrayed] (2).

[186] *NX*, also called *Nexo* (Nexus), is the name of the principal magazine of the Argentine gay community. Its paper format ceased publication in 2002 because of the economic crisis, but its online format continues, focusing on health issues. See the site <http://nexo.org/index.php/salud>.

[187] It is interesting that the practice of sadomasochism uses the English language to express itself, the result of importation and influence from the United States, to which it unhesitatingly submits.

activo, protector, bien dotado, para relación estable con sexo seguro'" [That's it. I sent it in. It's going to read: "30, 1.73 meters, 60 kilos, Latin type, good body, slave tendencies, very obedient sometimes. Seeking male master or friend, active, protective, well endowed, for a stable relationship with safe sex"] (55). His self-promotional effort highlights those aspects that make him stand out from all the other men who buy personal ads; he tries to stand out among the competition without lying but also without faithfully representing reality. The promotional nature of the text demands a certain lack of faithfulness to reality in order to pique interest and spark desire. Yet the effort is beset by failure. He hides the fact that he is HIV-positive (I have cited here only the most relevant example), encrypting it in the phrase "safe sex"—which is not the same as guaranteed sex—and the clarification later in the sentence ends up contradicting the intended effect of the deceptive tactic. "Pérez" calls these occurrences "rebotes telefónicos" [telephonic rejections] (139), but he also experiences rejection face-to-face.

Let's take a look at the process of self-promotion, which is interesting because of the combination of registers it produces. In this and other advertisements, biographical elements are condensed in a note that is less poetic than it is economical; the one ad that uses the verse form is only a sort of jingle (56–57). The texts' rhetorical strategy is that of marketing, "the science of constructing, dividing, targeting and mobilizing consumers" (Singer 38). The goal of the ads is to seduce with the right word or phrase, turning readers into potential consumers of sex and, eventually, into partners. But this last outcome will not come to pass, because the logic of consumption is governed by a desire for intensity that is difficult to maintain over time, a desire for the other that fades or disappears when consummated. And that instantaneous impetus is the mark of the culture of the new capitalism in which the desire for durability, claims Richard Sennett, has dwindled. The consumer, who was once a collector of objects that represented him and who therefore took care of them, is now a consumer modeled on the format of tourism, stimulated less by an object or a place itself than by the process of acquiring or visiting it, and by the possibility of repeating that acquisition or visit. Desire is thus directed not at a particular object but at desire itself, at the desire to keep desiring different objects, and it is for this reason, adds another sociologist, that the desirability of the object cannot last (Bauman 82).

It is this kind of consumer that is portrayed in *Un año sin amor*, one who even anticipates desire's *in situ* consummation and who, when confronted with reality, ends up being disappointed: "Entre la charla telefónica y el encuentro para conocernos," he notes in his diary, "me hago unas pajas fantásticas imaginándome como puede llegar a ser el tipo. Hasta ahora nunca coincidió lo que yo imaginaba con la realidad" [Between the telephone call and meeting each other, I jack off a couple of times, fantasizing about what the guy might be like. Up till now, my imagination has never matched reality] (98). The repetition of this error, this gap between the imagined—derived from a repeated process of masturbating to fantasies—and the disappointing reality confirms that technology, rather than aiding him in his search for a *stable partner*, will drive him to new masturbation: "Acabo de escuchar en el contestador un mensaje que me dejó un chico por un anuncio de *NX* al que contesté. Tiene una voz muy sensual. Por lo menos hasta que hablemos o hasta que lo conozca personalmente puedo soñar y hacerme la paja" [I just listened to a message that a guy left on the answering machine about an ad in *NX* that I answered. He has a really sexy voice. At least until we talk or until I meet him in person, I can dream and jack off] (112). The imagination, assisted by the recorded voice on the answering machine, stimulates desire and the possibility of *dreaming* about what is not at hand. Both exercises in solitary gratification—imagination and masturbation—are auxiliary forms of safe sex: fantasy arranges the sex scene like an advertisement to achieve maximum pleasure, and sex imagined or mediated by technology also provides enjoyment without the risk of contact with potentially dangerous fluids. But that completely safe sex is not the only sex: in addition to solitary masturbation, "Pérez" goes out to hook up casually with sexual partners, not always using condoms when impatience gets the upper hand. "Pérez" confesses to having let himself be penetrated once without protection.[188] "Yo no pude decirle que no porque estaba muy caliente y borracho" [I couldn't say no because I was really horny and drunk] (132), he explains. His is not a program of sexual abstinence, and this is the most potent aspect of his transgression. In response to an interview question regarding the scene quoted above, the author stated that he had wanted to remove that passage from his diary "porque iban a pensar que soy un enfermo mental" [because people were going to think I'm sick in the head], but that he deliberately chose to leave it so that people would know "que un seropositivo no está siempre guardado en su casa con abstinencia" [that an HIV-positive person is not always abstinently holed

---

[188] Argentine prevention campaigns did not include condoms until 2001. All the information came from the international campaigns.

up in his house] (Mazzini 54). Rejecting the idea of abstinence, even accepting the risks inherent in sex, "Pérez" documents the everyday life of an HIV-positive person,[189] convinced of the importance of his *unseemly* realistic approach and recognizing the difficulty he has staying at home and not seeking out sex. His enormous anxiety (a word that appears again and again throughout the diary) is due less to a lack of sexual opportunities than to the titular lack of love. And though Pérez uses the word *amor* without distinguishing it from the word *sexo*, when he titles his diary *Un año sin amor*, it is evident that he is referring to the loving companionship that complements sexual relationships. "Decidí dejar de buscar tanto el amor para encarar unos días de abstinencia," he says at the end of 1996, knowing that he will not be able to achieve what he has not achieved already. "Me cuesta mucho porque mi nivel de ansiedad me supera. Tengo que poder, a pesar del miedo de quedarme solo para siempre por estar cada vez más enfermo y menos atractivo. ¿Cómo hago para vivir tranquilamente con estas fantasías que me acosan? ¿Por qué creo que dejando de estar solo voy a estar mejor?" [I decided to stop searching for love so much, and to take a few days of abstinence. It's hard for me because I can't deal with my anxiety level. But I need to deal with it, despite my fear of being alone forever as I keep getting sicker and less attractive. How can I live in peace with these fantasies assaulting me? Why do I think that I'll be better if I'm no longer alone?] (177). Unlike most other protagonists in Latin American HIV-positive literature, "Pablo Pérez" spends that watershed year and the rest of his writing existence *thinking* that a lasting relationship is "la única medicina" [the only medicine] that can soothe his anguish (72). But the discourse on love, of the Apollonian sort "Pérez" claims to prefer, seems to be refuted by the libidinal economy that runs through his text. "Creo que en mí es algo cíclico, y que aunque me sienta muy inclinado hacia lo dionisíaco y orgiástico, este verano me sentí mucho más entregado al enigma del amor y lo apolíneo" [I think it's something cyclical in me, and that although I feel very drawn to the Dionysian and orgiastic, this summer I've felt more drawn to the mystery of love and the Apollonian], "Pérez" writes (37–38). Then, ever the unreliable narrator, he contradicts himself and recounts another of his adventures in the adult movie theater on Calle Laprida. The novel

---

[189] The novel appeared in bookstore windows with a yellow band (reminiscent of the armband worn by Jews in Nazi Germany) that announced, as if it were an advertising slogan, "VIH Positivo." (See notes 58 and 120.)

records endless Dionysian and orgiastic activity that takes place in parks, bathhouses, adult movie theaters, and S&M clubs, as well as in the written accounts after each encounter. It is *serial sex* in which the lovers' names are too generic to tell them apart; sometimes they are simply nameless lovers whose faces are lost in the darkness. They are bodies that engage in immediate sexual consumption that offers only fleeting satisfaction and then drives the lovers out in pursuit of more sex with new real or virtual bodies. Bodies that are merely functional, that need only provide instantaneous pleasure, the repetition of which pleasure is incessantly sought in other bodies.

Let there be no misunderstanding: this promiscuity is not the inverse of love, nor is it necessarily the opposite of the stable couple; it could function in the narrative as a means through which love operates, or even be part of a longer-lasting relationship. Yet this diary proposes only the empty mechanism of sexual satisfaction: sex as a search that does not find love and may even inhibit it. The rhetoric of love becomes suspect, coming from this unreliable narrator: it arises as an excuse that legitimizes the erotic compulsion. It even seems inarguable that the need for love suggested in the title is part of the marketing discourse of sex—as are the ads in *NX*, the messages, and the diary entries. The narrative is undergirded by the pursuit of a specific objective: the search for a satisfaction that substantiates the eternal promise of an ephemeral pleasure, whose value consists of being neither long-lasting nor real, is associated with the contradictory mechanism of contemporary capitalism (Singer 36–38). The situation must also be understood as a sign of the times. Some sociologists who study the present note that the current mechanism of consumption destroys the longing to possess, the longing for the long-lastingness of what we believe we deserve. They suggest that the idea that consuming without possessing makes us free is now predominant: "Freedom from possessiveness is also a kind of freedom," writes Sennett (150). And he also writes that giving up an object is experienced not as a loss but as the possibility of beginning to seek out new stimuli. The excitement of a new, unprecedented search, associated with capitalist consumption, thus resembles that of sex, transforming the scene of desire into one of the marketplace.

Happy Hour?

Another central issue in Pérez's writing is his regimented consumption. A repetitive, predictable consumption, like that of an addict. His existence is organized around what he desires because consumption gives him an order, distracts him from the equally predictable but lethal linearity of his existence during the first half of the *watershed year*. In the first months of 1996, death is still a concrete element of intimate reality: "Pérez" has watched several of his friends die in Paris, from which he has just returned.[190] The son of the aunt with whom he is living died in 1994, and during the time that he writes the diary, death carries off another Argentine friend. But the situation begins to change: with the cocktail, infected people's prospects gradually improve. Despite his reservations, the protagonist agrees to participate in the "happy hour" to halt the rapid drop in his T-cell count and the swift progression of opportunistic infections: a bothersome mycosis between his legs, a lung condition that sometimes suffocates him, overwhelming exhaustion. He starts taking an antiviral mini-cocktail.[191] The combination of medications and the strict schedule on which they must be taken constantly remind him of his illness. "Creo que tomar AZT y DDI hace que el sida esté presente en todo momento, que no pueda olvidarme de mi enfermedad, encerrado en mí mismo, siempre con la idea de que voy a morir pronto" [I think taking AZT and ddI makes it so AIDS is present at all times, so that I can't forget my illness, trapped in my own body, always with the idea that I'm going to die soon], he writes (*Un año* 118). Only sex, which he *consumes* regularly, can offer him relief from his harsh pharmaco-logical routine. This predictable, pleasurable form of consumption runs through the diary, making up for the other less pleasurable form that appears halfway through: now, says "Pérez," they both keep him alive.

This Argentine diary, initially conceived as a diary of death, begins to expand with the extension granted by the treatment, until it eventually becomes a diary of life. It is often said that writing puts life, and sometimes death, on hold; here, that metaphorical formulation becomes quite literal. The text, like any diary, describes everyday micropractices, episodes that particularize his situation and undermine

---

[190] Pablo Pérez's diary is an explicit homage to the renowned Parisian writer Hervé Guibert, a member of Michel Foucault's circle who, when he fell ill, wrote several diaries, each one shorter than the last, in which he recorded his desperate wish to be cured. Guibert died in 1991.

[191] The Argentine "happy hour" took place in two stages. The *mini-cocktail* of 1996 combined two drugs, the *cocktail* of 1997, three: the long-since-repudiated AZT (which, taken alone, promised to prolong life six months), ddI or ddC (which Pérez nicknamed DDT, like the main chemical compound in insecticides), and protease inhibitors. These last drugs only began to be used in Argentina in 1997, when Pérez's first diary was already finished.

HAPPY HOUR?, OR THE COCKTAIL ERA ❖ 213

the generalizations and abstractions imposed on the existence of HIV-positive individuals by the global account of the epidemic. It also details sex and its sadomasochistic trappings, and discusses the always only partial success of the cocktail. "Pérez's" happy hour is not an entirely *happy* situation: the medication might be a temporary improvement, but it is experienced as an existential crisis. The cocktail marks a split, dividing the diary into two parts and the protagonist into two mutually exclusive identities: "Pérez" the sick poet in the first part, and "Pérez" the uncomfortable, asymptomatic survivor in the second. Beginning a new life dominated by pharmacological routine is experienced as a shutting down of the creative mind. The single poem recorded in this diary is the long notice or "mensaje personal" [personal message] (56–57) that brings the first half of the book to a close, marking the interruption of the poetry and the irruption of the mini-cocktail. The loss of poetry is described as a grave matter, a moment of identity crisis: "No me siento muy identificado con mi nueva forma de vida y es en este punto donde emerge la crisis. Este Pablo que trabaja, este Pablo que acepta un tratamiento del que siempre habló pestes, no es Pablo" [I don't really identify with my new lifestyle, and that's where the crisis comes in. This Pablo who works, this Pablo who accepts a treatment that he always spoke ill of—he's not Pablo] (93). This Pablo, who writes mechanically in his diary as if he were "una especie de piloto automático de la poesía" [a sort of automatic pilot for poetry] (93), has entered the confines of a disciplined, hyperproductive society that forces him, now that he is healthy, to return to work as a professor and translator and become part of (and write about) a society of "muertos vivos" [living dead] (89). But the disappearance of the poet self does not promote resistance; indeed, it reinforces his resignation to belonging to a system from which he cannot escape and that he, in his way, puts into practice sexually. This is another contradiction out of which the diary constructs its poetics: "Pérez" seeks to elude the regimentation of medical and job-related routines through sex, which is gratuitous, an act of excess and intensity that makes him feel alive; yet sex also provokes a profound sense of loneliness from which he can only escape through vivifying sex, and so on and so forth.

Pablo Pérez writes, "Cada orgasmo es para mí como un golpe de electricidad que me revive…como un rayo que me trae de la muerte a la vida" [Every orgasm for me is like a jolt of electricity that revives me, like a bolt of lightning that brings me back to life] (64). And this Frankensteinian image turns out to be quite suggestive. "Pérez" is a maladapted individual who is looking for his place in the world, who is reinvigorated by other bodies (mere parts, genitals?). Collaborating in his resurrection are a medical technology (combination therapy) and another, let's say, *electrical* technology (the telephone and Internet chatting, which stand in for the jolt of electricity that brings Frankenstein to life). Like Mary Shelley's romantic character, "Pérez" comes back from certain death and begins searching for a love that in the narrative present he is unable to find. The need for (sexual) "electricity," mediated by the instruments of communication and of pharmacological research, suggests an individual who can become highly disciplined in order to make up for what is lacking. Therefore, despite his initial worry, after losing his identity as a poet (a publicist poet, the only poem in *Un año sin amor* suggests), Pérez soon buries himself in the routinized consumption of antiviral medications and the ritualized consumption of sex (routine and ritual here are basically interchangeable), as if pills and sex were two types of treatment for despair, as if "Pérez" must always receive new doses of both in order to continue functioning. In this consumptive tic, we can see the crisis of this text, as the protagonist's self disappears and he forgets the need to be part of a community. Under the spell of his objects, "Pérez" appears to be in the dilemma of the *dependent* individual, his willpower and his agency overpowered by the urge to consume. The logic of the object dominates the individual, subjugates him, determining his behavior and eventually separating him from everybody else. To go back to the beginning, to tie some of these threads together, we should note that although AIDS was seen as a pathology of the global system, although infection by the virus was linked to the technical advances of the twentieth century, here AIDS establishes a symbiotic relationship with the cultural processes of capitalism. The medicalization of the individual and his pleasure, linked to mechanisms of impatient consumption, establish a *mechanical relationship*, says Link, with the modes of social consumption.

The power invisibly at work in the *reasonable* discourse of health pervades the protagonist's life and is also buttressed in Link's reading of Pérez's diary. Despite his own doubts as to whether medication truly offers a way out, Link interprets "Pérez's" consent and its consequences not as a defeat in the face of the mechanisms of power but as a "strategic" measure that consists of taking the drugs so he can recover his strength (or his "calentura" [arousal], as "Pérez" puts it) and be able to continue the party (Link, "Enfermedad y cultura" 263–64). This recovery does take place, but in his analysis the Argentine writer and critic leaves out those instances in which "Pérez" claims to be trapped, even defeated, by the routine of pills that has *domesticated* him, as he puts it, because he must work to earn money to support his medicine consumption. This process by which the individual is mechanized and subjugated to the logic of the object is apparent in the writing itself. In a later text, *Diario. Septiembre/octubre* (2001; Diary: September/October), "Pérez" is completely committed to the orderliness of health and the disorderliness of sex as two kinds of routine. Early on in the photocopies that make up the provisional first edition of this *Diario*, written in the middle of the Argentine economic crisis, Pérez meticulously notes: "Hoy me desperté cerca de las once. Tomé el *coctail* de la mañana: 2 Indinavir, 1 3TC Complex, 1 Deltisona B4, y el Phophorus en bebida plus, además de un Redoxón; estos últimos dos para combatir el resfrío. . . . Almorcé media tortilla (3 papas, 1 cebolla, 1 diente de ajo, 4 huevos, aceite) con chauchas al natural con aceite de oliva" [Today I woke up around eleven. I had my morning cocktail: 2 indinavirs, 1 3TC complex, 1 Deltisona B4, and a homeopathic dilution of phosphorus, as well as a Redoxon—these last two to fight off a cold. . . . I had half a Spanish omelet for lunch (3 potatoes, 1 onion, 1 clove of garlic, 4 eggs, oil) with fresh green beans with olive oil] (*Diario* n.p.). The list of the omelet ingredients mimics the listing of the pills, as if lunch were another prescription for survival. A diary of death, and then of life, and now a detailed notebook of pharmacological and sexual medicine: the author's existence spills out in an inventory stripped of subjective experience.

Sex on the Screen

Daniel Link's *La ansiedad: Novela trash* (2004; Anxiety: A trash novel) is another Argentine text of the cocktail era, reflecting on the place of love and sexual desire in the HIV-positive community. The storyline features a situation already explored in Argentine AIDS literature: the main character's life is governed by the routine of his medications and the compulsion to pursue sex and writing in different formats. Like Pérez's diaries, *La ansiedad* is a novel of insatiability, contrasting the urgency of intense desire with the necessary slowness of a romantic consolidation that forms only gradually. But in this novel the search for love is soon undermined by the protagonist's inability to abide by the conventions of Apollonian fidelity that his partner demands: that definitionally monogamous love does not have enough power or *electricity* to sate or contain his urges. The details matter, here, though, so I will begin at the beginning: in the last months of 1998—well into the cocktail era—we observe the sexual adventures of Manuel Spitz, an HIV-positive homosexual in Buenos Aires. Through an email whose subject line reads "Amor" [Love], the protagonist documents his endless aimless wanderings through Buenos Aires bars and streets where sex is easily found. This ambler, whose pursuit of instant gratification is reminiscent of "Pérez's," first goes off with two "chonguitos" [Buenos Aires slang for attractive men] who are "negros como el pecado pero limpitos" [black as sin but nice and clean] (29), and then with a young cadet who approaches him on the street, offering sexual contact in exchange for money. Spitz does not dwell on economic issues, though the chronological context no doubt reminds readers of the massive collapse of Argentina's economy. This does not seem to worry him. His email focuses instead on the favorable erotic climate in Buenos Aires, where control over sexual commerce and homosexual encounters has loosened. Texts in email form (which predominate in the rest of *La ansiedad*) are brief and scarce here in 1998 and in the following year, suggesting, perhaps, the sporadic availability of that technology. The novel quickly dives into the year 2000 and the heart of the plot: Manuel's romantic encounter with Michel, an HIV-positive Frenchman, in a gay nightclub in Barcelona.

We see this transnational romance through an impassioned correspondence that has left paper behind and quickened its pace. In their accelerated back-and-forth, the two share feelings, bits of biographical information, and descriptions of their local and global difficulties in obtaining the tritherapy. Everything seems to be going well, at least for them, privileged survivors of the epidemic, but the emotional enterprise begins to wobble when Spitz *imports* Michel to Argentina and their long-distance affair becomes a partnership. But unlike the virtual relationship, the domestic routine is full of difficulties that soon exhaust and depress Spitz: "El mundo es cruel y es mucho" [The world is cruel, and it's too much], he explains to his friend Florencia, who is consoling him from New York. Life, in his view, has become a constant "luchar por conseguir: residencia, trabajo, medicamentos, etc." [struggle to acquire: a place to live, a job, medicine, etc.] (Link, *La ansiedad* 148). The French immigrant's impatience and nervousness run counter to the program of desire pursued by the Argentine, whose daily life demands erotic novelties to satisfy his longing for intense emotions: he seeks an "huida de la realidad" [flight from reality] (174) through the Internet, finding it relaxing to have the sensation of being (if only virtually) in many different places, talking with different strangers at once. The idea of *seeing* boys is exciting, offering him "esa cuota de ficción que necesito para seguir viviendo" [that quota of fiction I need in order to keep living] (174). This triggers jealousy in Michel, who follows the conventions of a monogamous couple.

Let's pause for a moment as the conjugal conflict advances and consider Spitz's pressing need to receive *electric* stimuli (a Pérezian metaphor that here curiously acquires a literal meaning). Spitz embodies the favored figure of urban gay culture, which celebrates cosmopolitanism and pushes it to its maximum virtualized expression: a culture that transcends the bounds of the nation, even of Latin America, and reflects a desire for a decidedly globalized yet also restricted world—not an open world but one that is online or lined up for those who have access to that *other plane* of reality. Throughout the year 2000, Spitz becomes competent in the technologies of the global era: the use of email, chatting and its multiple community spaces, discussion forums, sharing and consuming images. These new media place him, so to speak, several steps ahead of the "Pérez" of the diaries. Whereas "Pérez's" approach resembled certain modalities of consumption that were the product of the new capitalist culture, Spitz is completely functional in his system of subliminal seductions. Whereas "Pérez" thought of sex with strangers as a temporary undertaking that precedes love, Spitz finds in virtual sex an effective substitute for emotional and physical togetherness that begins to fall apart precisely because it conflicts with the definition of love that has allowed him to enjoy a stable relationship. But Spitz becomes more and more involved in social networks with strangers he never meets; it becomes impossible for him to function in the outside world. Like an addict, he shifts his wanderings to the screen, becoming a virtual *flâneur* and turning this contemporary epistolary novel into one of great instability on a number of levels.

The plot involves a variety of movements, never a pause or rest; it suggests the constancy of desire and merely ephemeral satisfactions. It also reveals a worldview that demands novelty and variety and not isolated companionship. The anxiety and impatience are paralleled in the very writing of the novel. The textual body has the appearance of screen shots of a variety of texts; it contains forms of dialogue in which the exchange of rapid messages does not allow for psychological identification or exploration. The author's strategy in constructing the novel weaves together a variety of text types like those found on the web, at those addresses also known, in a curious coincidence of terms, as *links*. There are endless electronic conversations full of typos and transmitted instantly; notes exchanged between two or more chat users who enter with their identities hidden, write, and then unexpectedly disappear; and hurried talk dominated by the frank language of computing but using jargon taken from English, recycled, translated, and synthesized: another "cocoliche espantoso" [horrible pidgin] like the one spoken by the central couple.[192] It is the emergence of a language that incorporates the speed of the new forms of communication into the novelistic imaginary.[193] The texts, mostly dialogues,[194] alternate with quotations from famous writers and critics from the Western and local canons on illness and love, and especially on the genre of correspondence (hypertexts that can also become part of the plot), and address communication as a topic and as a problem. I will skip the quotations and the descriptions of sexual encounters—there are many of them and they repeat the same themes—to note that all of those quotations and conversations refer, perhaps unintentionally, to new forms of relationships within the HIV-positive community. The literary text thus serves not only as a laboratory in which genres and methods of writing are ably combined, not only as a "novela de *técnica*" [novel of *technique*] (Sarlo 5), but also as a realm in which to imagine a community in motion, where the binding power of being together dissolves, where identity itself fractures and becomes mutable: Spitz is Manuel on the street, but on the Internet he is also <manu35>, <ansioso40>, <sm master>, <mann>.[195] His unstable self is in flux, and it is this suppression or simulacrum that sparks the anxiety of the text.

Even before the intimate relationship splits apart, the narrative discontinuity is the first thing that catches the reader's attention. The novel's hypercommunicative format emphasizes constant interruptions and an intensity that seems unable to sustain lasting connections. Love and serial onscreen sex are, as demonstrated by the tension between the couple, two speeds that correspond to two

---

[192] Spanish remains a local language: the couple uses it to communicate. "¿En qué idioma hablás con Michel?" [What language do you talk to Michel in?], asks Florencia. Manuel answers, "En castellano, pobre santo. . . . Entre yo y él hablamos un cocoliche espantoso" [In Spanish, poor guy. . . . Between the two of us we speak a horrible pidgin] (Link, *La ansiedad* 132).

[193] For an interesting reflection on the mix of text types, see Daniel Link's *La ansiedad* (132) and articles at his site <http://linkillo.blogspot.com>.

[194] The author includes as a prologue a fake interview with himself—the interview as another form of dialogue.

[195] *Mann* as an abbreviation of Manuel, a version of "man" in English, and as a reference to the author of *The Magic Mountain* (1924), far and away the novel most often quoted in *La ansiedad* because of its treatment of the relationship between love and illness in the nineteenth century.

different ways of thinking and, perhaps, to two planes of reality that Michel is unable to resolve on the plane of the romantic relationship. Spitz, on the other hand, embodies the new man accustomed to the instantaneous contacts of the Internet, to the collective relationships of chatting, to the simulated and *prerecorded* pleasures of the web, to masturbating "al calor de la computadora" [to the heat of the computer] (Link, "Arde"). In them he finds the intensity of safe, uncommitted sex. Living together day to day, with a single body that demands exclusivity, becomes unsustainable: faced with the *weight of reality*, he ends up escaping into the virtual space, where, as the author writes in an article on his blog, "hay de todo, pero sobre todo mucho sexo" [there's a little of everything, but especially a lot of sex].[196]

The substitution of the real relationship with the simulated one is what finally triggers the split between two men who symbolize two paradigms. "Tenés que entender," writes Manuel, heartbroken, in an email to the jealous Frenchman once they have broken up, "es pura ficción, el *chat*, pura literatura (para mí). Y alguna paja, claro, alguna vez, que es como decir: la ficción en su estado más puro" [You have to understand, chatting is pure fiction, pure literature (for me). And sure, jacking off from time to time—which is to say, fiction in its purest form] (Link, *La ansiedad* 188).

In a twist on the geopolitical powers that the two characters represent, it is the Argentine who longs to belong to that global community facilitated by technology, while the foreigner seems trapped in a rigid—*provincial*, in purely geographic terms; *retrograde*, if we accept the paradigm of progress that prevailed at the time—model of relationships. Michel appears as a character who objects to the sexual flexibility that Spitz proposes: "Alguien enamorado, como me dices que lo estas de mí, no pasaría tanto tiempo con el '*chat* gay', con fotos de chicos y otras cosas" [A person who was in love, like you say you are with me, wouldn't spend so much time "gay chatting," looking at

---

[196] Despite the celebratory tone of that article, Link notes instances of failed encounters created by this technology. He mentions an Internet relationship in which one of the men involved, after fevered electronic exchanges, wanted to meet his interlocutor to have sex for real, "como nunca" [better than ever], but the other rejected him because "¿qué onda podés llegar a tener con alguien cuya cara no viste nunca?" [How well can you really get along with someone whose face you've never seen?]. Link concludes that "la *humanidad* en internet tiene sus límites" [*humanity* on the Internet has its limits] ("Arde").

photos of guys, and that sort of thing] (69). The tireless "chiquititos" [little boys] (122) are available at all hours, and they cause Michel an anxiety that he rejects, as well as rejecting the arguments and Spitz himself as an intimate partner. For him, nothing that appears on the screen is fiction: instead, it is a simulation in which the real still persists. Echoing Baudrillard's notion, Michel understands that the virtual, too, is real, and from this perspective Spitz has broken the promise of fidelity. The Frenchman here embodies the rhetoric of possession, which, as Sennett would have it, has been left behind in the past. He rejects the promotion of any freedom that is not enslaved to possessiveness (Sennett). Michel's desire is to possess concretely, not to be stripped of his amorous belonging.

This couple, immersed in the spirit of the new technologies, represents tensions and contradictions within the community. Or, to use Pérez's metaphor, the couple manifests the possible electrification of private and group communication. In this most recent story, they are now inescapably surrounded by an online community that, rather than being present, is temporarily brought together. But in the background—and this is the political point of *La ansiedad*—there is a desire to meet someone who will fleetingly soothe those fears, someone with whom to truly connect. The technological utopia, a premise of late capitalism that survives by provoking continual consumption, here turns out to work against the protagonists' stated intentions. Far from linking consciousnesses and bodies, far from producing lasting satisfaction, the immediacy and infiniteness of the web distract and distort people's reality, promoting fictions of anxiety, impeding the concrete obtainment of affection, and provoking depression. Saccomanno's story describes a day of anxious loneliness temporarily soothed by pornography; Pérez's year and Link's nearly two end as they began, loveless, with loneliness relieved somewhat by the sexual possibilities offered by the new media—and with an excess of anguish. "Vivo en un estado de ansiedad permanente" [I live in a permanent state of anxiety], notes "Pablo Pérez" as he waits by the telephone (*Un año* 122). "Mi nivel de ansiedad me supera" [I can't deal with my anxiety level], he repeats toward the end of his diary (177).

Echoes of the same feeling appear in Link, who brings to the page/screen the same distressed mood: under the fitting title *La ansiedad*, we find increasing unease about disease and solitude. In addition to the cocktail, Spitz ends up taking tranquilizers, but after Michel leaves him, he sits down to chat with a number of different strangers at the same time, telling them all the same thing: "<ansioso40> Supongo que la ansiedad es sobre todo sexual. O afectiva.... <ansioso40>

No sé. . . . <ansioso40> No tengo paz, en todo caso" [<ansioso40> I guess anxiety is mostly sexual. Or emotional. . . . <ansioso40> I don't know. . . . <ansioso40> I'm not at peace, at any rate] (231). He writes about his emotional anxiety in disorderly parallel conversations, talking about the impossibility of believing in electronic words but simultaneously confessing his lack of trust to an anonymous interlocutor and concluding each of these dialogues with the exchange of names—never last names, just that fragment of their identities—and telephone numbers. It is therefore not difficult to identify that frenzied behavior as the "schizophrenia" indicated in the title of the second part of the novel. It is also the imbalance of a social mode that articulates not relationships but possibly contradictory desires. This is clearly an authorial nod to Gilles Deleuze and Felix Guattari, who in their monumental two-volume work *Capitalism and Schizophrenia* (1972–80) claimed that desire is the machine that produces reality, and that capitalism channels different types of desire into an economy that is organized around the abstraction of money and can function without the materiality and even the precise localization of the subjects. Capitalism as a system articulates instability, and despite evidence of impending crisis it continues—like Spitz—to push toward its limits, rejecting all limitations and surviving on the edge of collapse.

A Fictional Community

In reading these texts, one wonders about the forms of community described in the literary imaginary. This question always points, in its way, toward social issues: how, through fiction, to rethink the relationship between the close, the distant, and the intimate; in what terms to think about presence; what relationship there might be between discursive technologies and political formations in a context made up of a range of textual forms—direct speech, telephone conversations, telephone messages, movies, television and advertising, Internet messages—written and produced at a great distance from the place where they will be consumed. Despite their centrality in contemporary culture, these technologies, which inarguably put the community in touch, are not portrayed positively in the last narrative of the epidemic. Although bodies become ever more available for consumption, actual contact, lasting intimacy, the very possibility of love is always postponed; emotional commitment to others and responsibility regarding their bodies and fates are delayed until new notice. How to go about *living together*, a crucial topic in previous eras, is no longer expressed in the imaginary creation of a community joined together in voluntarily exile that seeks to establish itself away from the nation (Gombrowicz); nor is it the forcibly exiled community that comes back together and collectively rethinks homosexual literary genealogy (Arenas); nor is it the marginalized, transgressive, and politicized community that celebrates its dissidence and combats the extinction of a feminized performance (Perlongher, Arenas); nor an HIV-positive community that lives supportively or desperately but together in the institutional spaces of terminal confinement outlined by Copi, Severo Sarduy, or Mario Bellatin, all of which have been discussed throughout this book. Here instead is a *living apart*, even in isolation, while technology facilitates imagining a *virtual togetherness* in the unique present of telephone wires and screens: a community that exists within technology but not without it. Living in the word that is uttered or heard in that *other plane* of reality that also is real. Yet the reality of that community is called into question because it does not manage to sustain visions of the future or viable political projects. As if politics or the polis still required physical presence and present emotions that don't just tune in but make a commitment. As if the reality of the web were, in fact, only an alternative world in which "es otra la vida que uno construye, es otro el lugar desde el cual se habla, sin responsabilidades, sin coherencia. Una utopía libertaria [donde] el universo comunicacional de la red es puramente imaginario" [you build another life, talk from another place, without responsibilities, without coherence. A utopia of freedom (where) the communicational universe of the web is purely imaginary] (Link, "Arde"). This argument, which appears in an essay by Daniel Link but is also expressed in his novel by the *schizophrenic* Manuel Spitz, takes a critical look at that form of virtual community seen as *pure fiction*. Alternative fiction, writes Link; a simulacrum of reality, Baudrillard would add; ways of building a transnational virtual community that in Arjun Appadurai's words would comprise a variety of people known to be in more than one place—emotional or even virtual—at once. A community that, as Appadurai sees it, would be the product of a *plurality of consciousnesses*. But Link questions what Appadurai celebrates: the title of his novel refers not only to his anxiety about consumption but to the state of anxiety that controls and may also alienate even the most privileged members of the system. Spitz enjoys a class privilege that makes him a model of the expectations of the system, but he also suffers the disadvantage of illness, which prevents him from being able to simply revel in his advantage. He is well equipped to engage in the confusions of the hegemonic gaze to which he longs to belong, but his own geographic position and especially his HIV-positive condition become his greatest obstacle: Spitz's body contains the dramas and inequalities that characterize the system—that is the idea. His symptom: the impossibility of achieving and maintaining a romantic bond and the suffering that this impossibility causes him. His ailment, besides a virus kept precariously under control, is the anguish of not being with others, of having become disposable like any object of consumption—pure *effects* but no *affection*. Such seems to be the story of the utopia of the global community, which, like all dreamed-of territories, has neither place nor future. It remains in suspension, for now, on the opaque screen of an HIV-positive present.

BIBLIOGRAPHY

Agamben, Giorgio. *Homo Sacer: Foreign Power and Bare Life*. Trans. Daniel Heller-Roazen. Stanford, CA: Stanford University Press, 1998.

Almendros, Néstor, and Orlando Jiménez-Leal. *Conducta impropia*. Madrid: Playor, 1984.

Altman, Dennis. "Global Gaze/Global Gays." *GLQ* 3 (1997): 417–36.

———. "Globalization, Political Economy, and HIV/AIDS." *Theory and Society* 28.4 (1999): 559–84.

———. "Rupture or Continuity? The Internationalization of Gay Identities." *Post-Colonial Queer: Theoretical Intersections*. Ed. John C. Hawley. New York: State University of New York Press, 2001. 19–41.

Anderson, Benedict. *Imagined Communities*. Rev. ed. New York: Verso, 1991.

Appadurai, Arjun. *Modernity at Large: Cultural Dimensions of Globalization*. Minneapolis: University of Minnesota Press, 1997.

Arenas, Reinaldo. *Antes que anochezca*. Barcelona: Tusquets, 1992.

———. "Autoepitafio." *Poesida: An Anthology of AIDS Poetry from the United States, Latin America and Spain*. Ed. Carlos Antonio Rodríguez Matos. New York: Ollantay Press, 1995. 17.

———. *Before Night Falls*. Trans. Dolores M. Koch. London: Serpent's Tail, 2001.

———. *El color del verano o Nuevo jardín de las delicias*. Barcelona: Tusquets, 1999.

———. *The Color of Summer: Or the New Garden of Earthly Delights*. Trans. Andrew Hurley. New York: Penguin Books, 2001.

Arrieta, Ricardo. "Recuerdos obligatorios del olvido." *Toda esa gente solitaria: 18 cuentos cubanos sobre el sida*. Ed. Lourdes Zayón Jomolca and José Ramón Fajardo Atanes. Madrid: La Palma, 1997. 161–74.

Bachelard, Gaston. *The Poetics of Space*. Trans. M. Jolas. Boston: Beacon Press Books, 1994.

Barnett, Tony, and Alan Whiteside. *AIDS in the Twenty-First Century: Disease and Globalization*. New York: Palgrave, 2002.

Baudrillard, Jean. "The Precession of Simulacra." *A Postmodern Reader*. Ed. Joseph Natoli and Linda Hutcheon. Trans. Paul Foss, Paul Patton, and Philip Beitchman. New York: State University of New York Press, 1993. 342–75.

———. *La transparencia del mal: Ensayo sobre los fenómenos extremos*. Trans. Joaquín Jordá. Barcelona: Anagrama, 1991.

Bauman, Zygmunt. *Globalization: The Human Consequences.* Cambridge, UK: Polity Press, 1999.

Bazán, Osvaldo. *Historia de la homosexualidad en la Argentina: De la conquista de América al Siglo XXI.* Buenos Aires: Marea, 2004.

Bellatin, Mario. *Beauty Salon.* Trans. Kurt Hollander. San Francisco: City Lights, 2009

———. "Flores." *Se habla español: Voces latinas en USA.* Miami: Alfaguara, 2001. 63–68.

———. *Flores.* Barcelona: Anagrama, 2004.

———. *La jornada de la mona y el paciente.* Mexico: Almadía, 2006.

———. *Lecciones para una liebre muerta.* Barcelona: Anagrama, 2005.

———. *Salón de belleza.* Barcelona: Tusquets, 2000.

Bersani, Leo. "Is the Rectum a Grave?" *AIDS: Cultural Analysis/Cultural Activism.* Ed. Douglas Crimp. Boston, MA: MIT Press, 1988. 197–222.

Billard, Henri. "La desarticulación del prejuicio del personaje seropositivo en la narrativa de la generación McOndo." *En teoría hablamos de literatura.* III Congreso Internacional de Aleph. 3–7 Apr. 2006. Ed. César Antonio Morón Espinoza and José Manuel Luis Martínez. Granada: Dauro, 2007. 53–60.

Binnie, Jon. *The Globalization of Sexuality.* London: Sage Publications, 2004.

Blanco, Fernando. "Políticas de la ciudadanía sexual y la memoria en la escritura de Pedro Lemebel." *Desde aceras opuestas: La literatura/cultura gay y lesbiana en Latinoamérica.* Ed. Dieter Ingenschay. Madrid: Iberoamericana/Vervuert, 2006. 53–74.

———, ed. *Reinas de otro cielo: Modernidad y autoritarismo en la obra de Pedro Lemebel.* Santiago: Lom, 2004.

Blanco, Marta. *Maradentro.* Santiago: Alfaguara, 1997.

Boone, Joseph. "Vacation Cruises; or, the Homoerotics of Orientalism." *Colonialism and the Postcolonial Condition.* Spec. issue of *PMLA* 110.1 (1995): 89–107.

Boyarin, Daniel. "Homotopia: The Feminized Jewish Man and the Lives of Women in Late Antiquity." *Differences: A Journal of Feminist Cultural Studies* 7.2 (1995): 41–60.

Brookes, Les. *Gay Male Fiction since Stonewall: Ideology, Conflict, and Aesthetics.* New York: Routledge, 2009.

Brown, Stephen. "'Con discriminación y represión no hay democracia': The Lesbian and Gay Movement in Argentina." *Gender, Sexuality, and Same-Sex Desire in Latin America.* Spec. issue of *Latin American Perspectives* 29.2 (2002): 119–38.

Butler, Judith. *Bodies That Matter: On the Discursive Limits of Sex.* New York: Routledge, 1993.

———. *Gender Trouble: Feminism and the Subversion of Identity.* New York: Routledge, 1990.

———. "Sexual Inversions." *Discourses on Sexuality: From Aristotle to AIDS.* Ed. Domna C. Stanton. Ann Arbor: University of Michigan Press, 1992. 244–361.

Cacho, Lydia. *Muérdele el corazón*. Mexico: Plaza y Janés, 2006.

Camus, Albert. *The Plague*. Trans. Stuart Gilbert. New York: Random House, 1948.

Canese, Jorge. "Eminente peluquero visita nuestro país (¡Chake sida!)." *Stroessner Roto*. Asunción: Intento, 1987.

Canguilhem, Georges. *The Normal and the Pathological*. Trans. Carolyn R. Fawcett and Robert S. Cohen. New York: Zone Books, 1991.

Casas, Francisco. "Un transiberiano llamado sida." *Nuevos aires* (ca. 1990–1993): 18.

Charlesworth, Dacia. "Transmitters, Caregivers, and Flowerpots: Rhetorical Constructions of Women's Early Identities in the AIDS Pandemic." *Women's Studies in Communication* 26.1 (2003): 60–88.

Chekhov, Anton. *Uncle Vanya*. Trans. Max Bollinger. London: Sovereign, 2012.

Chocrón, Isaac. *Escrito y sellado*. Caracas: Ex Libris, 1993.

Contardo, Óscar. *Raro: Una historia gay de Chile*. Santiago: Planeta, 2011.

Copi (Raúl Natalio Damonte Taborda). *Una visita inoportuna*. Buenos Aires: Teatro Municipal General San Martín, 1993.

Cortázar, Julio. "Poema sin título." *Casa de las Américas* 67 (1971): 35–36.

Crimp, Douglas, ed. *AIDS: Cultural Analysis/Cultural Activism*. Boston, MA: MIT Press, 1988.

Cruz-Malavé, Arnaldo. "Towards an Art of Transvestism: Colonialism and Homosexuality in Puerto Rican Literature." *¿Entiendes? Queer Readings, Hispanic Writings*. Ed. Emilie Bergmann and Paul Julian Smith. Durham, NC: Duke University Press, 1995. 137–67.

Cruz-Malavé, Arnaldo, and Martin Manalansan IV, eds. *Queer Globalization: Citizenship and the Afterlife of Colonialism*. New York: New York University Press, 2002.

D'Emilio, John. "Capitalism and Gay Identity." *The Lesbian and Gay Studies Reader*. Ed. Henry Abelove, Michéle Aina Barale, and David Halperin. New York: Routledge, 1993. 467–76.

D'Halmar, Augusto. *El hermano errante: Antología de Augusto D'Halmar*. Ed. Enrique Espinoza. Santiago: Zigzag, 1963.

———. *Pasión y muerte del cura Deusto*. Santiago: Nascimento, 1938.

Davidovich, Carlos. "XI Conferencia Internacional Sobre el Sida en Vancouver." *Medicina* 56.5/1, n.d. Web. 1 May 2012 <http://www.medicinabuenosaires.com/revistas/vol56–96/5/vancouver.htm>.

Davidson, Diana. "Difficult Writings: AIDS and the Activist Aesthetic in Reinaldo Arenas' *Before Night Falls*." *Atenea* 23.2 (2003): 53–71.

de Certeau, Michel. *The Practice of Everyday Life*. Trans. Stephen Rendall. Berkeley: University of California Press, 1988.

de Ferrari, Guillermina. "Enfermedad, cuerpo y utopía en *Los pasos perdidos* de Alejo Carpentier y en *Pájaros de la playa* de Severo Sarduy." *Hispanic Review* 70 (2002): 219–41.

de Gordon, Antonio. "Living inside Cuba's Health Services: The Reality of Castro's Power inside and outside the Island." 2000. Web. 1 May 2012 <www.finlay-online.com/nicolasgutierrez/livinginsidecuba.htm>.

de Gordon, Antonio. "VIH-sida en Cuba. Actualización 2006." 2006. Web. 1 May 2012 <medicinacubana.blogspot.com/2006/02/vih-sida-en -cuba-ac-tualizacin-2006.html>.

de Lima, Paolo. "Peces enclaustrados, cuerpos putrefactos y espacios simbólicos marginales en una novela latinoamericana de fin de siglo." *Ciberayllú.* 31 Dec. 2004. Web. 1 May 2012 <www.andes.missouri.edu/andes /Especiales/PdL_Bellatin.html>.

de Navas-Walt, Carmen, Bernardette Proctor, and Cheryl Hill Lee. *Income, Poverty, and Health Insurance Coverage in the United States: 2005.* Washington, DC: Census Bureau, Department of Commerce, 2006.

Deleuze, Gilles, and Felix Guattari. *Anti-Oedipus: Capitalism and Schizophrenia.* Trans. Robert Hurley, Mark Seem, and Helen R. Lane. New York: Viking Press, 1987.

———. *A Thousand Plateaus: Capitalism and Schizophrenia.* Trans. Brian Massumi. Minneapolis: University of Minnesota Press, 1987.

Delgado, Verónica. "Las poéticas antirrepresentativas en la narrativa argentina de las últimas dos décadas: César Aira, Alberto Laiseca, Copi, Daniel Guebel." *Celehis, revista del Centro de Letras Hispanoamericanas de la Universidad de Mar del Plata* 6–8 (1996): 255–68.

Dillón, Marta. *Vivir con virus: Relatos de la vida cotidiana.* Buenos Aires: Norma, 2004.

Denneny, Michel. "AIDS Writing and the Creation of a Gay Culture." *Confronting AIDS through Literature: The Responsibilities of Representation.* Ed. Judith Laurence Pastore. Urbana: University of Illinois Press, 1993. 36–54.

Donoso, Jaime. "Comunidad y homoerotismo: La transgresión y la política en la crónica de Lemebel." *Taller de letras,* Pontificia Universidad Católica de Chile, Instituto de Letras 36 (2005): 73–97.

Donoso, José. *El lugar sin límites.* Santiago: Alfaguara, 1995.

———. *Lagartija sin cola.* Santiago: Alfaguara, 1995.

Epps, Brad. "Proper Conduct: Reinaldo Arenas, Fidel Castro, and the Politics of Homosexuality." *Journal of the History of Sexuality* 6.2 (1995): 231–83.

Epstein, Julia. *Altered Conditions: Disease, Medicine, and Storytelling.* New York: Routledge, 1995.

Eribon, Didier. *Michel Foucault.* Trans. Thomas Kauf. Barcelona: Anagrama, 1992.

Esquivel, Rosa. *Amor a la vida: Confesiones íntimas de enfermos de sida.* Mexico: Ediciones del Milenio, 1995.

Esterrich, Carmelo. "Locas, pájaros y demás mariconadas: El ciudadano sexual en Reinaldo Arenas." *Confluencia* 13.1 (1997): 178–93.

Figueroa, Blanca. "De peluqueros y peluquerías: Entre el margen y la afirmación." *De amores y de luchas: Diversidad sexual, derechos humanos y ciudadanía.* Ed. Jorge Bracamonte. Lima: Centro de la Mujer Peruana Flora Tristán, 2001. 193–211.

Foertsch, Jacqueline. "Angels in an Epidemic: Women as Negatives in Recent AIDS Literature." *South Central Review* 16.1 (1999): 57–72.

Fogwill, Rodolfo. *Vivir afuera*. Argentina: Sudamericana, 1998.

Foster, David William. "Argentine Intellectuals and Homoeroticism: Néstor Perlongher and Juan José Sebreli." *Hispania* 84.3 (2001): 441–50.

———. *Gay and Lesbian Themes in Latin American Writing*. Austin: University of Texas Press, 1991.

Foucault, Michel. *Birth of a Clinic*. Trans. Alan Sheridan. New York: Routledge, 2003.

———. *The History of Sexuality: An Introduction*. Trans. Robert Hurley. New York: Vintage Books, 1990.

———. "Of Other Spaces." Trans. Jay Miskowiec. *Diacritics* 16.1 (1986): 22–27.

Franco, Jean. "Angst global en la ciudad letrada." *Alteridades* 3.5 (1993): 21–33.

———. *The Decline and Fall of the Lettered City: Latin America in the Cold War*. Boston, MA: Harvard University Press, 2002.

Franco, Jorge. *Melodrama*. Bogotá: Planeta, 2006.

Frasca, Tim. *AIDS in Latin America*. New York: Palgrave, 2005.

———. "Men and Women: Still Far Apart on HIV/AIDS." *Reproductive Health Matters* 11.22 (2003): 12–20.

Galvão, Patrícia (Mara Lobos). *Parque industrial*. São Paulo: José Olympio, 2006.

Garber, Margorie. *Vested Interests: Cross-Dressing and Cultural Anxiety*. New York: Routledge, 1997.

García Canclini, Néstor. *La globalización imaginada*. Buenos Aires: Paidós, 1999.

Gasparini, Pablo. "Patria y filiatrias: Exilio y transnacionalidad en Gombrowicz, Copi y Perlongher." *Hispamérica* 35.105 (2006): 45–58.

Gilbert, Thomas. "The Emergence of HIV in the Americas and Beyond." *PNAS* 107.47 (2007): 18566–70. Web. 1 May 2012 <www.pnas.org/cgi/doi/10.1073/pnas.0705329104>.

Gillio, María Esther. "Manuel Puig a 10 años de su muerte." N.d. Web. 1 May 2012 <www.pagina12.com.ar/2000/00–09/00–09–18/pag15.htm>.

Gilman, Sander. "AIDS and Syphilis: The Iconography of Disease." *AIDS: Cultural Analysis/Cultural Activism*. Ed. Douglas Crimp. Boston, MA: MIT Press, 1988. 87–107.

———. *Disease and Representation: Images of Illness from Madness to AIDS*. Ithaca, NY: Cornell University Press, 1984.

Giorgi, Gabriel. "Diagnósticos del raro: Cuerpo masculino y nación en Osvaldo Lamborghini." *Heterotropías: Narrativas de identidad y alteridad latinoamericana*. Ed. Carlos Jáuregui and Juan Pablo Dabove. Pittsburgh, PA: Instituto Internacional de Literatura Iberoamericana, 2003. 321–42.

Giorgi, Gabriel. "Historias de la sexualidad en *Las afueras*: Las crónicas de Pedro Lemebel." Unpublished paper. 2002.

———. *Sueños de exterminio*. Rosario: Beatriz Viterbo, 2004.

Glantz, Margo. "Palabras para una fábula." *Historia de una mujer que caminó por la vida con zapatos de diseñador*. Barcelona: Anagrama, 2005. 151–90.

———. "Tres personas distintas. ¿Alguna verdadera?" *Excesos del cuerpo: Ficciones de contagio y enfermedad en América Latina*. Ed. Nathalie Bouzaglo and Javier Guerrero. Buenos Aires: Eterna Cadencia, 2009. 273–317.

Goffman, Ervin. *Stigma: Notes on the Management of Spoiled Identity*. New York: Touchstone, 1986.

Gombrowicz, Witold. *Diario argentino*. Trans. Sergio Pitol. Buenos Aires: Adriana Hidalgo Editora, 2006.

———. *Diary*. Trans. Lillian Vallee. New Haven, CT: Yale University Press, 2012.

———. *Trans-Atlántico*. Trans. Sergio Pitol and Kazimiersz Piekarec. Barcelona: Seix Barral, 2004.

———. *Trans-Atlantyk*. Trans. Carolyn French and Nina Karsov. New Haven, CT: Yale University Press, 1994.

Gómez, Sergio. "Hombres en habitaciones pequeñas." *Partes del cuerpo que no se tocan*. Santiago: Planeta, 1997. 121–36.

Gómez, Sonia, ed. *Sida en Colombia: "Nunca me imaginé que podría infectarme." Testimonios*. Medellín: Colina, 1988.

González Mateos, Adriana. "Las excepciones del panamericanismo: Salvador Novo y su viaje por Sudamérica (1933)." *Torre de papel* 9.2 (1999): 43.

Guerra Cunningham, Lucía. "Ciudad neoliberal y los devenires de la homosexualidad en las crónicas urbanas de Pedro Lemebel." *Signos literarios y lingüísticos* 2.1 (2000): 99–119.

Guibert, Hervé. *Cytomegalovirus: A Hospitalization Diary*. Trans. Clara Orban. New York: University Press of America, 1992.

———. *To the Friend Who Did Not Save My Life*. Trans. Linda Coverdale. New York: Atheneum, 1991.

Hammonds, Evelynn. "Gendering the Epidemic: Feminism and the Epidemic of HIV/AIDS in the United States 1981–1999." *Feminism in Twentieth Century Science, Technology, and Medicine*. Ed. Angela Creage, Elizabeth Lunbeck, and Londa Schiebinger. Chicago: University of Chicago Press, 2001. 231–44.

Haraway, Donna. "The Biopolitics of Postmodern Bodies: Determination of Self in Immune System Discourse." *Feminist Theory and the Body: A Reader*. Ed. Janet Price and Magrit Shildrick. New York: Routledge, 1999. 203–14.

Hardt, Michael, and Antonio Negri. *Empire*. Boston, MA: Harvard University Press, 2001.

Haver, William. *The Body of This Death: Historicity and Sociality in the Times of AIDS*. Stanford, CA: Stanford University Press, 1996.

Hawley, John, ed. *Post-Colonial Queer: Theoretical Intersections.* New York: State University of New York Press, 2001.

Hernández Adrián, Francisco Javier. "Sarduy, la isla nómada: Territorios queer, biopolítica, multitud." *Lecciones de disidencia: Ensayos de crítica homosexual.* Ed. Xosé María Buxán Bran. Madrid: Egales, 2006. 179–98.

Hurtado, Joaquín. *Crónica sero.* Nueva León: Consejo Nacional para la Cultura y las Artes, 2003.

———. *Laredo Song.* Nueva León: Consejo Nacional para la Cultura y las Artes, 1997.

Ingenschay, Dieter, ed. *Desde aceras opuestas: La literatura/cultura gay y lesbiana en Latinoamérica.* Madrid: Iberoamericana/Vervuert, 2006.

———. "Hemispheric Looks at Literary AIDS Discourses in Latin America." *Revista iberoamericana* 20 (2005): 141–58.

Kaplan, Caren. *Questions of Travel: Postmodern Discourses of Displacement.* Durham, NC: Duke University Press, 1996.

Klengel, Susanne. "Señalar lo ilusorio de todo: Entrevista con Severo Sarduy." *Vuelta* 206 (1994): 39–42.

Kramer, Larry. *The Normal Heart and The Destiny of Me.* New York: Grove Press, 2000.

La Fountain-Stokes, Lawrence. "Queer Ducks, Puerto Rican Patos, and Jewish-American Feygelekh: Birds and the Cultural Representation of Homosexuality." *Centro: Journal of the Center for Puerto Rican Studies* 19.1 (2007): 192–229.

Lancaster, Roger. "On Homosexualities in Latin America (and Other Places)." *American Ethnologist* 24.1 (1997): 193–202.

Lacey, Marc. "Vulnerable to HIV, Resistant to Labels." *The New York Times.* 7 Aug. 2008. Web. 19 Sept. 2013 <http://www.nytimes.com/2008/08/07/world/americas/07mexico.html?pagewanted=all&_r=0>.

Le Breton, David. *Adiós al cuerpo: Una teoría del cuerpo en el extremo contemporáneo.* Trans. Ociel Flores Flores. Mexico: La Cifra, 2001.

Lederer, Robert. "Origin and Spread of AIDS: Conclusion." *CovertAction* 29 (1988): 52–66.

———. "Origin and Spread of AIDS: Is the West Responsible?" *CovertAction* 28 (1987): 43–54.

Leiner, Marvin. *Sexual Politics in Cuba: Machismo, Homosexuality, and AIDS.* San Francisco: Westview Press, 1994.

Lemebel, Pedro. *Adiós mariquita linda.* Santiago: Sudamericana, 2005.

———. *De perlas y cicatrices: Crónicas radiales.* Santiago: Lom, 1998.

———. "Educación sexual para androides." *Nuevos aires* (ca. 1990–1993): 19.

———. *La esquina es mi corazón.* Santiago: Cuarto Propio, 1995.

———. *Loco afán: Crónicas del sidario.* Santiago: Lom, 1996.

———. *Loco afán: Crónicas del sidario.* Barcelona: Seix Barral, 2000.

Liguori, Ana Luisa. "Gender, Sexual Citizenship and HIV/AIDS." *Culture, Health and Sexuality* 5.1 (2006): 87–90.

Link, Daniel. *La ansiedad: Novela trash*. Buenos Aires: El Cuenco de Plata, 2004.

———. *Los años 90*. Buenos Aires: Adriana Hidalgo Editora, 2001.

———. "Arde Internet." *Página/12, Suplemento Futuro* (Buenos Aires). 17 Oct. 1998. Web. 1 May 2012 <www.bazaramericano.com/bazar/articulos/arde_link.htm>.

———. "Enfermedad y cultura: Política del monstruo." *Literatura, cultura, enfermedad*. Ed. Wolfgang Bongers and Tanja Olbrich. Colección Espacios del Saber. Barcelona: Paidós, 2006. 249–65.

Llamas, Ricardo. "La reconstrucción del cuerpo homosexual en tiempos del sida." *Construyendo identidades: Estudios desde el corazón de una pandemia*. Mexico: Siglo XXI, 1995. 141–71.

Lomeli, Felipe, and Luis Martín Ulloa. "El sida y la retórica del miedo." *Tierra adentro* 160 (2009): 9–14.

Lozada, Ángel. *No quiero quedarme sola y vacía*. Puerto Rico: Isla Negra, 2006.

MacCannel, Dean. *The Tourist: A New Theory of the Leisure Class*. New York: Schocken Books, 1989.

Marchant Lazcano, Jorge. *Sangre como la mía*. Santiago: Alfaguara, 2006.

Martin, Emily. "Toward an Anthropology of Immunology: The Body as Nation State." *The Science Studies Reader*. Ed. Mario Biaglioli. New York: Routledge, 1999. 358–71.

Massielo, Francine. *The Art of Transition: Latin American Culture and Neoliberal Crisis*. Durham, NC: Duke University Press, 2001.

Maturana, Andrea. "Enfermedad mortal." *No decir*. Santiago: Alfaguara, 2006. 163–71.

Mazzini, Martín. *Escrito en el cuerpo*. Buenos Aires: Veintitrés, 2001.

Menéndez, Ronaldo. "Una ciudad, un pájaro, una guagua." *El derecho a pataleo de los ahorcados*. Madrid: Lengua de Trapo, 1999. 41–69.

———. "La moneda, la bóveda, yo solo trato de alcanzar." *Toda esa gente solitaria: 18 cuentos cubanos sobre el sida*. Ed. Lourdes Zayón Jomolca and José Ramón Fajardo Atanes. Madrid: La Palma, 1997. 75–82.

Miller, James, ed. *Fluid Exchanges: Artists and Critics in the AIDS Crisis*. Toronto: University of Toronto Press, 1992.

Millot, Catherine. *Horsexe: Essay on Transsexuality*. Trans. Kenneth Hylton. New York: Autonomedia, 1990.

Moledo, Leonardo. Annex: "El sida en la Argentina." *El fantasma del sida*. By Néstor Perlongher. Buenos Aires: Punto Sur, 1988. 105–41.

Molloy, Sylvia. "La cuestión del género: Propuestas olvidadas y desafíos críticos." *Revista iberoamericana* 193 (2001): 815–20.

———. "Disappearing Acts: Reading Lesbian in Teresa de la Parra." *¿Entiendes? Queer Readings, Hispanic Writings*. Ed. Emilie Bergmann and Paul Julian Smith. Durham, NC: Duke University Press, 1995. 230–56.

———. "La flexión del género en el texto cultural latinoamericano." *Revista de crítica cultural* 21 (2004): 54–56.

————. "Of Queers and Castanets: Hispanidad, Orientalism, and Sexual Difference." *Queer Diasporas*. Ed. Cindy Patton and Benigno Sánchez-Eppler. Durham, NC: Duke University Press, 2000. 105–21.

————. "La política de la pose." *Las culturas de fin de siglo en América Latina*. Ed. Josefina Ludmer. Rosario: Beatriz Viterbo, 1994. 128–38.

Molloy, Sylvia, and Robert McKee. *Hispanisms and Homosexualities*. Durham, NC: Duke University Press, 1998.

Monsiváis, Carlos. "El amargo, relamido, brillante frenesí." n.d. Web. 1 May 2012 <www.letra2.s5.com/lemebel0311.htm>.

————. "El sida y el sentido de urgencia." *Sida: Aproximaciones éticas*. Ed. Mark Platts. Mexico: Fondo de Cultura Económica and Universidad Nacional Autónoma de México, 1996. 77–86.

Montaldo, Graciela. "Un argumento contraborgiano en la literatura argentina de los años '80 (sobre C. Aira, A. Laiseca y Copi)." *Hispamérica* 55 (1990): 105–12.

More, Thomas. *Utopia*. Trans. Paul Turner. London: Penguin Books, 2003.

Morris, David. *Illness and Culture in the Postmodern Age*. Berkeley: University of California Press, 1998.

Murphy, Timothy. "El VIH en las fronteras." *Sida: Aproximaciones éticas*. Ed. Mark Platts. Mexico: Fondo de Cultura Económica and Universidad Nacional Autónoma de México, 1996. 111–30.

Muslip, Eduardo. "Biografía, imagen de autor y género (gender) en 'Una visita inoportuna' de Copi." *Nuevas cartografías críticas: Problemas actuales de la literatura iberoamericana*. Actas del 1er Congreso Internacional del Instituto Internacional de Literatura Iberoamericana. Apr. 2007. Web. 1 May 2012 <http://www.geocities.ws/aularama/ponencias/lmn/musilip.htm>.

Nouzeilles, Gabriela. *Ficciones somáticas: Naturalismo, nacionalismo y políticas médicas del cuerpo (Argentina 1880–1910)*. Rosario: Beatriz Viterbo, 2000.

Novo, Salvador. "Continente vacío. Viaje a Sudamérica." *Viajes y ensayos I*. Mexico: Fondo de Cultura Económica, 1996. 703–803.

Ocasio, Rafael. "Gays and the Cuban Revolution: The Case of Reinaldo Arenas." *Gender, Sexuality, and Same-Sex Desire in Latin America*. Spec. issue of *Latin American Perspectives* 29.2 (2002): 78–98.

O'Neill, John. "AIDS as a Globalizing Panic." *Theory, Culture and Society* 7 (1990): 329–42.

Onetti, Juan Carlos. *La vida breve*. Barcelona: Seix Barral, 2007.

————. *Los adioses*. Barcelona: Seix Barral, 2007.

Ortiz, Ricardo. "Pleasure's Exile: Reinaldo Arenas's Last Writing." *Borders, Exiles, Diasporas*. Ed. Elazar Barkan and Marie-Denise Shelton. Stanford, CA: Stanford University Press, 1998. 92–111.

Ostrov, Andrea. "Las crónicas de Pedro Lemebel: Un mapa de las diferencias." *La fugitiva contemporaneidad: Narrativa latinoamericana 1990–2000*. Ed. Celina Manzoni. Buenos Aires: Corregidor, 2003. 99–119.

Oyarzún, Luis. *Diario íntimo*. Ed. Leonidas Morales. Santiago: Departamento de Estudios Humanísticos, Universidad de Chile, 1995.

Palaversich, Diana. "The Wounded Body of Proletarian Homosexuality in Pedro Lemebel's 'Loco Afán.'" Trans. Paul Allatson. *Gender, Sexuality, and Same-Sex Desire in Latin America*. Spec. issue of *Latin American Perspectives* 29.2 (2002): 99–118.

Pardo, Edmée. *El primo Javier*. México City: Planeta, 1996.

Parys, Jody. "La creación de (com)unidad mediante la hibridez: *Loco afán, Crónicas de sidario* de Pedro Lemebel." *Memoria histórica, género e interdisciplinariedad: Los estudios culturales hispánicos en el Siglo XXI*. Madrid: Biblioteca Nueva, 2008. 113–21.

Patton, Cindy. *Inventing AIDS*. New York: Routledge, 1990.

———. "Tremble, Hetero Swine." *Fear of a Queer Planet: Queer Politics and Social Theory*. Ed. Michael Warner. Minneapolis, MN: University of Minnesota Press, 1993. 143–77.

Patton, Cindy, and Benigno Sánchez-Epler, eds. *Queer Diasporas*. Durham, NC: Duke University Press, 2000.

Pérez, Pablo. *Un año sin amor: Diario del sida*. Buenos Aires: Libros del Perfil, 1998.

———. *Diario: Septiembre/octubre 2001*. Buenos Aires: Belleza y Felicidad (photocopied editions), 2001.

Perlongher, Néstor. *El fantasma del sida*. Buenos Aires: Punto Sur, 1988.

———. *Prosa plebeya: Ensayos 1980–1992*. Buenos Aires: Colihue, 1997.

Piglia, Ricardo. "¿Existe la literatura argentina?" *Espacios de crítica y producción* 6 (1987): 13–15.

Pratt, Mary Louise. *Imperial Eyes: Travel Writing and Transculturation*. 2nd ed. New York: Routledge, 2008.

———. "Tres incendios y dos mujeres extraviadas: El imaginario novelístico frente al nuevo contrato social." *Espacio urbano, comunicación y violencia en América Latina*. Ed. Mabel Moraña. Pittsburgh, PA: Instituto Internacional de Literatura Iberoamericana, 2002. 91–106.

———. "Why the Virgin of Zapopán Went to Los Angeles: Reflections on Mobility and Globality." *Images of Power, Iconography, and Culture and State in Latin America*. Ed. Jens Andermann and William Rowe. Oxford, UK: Berghahn Books, 2006. 271–91.

Prieto, René. "The Degraded Body in the Work of Severo Sarduy." *Body of Writing: Figuring Desire in Spanish-American Literature*. Durham, NC: Duke University Press, 2000. 135–72.

Povinelli, Elizabeth, and George Chauncey. "Thinking Sexuality Transnationally." *GLQ* 5.4 (1999): 439–48.

Puga, María Luisa. *Diario del dolor*. Mexico: Alfaguara and Conaculta, 2004.

Puig, Manuel. *El beso de la mujer araña*. Barcelona: Seix Barral, 2002.

———. *Pubis angelical*. Barcelona: Seix Barral, 2003.

Quiroga, José. *Tropics of Desire: Interventions from Queer Latino America*. New York: New York University Press, 2000.

Ramos Otero, Manuel. *Página en blanco y staccato*. Madrid: Playor, 1988.

Rivero, Giovanna. "Dueños de la arena." *Sangre dulce/Sweet Blood*. Santa Cruz, Bolivia: La Hoguera, 2006. 137–47.

Robles, Víctor Hugo. *Bandera hueca: Historia del movimiento homosexual de Chile*. Santiago: Cuarto Propio, 2008.

———. "History in the Making: The Homosexual Liberation Movement in Chile." *Nacla, Report on the Americas: Report on Sexual Politics* 31.4 (1998): 36–44.

Rosenberg, Charles. "What Is an Epidemic? AIDS in Historical Perspective." *Daedalus* 118.2 (1989): 1–17.

Saccomanno, Guillermo. "Deje su mensaje después de la señal." *Animales domésticos*. Buenos Aires: Planeta, 1994. 51–99.

Saer, Juan José. "La perspectiva exterior: Gombrowicz en la Argentina." *El concepto de ficción*. Buenos Aires: Seix Barral, 2004. 17–29.

Said, Edward. "In the Shadow of the West." *Wedge* 7–8 (1985): 4–11.

———. *Orientalism*. New York: Random House, 1978.

Saitta, Sylvia. "Costureritas y artistas pobres: Algunas variaciones sobre el mito romántico de la tuberculosis en la literatura argentina." *Literatura, cultura, enfermedad*. Ed. Wolfgang Bongers and Tanja Olbrich. Colección Espacios del Saber. Barcelona: Paidós, 2006. 95–114.

Saguier, Raquel. *La vera historia de Purificación*. Asunción: RP Ediciones, 1989.

Salas, Fabio. "Las Yeguas del Apocalipsis." *Cauce* 204.1–7 (1989): 26–29.

Salessi, Jorge. "The Argentine Dissemination of Homosexuality, 1890–1914." *Lesbian and Gay Histories*. Spec. issue, Part II, of *Journal of the History of Sexuality* 4.3 (1994): 337–68.

———. *Médicos, maleantes y maricas: Higiene, criminología y homosexualidad en la construcción de la nación argentina*. Rosario: Beatriz Viterbo, 1995.

Sandoval, Alberto. "Politizing Abjection: Towards the Articulation of a Latino AIDS Queer Identity." *Passing Lines: Sexuality and Immigration*. Ed. Brad Epps, Keja Valens, and Bill Johnson González. Boston, MA: Harvard University, David Rockefeller Center for Latin American Studies, 2005. 311–19.

Sarduy, Severo. *Beach Birds*. Trans. Suzannne Jill Levine and Carol Maier. Los Angeles, CA: Otis Books/Seismicity Editions, 2007.

———. *Christ on the Rue Jacob*. Trans. Suzanne Jill Levine and Carol Meier. San Francisco: Mercury House, 1995.

———. *Colibrí. Obra completa. Tomo I*. Buenos Aires: Sudamericana, 1984.

———. *El Cristo de la rue Jacob*. Barcelona: Ediciones del Mall, 1987.

———. "Diario de la peste." *Vuelta* 206 (1994): 33–35.

———. "El estampido de la vacuidad." *Vuelta* 206 (1994): 36–38.

———. *Pájaros de la Playa*. Barcelona: Tusquets, 1993.

———. "Para una biografía pulverizada en el número—que es pero no póstumo—de 'Quimera.'" *Severo Sarduy: Antología*. Mexico: Fondo de Cultura Económica, 2002. 20–26.

Sarlo, Beatriz. "Sujetos y tecnología: La novela después de la historia." *Punto de Vista* 86 (2006): 1–6.

Sedgwick, Eve Kosofsky. *Epistemology of the Closet.* Berkeley: University of California Press, 1990.

———. "Nationalisms and Sexualities in the Age of Wilde." *Nationalisms and Sexualities.* Ed. Andrew Parker, Frank Davey, Mary Russo, Doris Sommer, and Patricia Yaeger. New York: Routledge, 1992. 235–45.

Selden, Daniel. "Just When You Thought It Was Safe to Go Back in the Water." *The Lesbian and Gay Studies Reader.* Ed. Henry Abelove, Michéle Aina Barale, and David Halperin. New York: Routledge, 1993. 221–23.

Sennett, Richard. *The Culture of the New Capitalism.* New Haven, CT: Yale University Press, 2007.

Shilts, Randy. *And the Band Played On: Politics, People, and the AIDS Epidemic.* New York: Saint Martin Press, 1987.

Siebers, Tobin. "What Does Postmodernism Want? Utopia." *Heterotopia: Postmodern Utopia and the Body Politic.* Ed. Tobin Siebers. Ann Arbor, MI: Michigan University Press, 1994. 1–38.

Simmel, Georg. "Prostitution." *Georg Simmel on Individuality and Social Forms.* Ed. Donald Nathan. Chicago: University of Chicago Press, 1971. 121–26.

Singer, Linda. *Erotic Welfare: Sexual Theory and Politics in the Age of Epidemics.* New York: Routledge, 1993.

Smith, Paul Julian. *The Theatre of García Lorca: Text, Performance, Psychoanalysis.* New York: Cambridge University Press, 2008.

Sontag, Susan. *Illness as Metaphor and AIDS and Its Metaphors.* New York: Picador, 2001.

Sommer, Doris. *Foundational Fictions: The National Romances of Latin America.* Berkeley: University of California Press, 1991.

Suquet, Mirta. "Rostros femeninos del VIH/sida: La cara oculta de una epidemia." *Así hablan y escriben las mujeres.* Actas del Congreso Internacional. 11–13 June 2009. Bern: University of Bern, 2009.

Sutherland, Juan Pablo. "En ti confío." *Santo roto.* Santiago: Lom, 1999.

Tiffin, John. "The Hyperreality Paradigm." *Hyperreality: Paradigm for the Third Millennium.* New York: Routledge, 2001. 25–42.

Treichler, Paula. "AIDS and HIV Infection in the Third World: A First World Chronicle." *AIDS: The Making of a Chronic Disease.* Ed. Elizabeth Fee and Daniel Fox. Berkeley: University of California Press, 1992. 377–412.

———. "AIDS, Homophobia and Biomedical Discourse: An Epidemic of Signification." *American Literary Studies: A Methodological Reader.* Ed. Michael Elliot and Claudia Stoker. New York: New York University Press, 2003. 182–210.

———. *How to Have Theory in an Epidemic: Cultural Chronicles of AIDS.* Durham, NC: Duke University Press, 1999.

Treichler, Paula, and Catherine Warren. "Maybe Next Year: Feminist Silence and the AIDS Epidemic." *Gendered Epidemic: Representations of Women in the Age of AIDS*. Ed. Nancy Roth and Katie Hogan. New York: Routledge, 1998. 109–52.

Tuñón San Martín, Amparo. "El sida como factor noticiable en la construcción del acontecimiento cultural en cuatro diarios de calidad: *El País, La Vanguardia, Le Monde* y *The Times*." *Análisis. Cuaderno de comunicación y cultura* 16 (1994): 57–87.

Turner, Bryan. "Social Fluids: Metaphors and Meanings in Society." *Body and Society* 9.1 (2003): 1–10.

Ullán, José Miguel. "El jardín rojo de Severo Sarduy." *Sarduy: Obra completa. Tomo II*. Buenos Aires: Sudamericana, 1999. 1780–81.

Ulloa, Leonor Álvarez de, and Justo Ulloa. "La función del fragmento en 'Colibrí' de Sarduy." *Hispanic Issue. MLN* 109.2 (1994): 268–82.

Vaggione, Alicia. "Literatura/enfermedad: El cuerpo como desecho. Una lectura de *Salón de belleza* de Mario Bellatin." *Revista iberoamericana* 75.227 (2009): 475–86.

Valdelomar, Abraham. *La ciudad de los tísicos t otros relatos*. Lima: Mejía Baca, 1958.

Valdés, Zoé. *La nada cotidiana*. Barcelona: Planeta, 1995.

Vallejo, Fernando. *El desbarrancadero*. Barcelona: Alfaguara, 2001.

Van Den Abbeele, Georges. *Travel as Metaphor: From Montaigne to Rousseau*. Minneapolis, MN: University of Minnesota Press, 1991.

Vieira, Estela. "Writing the Present, Rewriting the Plague: José Saramago's *Ensaio sobre a cegueira* and Mario Bellatin's *Salón de belleza*." *Ciberletras*. 7 July 2002. Web. 1 May 2012 <www.lechman.cuny.edu/ciberletras /v07/vieira.html>.

Watney, Simon. "The Spectacle of AIDS." *AIDS: Cultural Analysis/Cultural Activism*. Ed. Douglas Crimp. Boston, MA: MIT Press, 1988. 71–86.

Watts, Sheldon. *Epidemics and History: Disease, Power and Imperialism*. London: Yale University Press, 1999.

Weiss, Meira. "Signifying the Pandemics: Metaphors of AIDS, Cancer, and Heart Disease." *Medical Anthropology Quarterly* 11.4 New Series (1997): 456–76.

Young, Rebecca, and Ilan Meyer. "The Trouble with 'MSM' and 'WSW': Erasure of the Sexual-Minority Person in Public Health Discourse." *American Journal of Public Health* 95.7 (2005): 1144–49.

Zapata, Luis. "Todo tipo de médicos." *Historias médicas: ¿Qué me pasa Doctor?* Ed. Viviana Paletta and Javier Sáez de Ibarra. Madrid: Páginas de Espuma, 2001. 31–42.

Zayón Jomolca, Lourdes, and José Ramón Fajardo Atanes, eds. *Toda esa gente solitaria: 18 cuentos cubanos sobre el sida*. Madrid: La Palma, 1997.

Zeiger, Claudio. *Adiós a la calle*. Buenos Aires: Emecé, 2006.

———. "Confesiones de invierno." *Página/12, Suplemento Radar* (Buenos Aires). 2 Sept. 2001. Web. 1 May 2012 <www.pagina12.com.ar/2001 /suple/Radar/01–09/01–09–02/pagina3.htm>.

———. "El virus nuestro de cada día." *Página/12, Suplemento Radar* (Buenos Aires). 3 Oct. 2004. Web. 1 May 2012 <www.pagina12

.com.ar/diario/suplementos/libros/subnotas/1249–176–2004–10–03 .html>.

————. "Y la banda siguió escribiendo." *Página/12, Suplemento Radar* (Buenos Aires). 3 Oct. 2004. Web. 1 May 2012 <www.pagina12.com.ar /diario/suplementos/libros/10–1249–2004–10–03.html>.

Index

AIDS
  Africa hypothesis, 44, 45–8, 119
  in Argentina, 60, 132n131,
    139n137, 149n146
  in Brazil, 17n14
  in Colombia, 47n54, 74
  comparison with Jewish
    Holocaust, 51n58, 122n120
  as a discursive epidemic, 10,
    11, 42
  and globalization, 9, 14–22,
    35–6, 45–6, 48, 51–5,
    59–60, 65, 107, 133, 140,
    151, 152n151, 214, 223
  history, 43n47, 199n115
  and homosexuals, 22, 43–4, 65,
    71, 163, 185, 193 (see also
    homosexuality)
  as an imperialistic discursive
    fabrication, 117, 117n117
  and the Internet, 214, 216,
    218–22
  as a masculine disease, 67–71
  metaphors, 3, 10–11, 18–20, 41
  open secret, 24, 39, 39n40
  origins, 8–9, 8n5, 14, 20n18, 117
  patient zero, 4, 46, 47, 113
  statistics, 8, 8n4, 68n76
  treatment, 54n61, 55, 67n75
    AZT, 54, 54n61, 55, 56, 57,
      62, 201, 212, 212n191
    cocktail era, 55, 56, 56n64,
      61, 201, 203–6, 207, 212,
      212n191, 213, 215–16, 220
  as a weapon of extermination,
    118, 118n114, 120–1
  women, 72–6, 175–99 (see also
    feminism)

capitalism
  and globalization, 15, 21, 63,
    79, 160
  and sexual emancipation, 3,
    11–13, 32, 73, 84,
    130–1, 158
  and the young radical, 13, 50
Catholicism, 128
  and sexual dissidence, 85, 129
Chile, 1, 2, 24, 26, 87, 127,
    129, 130–1
  AIDS in Chile, 34, 50n57,
    68n76, 128, 126–33,
    135n133, 135n134, 158,
    186–7
  Allende's government and sexual
    dissidence, 32, 134
  Chilean feminists, 184
  homosexuality, 126–32, 135–7
  as a model of neoliberalism,
    32–3, 129, 129n129, 187
  transition to democracy and
    AIDS, 185
  See also dictatorship, in Chile; in
    Chile, and sexual dissidence
Cuba, 2, 19, 29, 38, 88, 102,
    106, 110
  AIDS camps, 49, 73, 123,
    123n123, 128, 145, 152,
    152n150, 156, 168, 169,
    170, 170n167, 171, 172, 203
  AIDS in Cuba, 49, 51, 66–7,
    67n74, 73, 123, 123n123,
    152, 152n150, 156–7, 169,
    170, 170n167
  homosexuality, 38, 102,
    103–7, 157
  Período Especial, 66n73

Printed and bound in Great Britain by
CPI Group (UK) Ltd, Croydon, CR0 4YY